The Wreck

The
Wreck

A Daughter's Memoir
of Becoming a Mother

CASSANDRA JACKSON

VIKING

VIKING
An imprint of Penguin Random House LLC
penguinrandomhouse.com

LIBRARY OF CONGRESS CATALOGING-IN-PUBLICATION DATA
Names: Jackson, Cassandra, 1972– author.
Title: The wreck: a daughter's memoir of becoming a mother / Cassandra Jackson.
Description: New York: Viking, [2023]
Identifiers: LCCN 2022033440 | ISBN 9780593490020 (hardcover) |
ISBN 9780593490037 (ebook)
Subjects: LCSH: Jackson, Cassandra, 1972– | Jackson, Cassandra, 1972—Family. |
African American families—Biography. | African American mothers—Biography. |
Motherhood—United States. | Fertilization in vitro, Human—United States. |
Loss (Psychology)—United States. | African Americans—Social conditions.
Classification: LCC E185.97.J26 A3 2023 | DDC 306.85/08996073092
[B]—dc23/eng/20220928
LC record available at https://lccn.loc.gov/2022033440

Printed in the United States of America
2nd Printing

Designed by Cassandra Mueller

Some names and identifying characteristics have been
changed to protect the privacy of the individuals involved.

For my Daddy and his sugar dolls,
Satchel and Basie

But was it really like that? As painful as I remember? Only mildly. Or rather, it was a productive and fructifying pain.

—TONI MORRISON, *THE BLUEST EYE*

Where I was before I came here, that place is real. It's never going away. Even if the whole farm—every tree and grass blade of it dies. The picture is still there and what's more, if you go there—you who never was there—if you go there and stand in the place where it was, it will happen again; it will be there for you, waiting for you.

—TONI MORRISON, *BELOVED*

The Wreck

CHAPTER 1

My father knocks on the door of a house, and when the door opens, he waves for me and my mother to get out of the car. We hesitate for a moment. The house we're parked outside of looks more like a trailer whose wheels have been stolen than someone's home. But we walk across the patchy yard, go up a few steps, and follow him into a dim living room with bumpy linoleum floors and air thick with the smell of Noxzema and fried pork chops.

An old brown woman walks up to me and points. "This the baby?"

My father nods, but I am not a baby. I am five years old.

The old woman tries to smile, but the edges of her brown lips refuse to turn all the way up. Her eyes dart across my ashy knees, my long noodle arms, and the hook nose that is way too big for my narrow face. I already know what she will say—the same thing the last two old ladies we visited today did.

"Humph . . . She just like 'em. Ain't she?" The old woman shakes her head and goes into the kitchen while we sit down. She comes back with a piece of chocolate cake and a glass of icy red Kool-Aid. She puts both on the table in front of me and nods for me to eat.

I have to take a bite, even though the last old lady, the one who cracked her neck when she looked at me, already gave me sugar cookies and lemonade, and the tall one before her who whistled when she said my name gave me a dish of homemade caramels.

I press a fork into the cake and it gives like warm pudding. I put a small piece in my mouth. Now the old lady's eyes watch my throat to make sure that I swallow. I know what she is doing. She wants to make sure that I am a real girl who eats and not a ghost. One time, when we visited another old lady in the country, I didn't eat or drink anything, and she started telling my parents to watch out for ghosts that she called "haints," who slip out of their graves and into new bodies. My mother began to nod her head like she always does when old people are talking. But then she stopped. My father told that lady that there's no such thing as ghosts. And later in the car, my mother said the same thing to me. *You know that's just old people's nonsense, right?* I nodded, but I do not know this for sure. Some of the old ladies we visit talk about bad hips and gas prices and those are real.

I hold the sweet chocolate in my mouth for as long as I can without swallowing and watch the old lady trying to pay attention to my father and keep an eye on me at the same time. He asks her questions about how other old people are doing, and if that storm that came through last week did much damage out here in the country. The lady tells him who died and who is about to die. My mother says that's a shame and when the old lady looks at her and moans "mm-hmm," I swallow the cake.

My father lets out a long "well" that means it is time to go.

The old lady says that it is too soon for us to leave, we just got here. But my father, who cannot bear to sit in anyone else's house for very long, stands up and says we have to be getting on back down the road 'cause we have a drive ahead of us.

The old lady turns to me with yellowing eyes and her mouth opens, but no words come out. I pick up the glass of Kool-Aid and watch a shiver pass through the old lady's body. I fill myself with sugary redness. When I put the glass down, she smiles at me for the first time since we arrived.

We all file out of the house with the old lady trailing behind, saying she can't remember the last time she saw us and that we need to visit more often because she's old and will be dead before we know it. I worry that she will try to hug me and her old lady smell will turn my full stomach. But when I turn around to say goodbye, she squints and shakes her head at me like I have given her bad news.

"That's something ain't it? That she could look that much like Maggie 'nem."

We get in our car and wave as we pull away. We are done visiting today and I do not know when my father will pick another Sunday afternoon and say, *Let's take a ride to the country.* Sometimes we travel out here every few weeks and other times months pass before we drive this way again. I do not know if we will see the same old ladies or other ones because I do not know which ones are cousins, which ones are friends, or which ones will die before we return. All I know is that when my father says, "Let's take a ride," my eighteen-year-old sister and my sixteen-year-old brother, who both know how to drive their own cars, will have somewhere else to go and I will climb into the green Oldsmobile and ride for a while, so that an old lady the color of pennies or pine cones or margarine can stare into my face again.

Today, my father drives most of the way home in silence while my mother talks about which old ladies looked sick and which ones looked well. Tired and full, I close my eyes in the back seat until I hear my mother ask my father, "Which one does she look like, your mama or your sister?"

I open my eyes and see my mother frowning at me like I am fruit that is starting to go bad.

"Mostly like Maggie, but Maggie looked like Mama. San looked different, you know, 'cause of all that red hair. But she had big eyes too, just like them," he says.

"So she kind of looks like all of them?" my mother says.

"Yeah. Just like them," he says.

Experiment Number One: In the kitchen, I crack a brown egg and shift the yolk from one half of the shell to the other, letting the clear thick snot of the white stream into a bowl. I suck the goo up with a yellow medicine dropper that looks like a shrunken turkey baster. I carry the full dropper to my bedroom, where I lie down next to my husband, Reginald, and insert the albumen of a chicken egg into my vagina. I feel the slime sliding back out even before I can squeeze the last bit of liquid out of the dropper.

"I think we better hurry," I say.

I am thirty-six years old, and I have been trying to get pregnant for six months. All my reading and research has only alerted me to the fact that at my age, my fertility is plummeting like a drop tower ride at an amusement park, one that falls so fast that the riders' screams hang in the air longer than the ride.

I know that mine is a shit-or-get-off-the pot situation and I am de-termined to shit. I have spent the last decade in academia, where in-fertility is the honorary faculty member who never misses a department meeting. The explanation is simple: many women postpone having children to complete PhDs and secure tenure, both of which take many years. Women who have children prior to completing degrees or before publishing enough research to get tenure sometimes lose the support of mentors and colleagues, who perceive them as lacking the necessary commitment to be a scholar. Of course, there are women professors who are childless by choice. Nonetheless, academic hallways are thick with the twin anxieties of research production and human reproduction. At the obligatory dinner parties I attended while in graduate school, I listened to white women debate over frittatas and white wine the best time to have a baby—searching for a moment that won't impair one's ability to finish the PhD or leave one visibly pregnant while on the job market. When I became a professor in a department where most of the women led fulfilling, adult-centered lives, it was impossible to know who had chosen not to have children, whose bodies refused to have them, and whose ambivalence had morphed into medical impossibility. Some of the women joked that while they had not had babies, they had given birth to books. But many of these same women were just a glass of wine and a cheese plate away from disclosing other women's losses: *You know she tried, right? Miscarriage. Twice.*

I scour infertility blogs and discussion boards and discover tons of women seeking at-home conception solutions, some of them in their kitchens. That's how I discovered that, apparently, egg whites can create the perfect highway for sperm, making their journey as fast and smooth as a high-speed rail. If a woman is not producing enough mucus to get her partner's guys to the target and this hypothetical woman is willing to take the risk of contracting vaginal salmonella, the egg whites could be a cheap and simple solution to infertility. It makes sense, as stupid ideas often do. Numerous women in cyber-land claim that it worked for them, and their avatars are pictures of grinning babies.

None of these blog posts mention that heterosexual sex with egg whites is like a pogo stick race on a bed of Jell-O—bungling and sloppy. When we are done, I must lie in bed for thirty minutes to give the sperm their best chance to complete their journey. My husband runs for a towel, but its absorbency is no match for the sticky mess and we are both laughing at the unexpected tenaciousness of egg whites.

I feel something light, like a balloon rising in my chest. Hope. I stamp it down. I may be foolish enough to lie in bed with egg whites running down my legs, but I don't dare admit that I think this trick could work.

My mother talks in a loud, high-pitched voice to a baby in the arms of his mother, the wife of a new hire at the factory where my father works. They sit on our plaid love seat. I kneel on the plush carpeted floor in front of them to get a close look at the baby's fingers that curl like a doll's. My mother tells the woman to tilt the baby up so he can see me. "Babies like San," she tells the woman. I do not know why she says this. I am nine years old, and I do not have a little brother or sister. I have never held a baby and the ones that I have seen at church scare me with their wobbly heads and screams that go off like stray bombs. I smile at the babies because my mother always grins at them in public and criticizes anyone who fails to do so. *Did you see her standing there with her mouth poked out? Some folks so awful they don't even smile at kids.* Good people like babies or pretend to, and in turn the babies are supposed to like them back. The woman tilts the baby up so he can see me sitting on the floor, but his eyeballs drift in different directions like Cookie Monster's.

"See," my mother says. "Ain't that something—how they know other kids when they see them."

The woman nods and returns the baby to a resting position in her arms. They talk, and the woman asks my mother questions, like which churches are Baptist and which grocery stores have the best prices on meat. Between answers, my mother leans toward the baby and talks nonsense in her funny baby voice. His face does not react, but he turns his head away from her. This makes my mother laugh and talk to him even louder.

"I bet you looking at me thinking who is this crazy lady here?" she says.

The woman asks to use the bathroom and settles the baby in my mother's arms. My mother continues to talk to the baby, asking him ridiculous questions, until she hears the bathroom door close.

"Watch this," my mother says in a loud whisper. She cradles the baby and presses his head to her breast. He opens his mouth and shakes his head left and right in search of a nipple, but he gets a mouth full of my mother's polyester blouse instead. He shakes his head again. This time he is frantic. His mouth opens wider, searching.

"They all do that when they're little," my mother says.

She turns to the now squirming baby and says, as if she and the baby are arguing, "I don't have any milk for you. I'm not your mama."

The baby's mouth closes and opens into a wide grimace like an angry gargoyle. The cry that comes out makes me want to run.

When the woman returns, she looks confused at the sight of her transformed baby.

My mother hands him to her. "I think he's hungry," she says.

Experiment Number Two: I dig out a disposable menstrual cup still pristine in its plastic wrapper from the bottom of a drawer of tampons and pads. According to a new thread on one of the many infertility discussion boards I visit, I could either insert the cup post-coitus or get my husband to make a direct deposit into the cup and then insert it into my body. I have the flu, so I choose the latter. The idea is to trap the sperm at the opening of the cervix, thereby increasing the chances that one of the swimmers will land and make it to shore. Improbable as this method sounds, I'd heard the occasional claim that a virgin had gotten pregnant by simply lying too close to the one-eyed snake. So why wouldn't trapping sperm near the cervix have a chance at producing a pregnancy?

I hand the cup to Reginald and he turns it over and examines it, laughing before disappearing into the bathroom down the hall.

No one explained exactly how I was supposed to insert the menstrual cup without spilling the precious contents. Never mind that I'd never figured out how to insert the hard, painful contraption even when it was empty.

When he returns with the cup, I look down at the few drops of cloudy liquid in the bottom. "Is that all there is?"

He smiles and rolls his eyes at me.

"You've always been a cup-half-empty kind of person."

He is only half joking. Unlike me, Reginald believes in things. He has always felt like he was not meant to be here alone. He shared a womb with a baby girl, who died when she was two months old, and he has spent his whole life missing this girl, whom he only knows by feeling and from a few pictures. He believes that my birth around the time of her death is a sign that we belong together. He swears he saw me in a dream when he was a boy, long before we ever met, right down to the color of my skin and the texture of my hair. He is sure that dead ancestors who love him look out for him and that all things work out, and that if they don't, he can limp along until he finds another way.

His optimism annoys me and buoys me at the same time.

I turn my head away to cough.

"Watch it," he says. "You wouldn't want your cup to runneth over."

I try to look disgusted, but I laugh in spite of myself. I carry the cup to the bathroom, afraid to say what I am thinking: he would be a good father.

I am seven years old in my room, styling the deep black hair of my Marie Osmond doll when my father calls me. "San! San!"

I put the brush down and walk out of my room, closing the door behind me. Then I run through the long hallway, letting the thick, springy carpet add bounce to each stride. I guess that my father is probably going to tell me that there is a show on TV that I will want to watch while he cooks dinner, or he wants to ask me if I want him to boil the corn or fry it.

But I find him with his limbs hanging over the edges of the maroon leather recliner.

"Daddy?"

His body jerks and his eyelids open. He stares at me with cloudy red eyes and wrinkled brows as if he is not sure I am real. His lids grow heavy and close again.

"San," he mumbles, softer this time, like a question, then he begins to snore. He is not talking to me. He is talking to the dead girl again. I should have known. He does this sometimes when he's been drinking. And lately, he's been drinking every day. He pours a glass of whiskey while he cooks, and then sits down in his big chair to watch TV while he waits for my mother to come home. He stretches his body out and falls asleep. When he talks in his sleep, he sounds so awake that I can never tell if he is calling me or the girl I am named for.

I never met the other San. She died in the wreck with a bunch of other people. We have a photo of her in the back of the red photo album. She is all eyes: wet, glassy, and sad. She leans on the shoulder of her older sister, Liza, like she is tired. They wear white dresses that pop out of the green tint of the photo. Liza smiles with tight lips, but San stares into the camera, the edges of her tiny mouth turned down. Dark shadows hover on the wall behind them.

When the dead girl comes to life, my father becomes a shaky dam, trying to hold back a string of disasters. He tells someone to stop, another to slow down. He warns Bumpy, the white man who works with him at the metal plant, that he is about to get himself killed. In my father's dreams, a giant pot of hot metal is always about to boil over and someone is about to be cooked alive.

I do not want to leave him, scared and waiting for bad things to happen. If she were here, my mother would wake him, rapping hard on the crown of his head and meeting his confused eyes with a sharp laugh before mimicking his expressions. Once he would fully wake, she would frown. *That's why you need to stop drinking. You make a fool of yourself.* But I cannot wake my father like that. I do not want to hurt him, and besides, I am afraid of his bloodshot eyes that look at me like I am not supposed to be here, like someone cut me out of an old photo and placed me here, in the wrong time period.

I run to my room, grab the brush and a coffee can my sister has covered with blue wrapping paper, and head back to the den. Marie Osmond will have to wait. I will style my father's short afro instead. Kneeling on the shaggy brown carpet, next to my father's chair, I open the can and pour out the hair bows inside. I sort them by color and type and begin selecting the largest and most colorful ones: Pink plastic hippos. Yellow-and-white striped ribbons. Red-white-and-blue clips.

I walk behind him and take a soft, cottony tuft of hair in my hands, divide it into three strands, and make a small braid. I wish I could cornrow short hair like my brother does, but plaiting will have to do. At the end, I place a purple elephant. I part his hair and braid another section. This time I tie a yellow ribbon on the end. With my hands in his hair, he eases into quiet sleep.

When I am finished, I stand back to take a look at my creation. His head leans back and his mouth opens wide. Above his head is a gorgeous halo of colors. He is a beautiful peacock. When my mother comes home, his beauty will make her laugh, and she will not have a chance to get angry and complain that he drinks too much.

Thirsty, I grab the glass of ice on the floor next to my father and drink the dribs of water in the bottom. I gag as whiskey sets my throat on fire.

Experiment Number Three: I take an over-the-counter drug called guaifenesin, which is used to thin mucus in the nasal passages and respiratory tract. The theory behind using this drug for fertility is that if it can help thin out nasal mucus, it can also thin other kinds of mucus. Thinner vaginal mucus would create a luge experience for sperm. The problem with this method is that guaifenesin does not target just one kind of mucus. Within days, the drug summons slippery fluids from every bit of spongy flesh in my body. I am a snotty, disgusting mess.

Reginald ignores the strange seepage in the corners of my eyes and we soldier on with sex. By the time my period arrives, my throat is swollen and sore from postnasal drip.

I am sitting on the kitchen counter while my father fries a chicken so slowly that the grease barely makes a sound. He sips from his glass of Old Forester whiskey and sings songs that he says are old church songs from his childhood in "the country," which is what everyone calls the nearby Alabama farmlands where he grew up. I have never heard any of these songs sung by anyone in or out of a church.

My sister walks in wearing her Shoney's waitress uniform and goes to her room to change. As she passes by my mother in the hall, my sister blurts out, "He's at work." She is talking about my brother, who never seems to be at home. He is probably at his girlfriend's, but "work" is so sacred to my parents that neither of them would dare call the grocery store to check to see if my brother is really there. *You don't ever call no man on his job.*

My sister returns to the kitchen dressed in street clothes, and we all sit down at the L-shaped bar with plates of chicken, greens, sweet potatoes, and cornbread. My mother mentions a woman she ran into on her lunch break. "She's a sweet person," she says. "But the poor thing has really let herself go."

My father nods without looking up from his plate.

"You know who I'm talking about, don't you, John?" she says. "Curly's wife. Her sister used to work at that gas station up by Huntsville Road."

My father chews and shakes his head.

She turns to my sister. "You know who I'm talking about, don't you?"

My sister nods. "The one with a scar through her eyebrow?"

"Yeah, that's her. John, you used to see her at Nate's ball games all the time. Her son was in the same grade with Nate."

My father ignores my mother as if she is the bird in a malfunctioning cuckoo clock. He lifts gigantic forkfuls of greens to his mouth with one hand and holds a chunk of cornbread in the other.

My mother's eyes dart back and forth between my plate and my sister's like she is not sure which of us is the bigger problem, me eating too little or my sister eating too much. Both of our bodies are all wrong. My twenty-year-old sister is fat and beautiful, and my mother is sure that *if she just lost some of that weight, went down by a couple dress sizes, she'd be so much happier 'cause men just don't like great big fat women anymore like they used to.* My mother tries to get my sister to eat all her meals from a saucer, but my sister uses a regular plate. After dinner, she tells my sister to come walk with her to the local park for exercise. Sometimes I go with them, but I don't like that the highway we walk along has no sidewalks and we have to walk fast and jump out of the way to keep from getting hit by cars.

Other times, my mother drives my sister to a class called Jazzercise at the recreation center. I picture them dancing with glamorous white ladies dressed like Wonder Woman and I beg my mother to let me go. But she says kids are not allowed at Jazzercise. I am not sure if this is true, but I am sure that my mother wouldn't let me go if kids were allowed because my body is too skinny. *Men don't like real skinny women. They like big legs. You need to fill out.* To help me gain weight, my mother buys family-size bags of cheese curls, Oreo cookies, and Reese's peanut butter cups. I can have as much as I want, but I have to stash the junk food in my room so my sister won't eat it. At school, I skip the greasy cafeteria pizza and the soggy peanut butter and jelly sandwiches that my mother packs and wait until I get home to fill up on candy bars and chips after school. But no matter how much junk I eat, I grow straight up instead of out.

When my sister and I are together, even though she is thirteen years older than me, someone always points out that I am skinny and she is fat like they want us to explain why. My sister ignores them. I tell them the truth, that my sister took after my mother's mother and I am like my father's family. But I do not say this in front of our mother because she will frown at me for answering a question from *a fool.* *People really should have more sense than to ask why somebody is fat and why their sister isn't.*

We do not talk about the fact that my sister and I look different because we already know something is wrong with both of us. My mother tries to make us look better. She buys us nice clothes from the department stores, never Kmart. She comes home from the mall smiling and plops big bags of clothes on our beds. We try them on and model each outfit for her. Sometimes she says we look nice. But mostly she frowns. The pants that fit my waist are too short for my legs and the ones that are long enough for my legs are too big in the waist. My sister can never seem to fit into the skirts and jackets in the bright green and yellow fabrics my mother favors. For some reason the clothes that fit her always seem to be dull khaki or navy. My mother bags up most of the clothes and returns them to the mall, but she does not give up. She always comes home with more to try on.

My mother's eyes settle on my plate. "John, she ain't eating nothing. Look!"

I push my food around to try to make it look like I am eating. My fingernails are still orange from the family-size bag of Doritos I ate after school.

"She'll be fine," my father says, bringing a chicken breast to his mouth.

"She's not going to gain any weight eating like that." Bits of food shoot out of my mother's mouth like tiny wet rockets.

My sister tries to sneak a second piece of chicken, but my mother stops her. "You can't eat everything you want."

"Yes, she can," my father says, without looking up from his plate. "Now eat!"

My sister grabs a thigh and eats with her eyes on her plate.

"That's why she's so big, John. She's gonna keep getting bigger and fatter and it's gonna be your fault. I tried to stop her when she was little, and you just wouldn't listen. Now look at her."

My father does not answer and silence swallows us for a few moments that feel like mercy. But my mother's eyes continue to dart back and forth between my plate and my sister's while she eats and I pretend to.

My father leans toward me and shoots me a quick smile. "My mama and my sister Maggie Jo weren't any bigger than you."

My mother makes a "humph" sound but says nothing. There is no good way to argue over dead women.

"Really?" I say.

"Yup. Maggie barely weighed a hundred pounds grown, and Mama didn't weigh much more when she died."

"Am I really like them?"

"Not in personality. They had some terrible tempers, now. Would get so mad you didn't know what they might do."

I want to ask more questions, but the pinched look on my mother's face tells me that it is wrong to ask about things that hurt. She starts to mumble something, and my father interrupts.

"You look just like them though." His eyes appear wet, but his voice is dry and matter-of-fact.

Experiment Number Four: While lurking on still more internet discussion boards, I discover a book cited hundreds of times, a sort of hippy fertility bible. I study it and put its central premise, cycle tracking, into action. Each day, I wake up and stick a thermometer in my mouth before I do anything else. According to the book, too much moving around will invalidate the results. Next, I reach for a chart I printed out from the internet and plot my temperature on it. The inclining, peaking, and falling temperatures indicate that I am ovulating regularly.

This method relies on the same ideas as the rhythm method of birth control to pinpoint fertile times, except rather than avoiding sex during these times, I am trying to have as much sex as possible. For years, I ridiculed any semi-educated woman I knew who mentioned the rhythm method. I know too many women who have gotten pregnant while using this method for me to believe in it. But I am so desperate to get pregnant that I would follow the hand-signaled advice of a street mime as long as she was pregnant.

On the days that the chart says that I am fertile, we have sex twice. At first, this is fun.

Since I was twenty years old, I have been excited by my husband's body; he's tall, lean, with a square jawline, saved from being too masculine by huge dimples. I enjoyed approaching him with a mixture of play and desire and he still grinned at me like I was new every time I came. But now as we learn how to have sex for the purpose of conception, I feel us slipping into new roles. I am the director of reproductive sexual relations, tracking ovulation, scheduling sex, and testing to find out if the production target was met. Reginald is no longer my lover, but my compliant worker who wants to be a father and who trusts that I know what I'm doing with an ovulation chart. We have gone from play to purpose, appetite to ambition. Sometimes this shift changes the easy way in which our bodies have always made shapes together into a more bumbling, amateurish kind of dance. We sally forth, half joking about how this peculiar version of sex makes us weary and recalling our younger selves who never could have imagined such a thing.

Reginald has always teasingly described our relationship with the insipid language of corporate America to make me laugh: "We are a team. There's no *I* in team." And I always respond with a laugh and an eye roll because we know that we are not a team, some artificial unit of mostly strangers formed in the name of corporate profit. We are two people trying to share our whole lives with each other until death. When we are successful, we are one. When we are not, we are still trying to be one. But the failure to conceive does not allow for that theory of marriage because natural conception requires two separate bodies with working reproductive parts. And when the parts don't work, we wonder quietly and sometimes aloud if something is wrong with one of our bodies. Neither of us wants our body to be the problem. But that also means secretly hoping that whatever is wrong lives in the other's body.

• • •

I have not always been this woman longing for a biological child. Once, when a colleague in her forties told me she was undergoing fertility treatments, I asked her if she had considered adoption. When she replied that adoption was not the right path for her, I judged her, thinking how conventional she was despite all her flowing hippy skirts and wild hair. She asked if I wanted children, and I told her maybe, but that I was in no hurry since I would be fine with adoption. I would later describe her to a friend as in love with her own genetic material.

Now I am the one who is in love with my own genetic material. I stare in the mirror at my face, the mouth and nose that take up too much space, the eyes that make me look surprised even when I am sleepy. And I see my father's mother, my grandmother Bernice, looking back at me in black-and-white, the only colors I have seen her in.

I call my mother and ask her to send me a photo of my paternal grandmother. When a brown envelope arrives in the mail, there are two photos inside. One of my maternal grandmother, plump and pleasant-faced, and also the photo that I have been waiting for: a portrait of Bernice, who stares back at the camera with her lips pressed together in a straight line as if smiles had yet to be invented. Her dark hair is parted down the middle and smoothed into two tight braids that loop. Her enormous eyes on her narrow triangular face might have made her look alien were it not for the liquid-y sad shine of her gaze that says, *I am alive in spite of something.*

When I show the photo to my husband, he takes two steps back and stares as if Bernice might jump out and strike him.

"It's like seeing you, just in another time."

I recognize the mixture of wonder and fear on his face. I have seen it my whole life every time I encountered old people who had known my grandmother and aunt.

I snap a photo of the picture and send it to a friend with no message. She texts back, a string of blue-faced wow emojis.

"My grandmother," I write back.

She texts: "No—you!"

I frame the photo and put it on the nightstand next to my bed. I want to wake up to this proof of belonging, this resemblance that made old Black women who knew there was more to this world than flesh and dirt look at me and see the ghosts of my ancestors. I talk to my grandmother without words, asking her to send me another one of us.

I am eight years old and I keep having the same dream that my mother has died. I sit on a church pew in front of an open, shiny green casket, the same color as the Thunderbird she drives. The church is empty except for me and her body. I cry until my body shakes me awake. But even awake, I am still certain that she is dead. I lie in bed until morning light bleeds through the heavy pink drapes, making my room glow like the inside of an oven. I get up and walk into the hallway, dreading the moment that someone will appear and tell me that she is really gone.

When I find her sitting on the sofa with a head full of pink rollers, I wrap my arms around her and tell her that I love her.

She pulls away. "What has gotten into you? You too old for this nonsense," she says.

I am six years old and standing next to a gravestone with my name on it. The little girl with my name is buried here along with her mom, who was my father's sister, and her dad. There were others who died in the wreck too, some who are buried here, and some who are buried at the other cemetery that looks just like this one. I cannot keep up with all the dead people. I am not sure how many there are because I have never heard anyone list all their names at once or tick them off on their fingers one by one. I do not ask what happened to the girl because I already know what my father will say, the same thing he said when I asked why I have just one grandmother. *The wreck.*

I try hard to imagine this thing called "wreck." I see toy race cars in the hands of a giant toddler who bangs them together, stretching the word "wreck" into a sound effect. But the bodies. I cannot picture what happens to the bodies. In my mind, they transform instantly into something glittery like the floating orb that turns into Glinda the Good Witch in *The Wizard of Oz*. But that cannot be true because the bodies are here in the red dirt under our feet.

My father presses the metal legs of a large spray of red and white fake carnations into his sister's grave, grunting at the resistance of the dry, hard ground.

My mother places a smaller arrangement on San's grave. "These really are pretty flowers, ain't they?" she says.

"Um-hmm." My father nods. He steps back to make sure the flower stand is straight.

"San's hair was real red," my mother says. "Wasn't it, John? Not like sandy red either. Real red, like white folks' hair. Right, John?"

"Yup." My father nods.

I do not understand why my mother is asking these questions even though she knows all the answers. When we came here the last time on Mother's Day, or Father's Day, or whenever it was, she asked the same questions and my father gave the same answers. At home she tells her own stories, mostly about when she was a little girl playing with her brothers and all the crazy things they did, like swinging on a rope over a deep ditch filled with dirty water even though they couldn't swim, or the time she was playing at a neighbor's house and their dog attacked her but everyone in the house was too drunk to hear her screams. *It's really a wonder none of us got killed,* she'd say at the end. But Daddy's family did get killed. Maybe this is why my mother does not tell stories here. She just recites information, going on and on about what they looked like.

"Her mama—Maggie Jo's hair wasn't like that, was it?" my mother asks. "Where do you think she got it from?"

"Some of Daddy's people had that hair. You know my cousin Rose and them got a bit of it too," my father says.

Today we are alone, but the last time we were here, a man and a woman were at the other end of the cemetery with their backs to us. The man was squatting in front of a grave of loose red dirt and the woman stood over him, her shoulders shaking. The man was saying something, and the woman said something back and started making a keening sound. I could not hear his words, but I bet he was not talking about the color of a dead girl's hair. My parents glanced at them and looked away like they did when we saw a man and a woman kissing in line at the Kmart.

"How tall was your sister?" my mother asks. "Was she tall like your mama?"

I can do whatever I want now. I am hidden without having to hide. I walk behind the grave marker and lean over to look at my name upside down.

CHAPTER 2

I am ten years old when, one morning, I climb into the car with my mother as usual to be dropped off at school before she heads to work. But today, my mother backs out of the driveway and heads in the opposite direction of my school.

"Where are we going?" I ask.

"To see Dr. M."

I had been to the doctor less than a month before when I was sick with a fever, and again a few months before that for my checkup. "What for?"

"To talk about your weight. You look like a gnat. The doctor can give you something, like a pill to make you gain some weight."

I picture my pediatrician, Dr. M., a smiling gray-haired white man, handing me a glowing pill that could transform me from skinny to round. A new me, curvy like my mother, emerges from the golden light. I like the way she looks, but my stomach trembles at the idea of losing the thing that makes me special, a body that looks like my father's family. I shake off this feeling because I know that Dr. M. can't really transform me. My mother believes that doctors know everything. But I have been seeing Dr. M. since I was little, and at nearly every appointment, he can't even remember where he left his pen.

When we arrive, a nurse takes us to an examining room. She checks my blood pressure, measures my height, and weighs me while my mother sits in a chair in the corner humming. When the nurse is done, she announces that Dr. M. is not in today. A new doctor, Dr. G., who has just joined the practice, will be filling in today.

We wait, but Dr. G. does not come. My mother checks her watch and worries her hands.

Finally, a young man with a head full of dark hair walks in and says hello without looking up from his chart.

"What seems to be the problem?"

My mother answers from the little chair she sits in behind him. "She's not gaining any weight, Doctor. Do you think you could give her something to make her eat?"

The doctor spins on his heels to face her and flips through the papers in his folder. "She showed normal weight gain and growth in the last year and every year."

My mother starts to speak but hesitates.

"Well?" the doctor says.

"She's not eating. You see how skinny she is? Do you think she's eating enough?" My mother is talking, but her voice is small and faint like a child's echo.

"She's eating something or she wouldn't be sitting here now, would she?"

"But I can't get her to eat her dinner."

The doctor scans my mother's plump body and shakes his head in exasperation.

Finally, he turns to look at me. "So you didn't eat your dinner yesterday?"

"I ate some of it," I say.

"What did you eat instead of dinner?"

"Oreo cookies and potato chips."

"And where, pray tell, did you get that?" he asks.

I look down, aware that he already knows the answer. "From my mother," I mumble into my chest. I had gotten the snacks from the stash of junk food she gave me.

He spins back toward my mother. "Well, there you have it! Mystery solved! Stop giving her the junk, and she'll eat her dinner. Now, is there anything else I can help *you* with today?"

My mother shrinks smaller into the chair, and says in a little-girl voice, "Can you maybe give her an iron pill to help with her appetite?"

He sighs and walks toward the door. "You can get some Geritol at the drugstore, but if she won't eat dinner, I'm not sure how you're going to get her to take that stuff."

He walks out and closes the door behind him.

My mother stares at the door as if she is expecting him to come back and say that he is playing a practical joke on us.

I jump off the table and reach for my jacket in her lap. She pulls back at the sight of my hand.

"My jacket," I say. "I just want my jacket."

She gives it to me, still frowning at the door.

"We better go," I say.

When we get in the car, she drives away in silence, her grip opening and closing on the steering wheel.

I want to be happy that the doctor has taken my side and said there is nothing wrong with me or my body. But my stomach lurches as if the car is filled with the stench of rotten meat. I cannot name the thing that is wrong with Dr. G.'s "Well?" or explain how he stopped some of my mother's thoughts in her throat and made the rest into questions. But by age ten, I have already bought candy from white cashiers who put my change on the counter to avoid touching my hands. I have sat in the car with my mother at a red light while Klansmen in full regalia handed out pamphlets with the earnestness of Jehovah's Witnesses trying to save souls. I have heard Dr. G.'s tone before from white men and women in car dealerships, parks, malls, restaurants—a tone that says, *I did not work this hard to have to deal with the likes of you.* I know that Dr. G. probably wishes he didn't have to see me or my mother or anyone Black. And I know my mother made a mistake when she asked him for help.

I do not want to think about how he treated my mother, so I try to concentrate on what he said about me—that there is nothing wrong with me. I am not an insect in need of transformation. But to the doctor, my mother and I are both just gnats.

At my gynecologist's office, I wait in a room painted a salmon pink vaguely reminiscent of the vaginal canals pictured in the anatomical diagrams on the walls. When a nurse finally calls my name, I follow her down the hallway to an examination room where she weighs me and leaves me to undress. I put on a blue gown and pull out the charts I created to track my ovulation. They are strangely beautiful with colorful dots and lines rising and falling, like the musical notes of a predictable melody. The graphs prove that I am ovulating like clockwork.

A hard knock on the door and Dr. O. sweeps in and says in a loud voice, "Well, hello there!" Her smile is enormous, huge white teeth against smooth, dark brown skin.

"How have you been and what brings you in today? You're not due for a while," she says.

"I'm good, but I'm trying to get pregnant and—"

"Oh, that's wonderful! Now, you know I don't deliver babies any-more. So once you are six weeks along, I'll pass you on to an OB. Okay?"

"Yes, of course. But I wanted to see you because I think something might be wrong."

Dr. O. looks from the chart in her hand to the homemade charts in mine. "What are those?" she says.

"They're basal body temperature charts."

"What? You know better than that nonsense. Why are you doing this?" she says.

"I wanted to make sure that everything was working, and I read a book that said charting was the easiest way to be sure I'm ovulating."

"Can I see those?"

I hand the charts to her, and she shuffles through the papers, frowning at each one like it is a vulgar note passed between sixth graders.

"I can't believe you're doing this. It's just voodoo! Do you know how many babies are running around here because books like that told someone that they couldn't get pregnant at certain times? What makes you think they can tell you when you'll get pregnant when they can't even tell you when you won't?"

"Well, they aren't telling me. I keep track of my temperatures. The idea is to empower yourself by better understanding your own body."

She waves the papers at me. "This is only going to keep you from getting pregnant by causing anxiety! How long have you been trying?"

"Six months."

She lets out a half laugh and says through her smile, "Six months is nothing. Look, my advice is to stop trying to plan everything and enjoy your husband."

"I'd love to, but I have to be realistic. I'm thirty-six years old. In my field, I see it all the time: women my age who've delayed pregnancy and by the time they start trying, it's too late."

"They are thirty-six-year-old *white* women. Most of them were probably infertile by thirty. That doesn't have anything to do with us."

I open my mouth to object, to try to convince her that I need help even though I am Black, but she puts down the charts and holds up her hand.

"The main reason why middle-class Black women are always in my office complaining that they can't get pregnant is that they just aren't having enough sex. They are working hard and thinking hard, and they are too busy scouring the internet and reading books about getting pregnant to have sex. Ever notice you don't see poor Black women in the same age range having this problem? That's because they are having sex instead of plotting to take over the world. You are not infertile, just impatient."

Voices inside me begin to argue with her, to accuse her of stereotyping middle-class Black women as blindly ambitious and poor Black women as oversexed, but I say none of this because this is the first time anyone has ever told me that Blackness, rather than making me vulnerable, could instead protect me from something: infertility.

She sits down on a stool in front of me, inhales deeply, and lets out another loud sigh. "Listen," she says in a soft voice I have never heard her use. "You can't study for this. It's not like writing a book where you get to plan everything. Getting pregnant isn't like that, and neither are babies. Be patient. You've got to let go." She waves the charts at me. "Now I'm going to tear these up. Okay? They're just going to make things worse."

I hesitate. The charts are lovely and reassuring. But so is she, this beautiful woman who refuses to even consider the possibility that I might be infertile.

"Okay?" she says, folding the charts in half.

I nod and relief passes over my body as I decide to believe her.

My friend Rowan says there is some "magic" at work in the conception of a human baby. Right now, as we eat lunch at his dining room table that I once sat on at the Crate and Barrel outlet to ward off eager bargain shoppers, a surrogate is carrying his and his partner's unborn child.

"With all this science, I never thought it would take us three tries at IVF to get pregnant, but it did," he says. "And just look at Morgan. How do you explain that she got pregnant by accident, after conceiving her first two kids through IVF?" With Rowan's surrogate on the opposite coast, our friend Morgan, whose baby is due the same month as Rowan's baby, serves as a model, helping him to imagine the changing body of the surrogate.

He pauses for a moment, swallowing with closed eyes like he is trying not to choke. He is not thinking about his baby or Morgan's. He is thinking about the one who will never be born. At their first ultrasound, a doctor had told him and his partner that they were having twins. By the next ultrasound, one of the fetuses had disappeared. The doctor called the disappearance "vanishing twin syndrome," but he offered little explanation. This omission sent Rowan on a whirlwind of research to learn more about why and how a fetus could vanish.

I study Rowan's face, at once happy and mournful.

"Magic," he says with a half smile and a shrug. "It's the only way to explain that even with all this technology, there's still so much that we don't know."

I put down my fork, ready to argue for science, even though I know what he is talking about. I think of a baby recently born to another friend who had been told that her chances of getting pregnant and carrying a child to term were less than 1 percent. In the end, all it had taken for her to reproduce was a martini and a horny husband. Didn't we all know of babies like this? Nearly everyone I know who is the third born, including me, had been what is politely termed "a surprise" and, impolitely, "an accident."

But the idea of magic frustrates me because I cannot see, control, or even be sure of such a nebulous force. Magic cannot be graphed like body temperatures on an ovulation chart, or disciplined like sex timed to the hour of peak fertility. "Magic" sounds too much like a mystery, something random, unsolvable. I have little reference for this hippy version of the occult. I picture a god dressed in a top hat and tails shaping lives with giant jazz hands. I talk to my ancestors regularly now, but they are not a sideshow magic act. Like me, they are evidence of a legacy of survival among people who were never meant to survive. They are dead, but don't they also live in me, still as visible in my body as they had been when I was a little girl, following my father from one old lady's house to another? My ancestors are not magic. They are facts. They lived long enough to create new generations because they battled the poverty and violence of the Jim Crow South.

If I tell Rowan these things in my clunky words, he will think that I am endorsing his idea of "magic," or worse, that I am losing my mind. So I tell him about Dr. O. instead.

"My doctor says that I am fertile. That Black women do not have to worry as much about infertility as they age as white women do." As I repeat my doctor's words, I can hear the false note in my own voice, conveying a question instead of a statement.

Rowan sips from a glass of water and shoots me a sad look. For a moment I am back in Dr. O.'s office, but this time the light that bounces off her white teeth, reassuring me, blinks like a cheap neon sign at a gas station.

"Listen," he says. "Every woman I've talked to about this infertility road has said the same thing. A gynecologist swore that they were fertile. Maybe you are. But after experiencing two failed procedures, despite genetic testing to determine the embryos were viable, I don't even know what doctors mean by 'fertile' anymore."

Other people would have heard Rowan saying there's an element of getting pregnant that goes beyond science. That I should wait for the magic. But I am my mother's daughter. *If something is wrong, you go to the doctor.* I decide to get another doctor, a better doctor, a specialist, fast.

I go home and research fertility doctors in my area. All of them report their in vitro fertilization success rates to the CDC, which then publishes these numbers on the internet. I locate a well-regarded reproductive endocrinologist who trained in New York City, aka the land of the over-forty first-time mom.

As I dial the number, I hear Dr. O. scolding me, "You are not infertile, just impatient," the words like a shield slipping from my grip. A woman answers, announcing the name of the fertility clinic. She puts me on hold, and I reason with myself in a whisper while I wait: "I'm impatient. It's true. But what if that's not the only thing wrong with me?"

The receptionist interrupts. "Hello? Can I help you?" I schedule the soonest available appointment, which is over a month away, as if I have all the time in the world to spare. I hang up and tell myself that I will probably be pregnant by then.

• • •

Weeks pass, during which I must submit to a battery of tests that seem as rigorous as those used to clear an astronaut for takeoff. I fill vial after vial with blood and urine. Yet all Reginald has to do is jack off in a cup and give one measly blood sample. The bodily fluids that have been collected are dispatched to various labs and technicians, and results shared with the fertility clinic before we even arrive for our first appointment with the doctor.

At the appointment at last, I sit on a table covered in noisy paper and wait for the doctor while Reginald sits in a chair beside me. Next to his chair is a small end table with magazines. All of them are parenting magazines with pictures of round-faced babies grinning maniacally on the front. We had already passed by two bulletin boards covered in redheaded babies, bald-headed babies, and an uncanny number of twins, each one goofily unaware of its doppelgänger.

A quick knock and Dr. Z., a dark-haired woman with a bob and a quick smile, walks in. She moves across the room in reasonable black pumps that tap like toy hammers on the tile floor. She stops in front of me and sticks her hand out with a little bounce like a cheerleader. Her hand feels soft and warm in mine.

She asks me to put my feet in stirrups and recline. Then she turns the lights off and picks up a fat probe, which she covers with a large dollop of clear gel and slides into my body. Next to the table I am lying on is a computer screen that lights up with a fuzzy image that looks like a video of outer space. She uses one hand to shift the probe around inside my body while using the other hand to maneuver a computer mouse that draws lines and measurements on the screen.

I watch the image on the screen as if it is someone else's body even though I can feel the probe pressing and pinching my insides.

"You have cysts on your ovaries, large ones on both sides." She points to two blobs on the screen.

Reginald leans toward the fuzzy screen from his chair.

"What kind of cysts?" I say.

"Well, cysts are pretty normal after ovulation. When an egg bursts from the ovary, sometimes it leaves a cyst behind, but it shouldn't last. We'll need to monitor these to make sure they go away before we can stimulate your ovaries."

"Stimulate my ovaries?"

"Normally, we'd give you a Clomid challenge test, to see how many eggs you have and whether they are viable. We administer a drug called Clomid to see how your body responds. If you respond well, we can then use the same drug to stimulate the egg follicles before we inseminate you with your husband's sperm. But we can't administer that drug with cysts on your ovaries. They could rupture."

"What's in the cysts?" I ask.

"Could be fluid. Could be solid. We don't really know until we go in to see." She removes the probe and turns on the lights. "We're going to monitor the cysts first to see if they go away on their own. Maybe we go in, but hopefully we do nothing."

She offers me a thin smile, but I am already drowning in her words. My body shifts from side to side like pondweed each time she hedges.

"What do you mean by 'go in'?" I say.

"We have time to wait since you still have more testing to do anyway. Why don't you get dressed, and we'll talk about the options in my office."

I want to tell her that I am not infertile, that my doctor said so, that I am just here for a little boost or for her to find out what is wrong with my husband's sperm. I am not here to discuss surgery. But before I can form the words, she slips out the door.

I stare at Reginald, tears already collecting in the corners of my eyes. "What is she talking about?"

He sucks in a breath, hands me my pants, and says, "I don't know. Let's go see."

I rise from the table, a wet thing leaning where I had walked in straight and true just ten minutes before. My back aches as I step into my pants. I had come to the doctor feeling fine and, with a word, she has transformed me into a patient.

In her office, Dr. Z. sits behind a large desk. We sit down across from her, and she smiles at us like we are contestants on a game show.

"Are you talking about surgery?" I ask.

"Well, not necessarily," she replies, looking at Reginald as if he is the one who asked the question. "We don't know if surgery will be required."

Even though I have heard this strange "we" that doctors sometimes use, I have never felt the cruel deception in it as sharply as I do now. She is pretending that we will arrive at a decision together, but only one of us has a medical degree, a medical license, and the ability to determine whether I will require surgery before she will treat me for infertility. If there was a real "we," I'd probably say let's chance it with the cysts. But she would have never mentioned surgery if she thought that was a safe option. Maybe the "we" is intended to be kind, to make me feel empowered, which would be fine if she was talking about acne creams. But there is no "we" in a surgery. One of us would be under general anesthesia, the other cutting through muscle and fat.

Dr. Z. keeps talking about an additional test I need while I struggle to focus. My mind keeps backtracking to the idea that I might have to have surgery. Until now, surgery has been something that happens to other bodies, sick bodies, not my body. Am I sick? My belly cramps as if I am.

Reginald's hand squeezes mine and I try to make my way back into the room.

"In the meantime," Dr. Z. says, "I'm going to need one more test from you, an HSG. It stands for hysterosalpingogram. It's a test where we put dye in your uterus and fallopian tubes to make sure you don't have any blockages. The good thing, though, is that if you do have blockages, the pressure from the dye will usually clear them."

"So there's a possibility that blocked tubes could be the problem?" I ask.

"Well, that's what we have to figure out. You see, your FSH numbers are low."

"What does that mean?" Reginald says.

"FSH is a hormone. Low FSH numbers mean that a woman is fertile. High FSH indicates that egg reserves are low. If the FSH is really high, it points to menopause."

"So my FSH is good?" I say.

"Right. But we can't do the testing to confirm your egg reserves with cysts present. If one of them were to rupture, it could damage the ovaries."

I struggle to follow the circling list of what is right and wrong with my body, but my fear tightens the muscle in my chest until I feel like I am in a house on fire, darting from one room of flames to the other. I have cysts that are bad, but my hormones are good. My eggs might be good too, but I can't find out for sure because the test might rupture my ovaries and damage my eggs.

"Could the cysts rupture on their own?" I say.

"Well, they could, but we are getting ahead of ourselves. First, we need to set you up with an HSG test to see if there are blockages and clear them. That might be enough to get you pregnant."

"But what about the cysts?" I say.

"They won't interfere with the HSG test."

"So they can stay?" I say.

"Well, we hope they go away on their own."

"And if they don't?"

She fidgets in her chair for a moment before answering, "Then, yes, we would need to remove them surgically."

I take a deep breath, but when I let it out, my shoulders do not fall. Reginald looks at me and presses his lips into a weak smile.

"Before we worry about surgery, let's get this HSG test taken care of so we can move forward."

She writes out two prescriptions and hands them to me. "The first is for an antibiotic to make sure you don't develop an infection from the dye. The second is for one Valium. You should take it one hour prior to the HSG, just to help you relax. Tends to make things a little easier."

"So the test is painful?"

"No, no. It's not painful, but some patients report discomfort. The Valium will help you relax to make the whole process more comfortable."

She smiles and says, "Okay. Let's get you pregnant." This is our cue to leave.

Reginald stands up and thanks her. I nod and smile, but I keep sitting as if I am waiting for further instructions. Dr. Z. stands up with her face still frozen in a smile and puts her hands in the pockets of her white coat. I have no questions other than the ones I've already asked, but I do not feel like I am finished, even though clearly she is. I am in a cross-country race in junior high school again, competing against the one girl who could always outrun me. We just ran side by side for two miles, but now, halfway through mile three, she pulls away, her strides getting longer, faster, while I struggle just to maintain my pace. This is where Dr. Z. and I are now, mile three, and she has left me plodding along in the dirt. I will my body out of the chair, moving like a woman who knows she has already lost a race.

O n the day of the HSG appointment, I am sure that it will be the cure for my infertility. On the internet, I found tons of accounts from women who had gotten pregnant soon after the procedure. A friend once mentioned that she had this test and that it was painful, but she got pregnant shortly after without even trying. I scoured the internet to see if others reported pain, but the responses varied. Some said they felt nothing; others described uncomfortable pressure; still others reported terrifying pain. The one thing they all agreed on was that the test took around five minutes, and I am sure that I can survive five minutes of dye being shot into my privates.

Reginald and I arrive at an office that is bigger and even more luxurious than Dr. Z.'s regular office. There is a large fish tank, plush seating, and big colorful artwork on the walls. I walk up to a young woman at an enormous circular desk and hand her the prescription that Dr. Z. had given me.

"Oh," she says, "we don't do the HSG test in this building. You'll have to go outside. Just follow the walkway to your right and you'll see the correct building."

We head back out and walk about one and a half city blocks to another door. Inside, we find a sparse clinical space filled with small plastic chairs. Unlike the tasteful carpets in the other waiting room, the floor of this one is covered in shiny brown synthetic tiles. Instead of the bright, broad custom blinds that cover the windows of the main office, this one has crooked brown standard-size blinds hanging row after row over the large windows. All the blinds are closed. A fake wood desk sits against the wall, but no one sits behind it. We take a seat in the empty waiting area, wondering aloud if this could be the right place.

A smiling woman in yellow scrubs steps out of the door behind the desk. "You must be Cassandra," she says. "I'm Julie. We're ready for you. What time did you take your Valium?"

"About fifty minutes ago. But I don't feel anything."

"That's okay. It's a small dose, just to help you relax a little. Come this way."

Reginald stands up to follow me, but Julie explains that he'll have to stay in the waiting area.

I follow her through a door and am surprised to see that there is no long corridor, but instead we're quickly in one large room with a table, a device that looks like an X-ray machine, and a curtained area off to the side.

She points to the curtain and tells me to go remove my clothes and put on a gown. When I step out, another smiling woman, a fair redhead with cheerful freckles, is standing next to Julie. She introduces herself as Melissa and gestures for me to lie on the table.

I lie down and look up at the two of them. The weirdness of the whole scene registers. I am alone with these two women, and I am not even sure who they are. They definitely are not doctors or nurses or they would have introduced themselves that way. Perhaps they are like X-ray techs, the two of them alone taking pictures of uteruses all day. But the waiting room is empty except for Reginald. For a brief moment, I wonder if I am in the right place, or if I have wandered into someone else's appointment for some procedure that I know nothing about.

"The first part of the procedure is like a Pap smear," Julie explains. "I'm going to insert a speculum. Then I'll use a catheter to inject the dye. You may feel some pressure. Then I'm going to take a few pictures, to see if the dye is making it through. Okay?"

Melissa nods at me but does not explain her role.

I feel the speculum and an uncomfortable pinch that I assume is the catheter. The X-ray machine hums louder. I feel pressure and then cramping in my abdomen, worse than any menstrual cramps I have ever had. The pain increases, and I grit my teeth as I feel myself becoming something else. I try to hang on, to be me and not just a body. I grunt: "If this is what having a baby feels like, maybe I don't want one." Instead of laughing, the women look at each other wide-eyed with somber expressions.

I open my mouth to speak again, but my voice cracks, and I scream as my belly explodes with pain. Then I am the pain. I see Julie's mouth moving, and I see Melissa's eyes widen even more. She tries to say something like "Just a little longer." But her voice fades and all I can hear is the loud hum of the X-ray machine and my own screams.

Then it ends. The room goes silent, but I do not move. Fear holds me fast to the table. I almost suspect that nothing real has happened. Only the sad look in Melissa's eyes confirms that the pain was real.

Julie sticks out her hand to help me up. I see my hand take hers and feel myself being pulled upright. I look down at the table, expecting to see the screaming woman still lying there.

"There are pads on the little table in there behind the curtain. You'll need them because the dye will start to leak," Melissa says.

I dress, already feeling the warm liquid leaving my body. As I step out from behind the curtain, I stare again at the table where I had become one long scream. Julie leads me to the door and back into the waiting area.

"My god, are you okay?" Reginald says. "I could hear you screaming!"

"I think so," I say.

"I nearly came running back there!" His eyes move from me to Julie, who is still standing next to me.

Julie ignores him and walks behind the desk. A printer begins to buzz. She hands me a black-and-white image of my uterus. It looks like a negative with dark fluid floating through two curved tubes.

"It looks clear," she says through a wide smile. "The doctor will talk to you about it, but you seem to have good dispersion." When I don't respond she leans toward me and says louder, "It's good news."

"Don't forget to continue with your antibiotic tomorrow, and you might have some mild cramping," she continues. "Good luck." She disappears behind the door, leaving me and Reginald standing in the waiting area.

"Do you need to sit down?" Reginald says.

I need to sit down, but I also want to leave this isolated building— the twisted blinds that hide bodies, the empty waiting room that traps screams, and the exam table that is also the scene of crimes.

I make my way to the door and Reginald opens it for me. But before I cross the threshold, I feel the first of the cramps that Julie warned me about. Unlike the pain I'd experienced on the table, this wringing out of my belly like a dirty dishrag feels familiar. This is the pain that has pursued me for twenty-two years, month after month, with the persistence of a stalker.

I am fourteen years old when pain wakes me. First a dull ache in my back, then the pain radiates to my abdomen, curling my body into a C. I climb out of bed, hoping that movement will help, but a wave of nausea carries me to the bathroom. I stare at the toilet but nothing happens. I sit down to pee and sticky redness greets me.

I smile even in the midst of this pain because I have been waiting for this moment. I am the very last of my friends to get a period. I have stockpiled menstrual pads, samples given out yearly at school by the female PE teachers to the students in the girls-only health classes since the fourth grade. They told us that we could have "discomfort." But no one said a period could make me feel like my body was collapsing from the inside out.

I take Tylenol, but it does not touch the long spasms that consume me.

My mother notices that I am dragging one leg behind me as if I have been struck by shrapnel.

"You got that from me, for sure," she says. She talks about period pains that prevented her from going to school or work. The telling carries her away and she closes her eyes and winces, even though she has not had a period since her hysterectomy soon after I was born.

"Men don't know a thing about what us women go through. You sure got that from me. I was just like that." She talks in the same excited voice she uses when she sees me in gold hoop earrings. *You look like me some. I don't care what they say.* Or when my clothes create the illusion that I have gained weight. *You look a little better. I used to be skinny until I got grown and started filling out.* It is as if she is trying to reclaim my body as something that belongs to her, not my father and his dead family. Other times, it seems like my body is a ghost, a reminder of a broader past that she also wants to forget. *Most Black folks was skinny back then 'cause we didn't have enough to eat. Couldn't get no kind of help either 'cause white folks wouldn't even let you stand in line with them for government help.* Either way, I always recognize her contempt for my body. But now I am hurting too much to tell her that I am not like her and that we both know who I am like.

For three days the pain worsens until suddenly it and the blood are gone.

I buy a small calendar with a picture of kittens on the front, and I try to plot out the days so that I might prepare myself before my period comes back. But my period does not know about the calendar and shows up whenever it pleases, each cycle hurting me more than the one before. Now from the first sight of blood until it disappears, I hold my swollen belly as if it were as separate from me as a baby.

My mother makes an appointment for me to see her gynecologist, Dr. B. Even though I don't remember him, I know Dr. B. by reputation because my mother, who admires all doctors, brags about him most. He is the dashing young doctor who delivered me, even though he was not at the time her doctor. Her usual ob-gyn and a few other doctors at the hospital were debating a C-section when someone decided to consult the new doctor right out of med school. Dr. B. was confident that though I was breech, he could get me out without cutting my mother open. The others decided to let the young doctor try his hand,

and with my mother knocked out cold, he pulled my body out of hers with forceps that left a permanent bite mark on my ass. Since then, she has worshipped him as the doctor who saved her from the knife.

Every time my mother praises Dr. B., my sister's whole body goes still. She stopped seeing Dr. B. as soon as she was grown enough to move out of the house. My mother accuses my sister of not liking him because *he gets on you about getting fat. You know, it's not just you. He's gotten on me about my weight too. And my friend Lana too.* My sister frowns but never responds.

On the day of the appointment, my mother stays in the examining room while I undress and put on a gown. When the doctor comes in, she greets him, but he barely looks up at the two of us. He stares at an open folder in his hand, and I stare at a man much older than I was expecting.

"So, you've been having some issues with cramping?" he says.

I say yes, but before I can explain, my mother chimes in. Her voice is so high and shaky that I cannot make out all the words. When she finishes, she clenches her fists at her sides and swings them like a little kid in trouble.

"You can step out now, so I can do the exam," he says to her.

My mother nods and walks out the door.

He directs me to lean back and put my feet in the stirrups. I lie down and feel damp, cold steel touching me and then burning pain between my legs.

"Relax," he says.

But I do not know how to relax. My hands clench the edges of the table and my breath catches somewhere between my chest and my throat. Metal squeaks against metal, and the pain increases, and then a sharp pinch grips me from inside.

He withdraws the speculum, and before I can let out a breath of relief, he shoves a wet hand into my anus. I let out a yelp and try to regain control of my bowels.

"Relax!" he barks.

But I cannot stop hanging on to the table. I feel his hand pressing on the wall between my anus and uterus, stretching me out like I am a new balloon.

Finally, he withdraws his hand and walks over to a sink, where he washes. As he walks out the door, he says over his shoulder, "Get dressed."

The door closes behind him, and I stand up and wipe myself with the gown. The burning between my legs is still there. I try to put my underwear on while standing up, but the muscles in my thighs feel loose and out of control. I sit down on a chair and dress.

A nurse sticks her head in the door and tells me the doctor will be back in a moment and that she will go get my mother.

My mother arrives before the doctor does. She gives me a quick nod and looks away like she does when we are at the mall and a Black man she does not know greets her. I look at her, questions rising from deep in my belly and crashing into one another in my throat until what comes out is "Why didn't you tell me?"

She stares at her fingers, bending and stretching all ten as if she has just learned how they work. "That's just part of it," she says. "You'll get used to it. Part of growing up."

I am about to object when Dr. B. walks in with a vague smile on his face and announces that he will write a prescription for a painkiller stronger than any of the over-the-counter ones available at the drugstore.

With the angry hand that was just inside my ass, he writes a prescription and gives it to my mother. "Make sure she doesn't take more than one every four hours or so or her stomach might hurt," he says.

"What is it?" I ask.

"It's called ibuprofen," he says.

"Isn't that just Advil, like at the store?"

My mother side-eyes me like I have called the doctor a shyster to his face.

He turns back to my mother. "It's stronger than you can buy over the counter, and with a prescription, your insurance will cover it."

She nods like she has been blessed by a holy man and slips the prescription into the side pocket of her purse.

Try to relax your muscles," Dr. Z. says. She is standing between my legs attempting to insert a probe while Reginald sits nearby. But my body is refusing the probe as if it has a memory and a will of its own. It is still on another paper-covered table waiting for Julie and Melissa to push a button.

Dr. Z. wiggles the slippery probe past my body's resistance. She moves the probe around my uterus and frowns at the screen.

"Cysts?" I ask.

"Yes. I'm afraid so. And they are not small," she says.

Reginald reaches over and grabs my hand.

"Get dressed and we will talk about this and your test results in my office," she says. She walks out.

I want to run out. I swallow a deep sob.

"I feel sick," I say to Reginald.

"Wait," Reginald says. "Let's just see what she has to say. It's going to be all right."

She is sitting behind her desk when we arrive in her office.

"So the HSG results look fine," she says. "Your tubes are open."

She combs through a file on her desk and pulls out a picture of my uterus, identical to the one that Julie had given me.

"But the pain," I say. "Something must have been blocked."

"You may have experienced some discomfort—"

"No. It was not discomfort. I was screaming in pain!"

She reaches for the picture and holds it up to the light. "Well, your tubes are a bit blunted. Sometimes that can make it—" She pauses. "Uncomfortable."

"I could hear her screaming from the lobby," Reginald says.

Dr. Z. blinks and swallows hard at the sound of his voice. But her eyes are blank, as if she cannot see us.

"Well, at any rate, what I would recommend is that we proceed with IUI, intrauterine insemination. That's when we stimulate the ovaries and then inject sperm at the right time. But before we can do that, we have to do something about these cysts." She glances at a computer screen to her right. "Looks like you've had two periods since I first saw you, and the cysts didn't shed. We can't safely stimulate your ovaries and risk rupturing cysts. We need to remove them."

She picks up a little plastic replica of a human abdomen from a table behind her. "The incisions would be here and here." She points to the corners where the abdomen and thigh meet. "In rare cases, the ovaries can be damaged from surgery, but with cysts this size, we couldn't possibly put you on ovary-stimulating drugs otherwise. This surgery is the only way to proceed with getting you pregnant."

"Is there any chance that these cysts could be cancerous?" Reginald says.

"Oh god," I say. Why hadn't that occurred to me?

Dr. Z. purses her lips. "Yes, but it is not likely."

I glance over at her bookshelf, which is not filled with books but with awards and pictures of a little girl who looks like her.

"What happens if I don't have the surgery?"

"Well, we could wait and monitor the cysts after your next couple of periods to see if your body sheds them. But we'd be postponing fertility treatment. You're . . ." She turns back to her computer screen. "Thirty-six, right?" She frowns at the screen like it just blew cigarette smoke in her face. "Turning thirty-seven in three months."

"Yes," I say in a voice that says, *Look at me, not your computer.*

"Well, if you wait and we have to do surgery later, plus the time you'll need to heal and start getting regular periods, we could be delaying your treatment quite a bit."

I stare down at my lap, trying to imagine what these cysts look like. Reginald asks questions about the surgery and the recovery while I picture an incision in my abdomen that would make it open like the little plastic abdomen in the doctor's hands. I can see them, little balls of fleshy tissue nestled alongside my ovaries, not really bothering anyone, just cozying next to two little egg pouches. But everything seems so small that I am not sure how anyone could cut the cysts without slicing through the eggs too.

"I'll just need you to sign these." Dr. Z. passes papers across her desk to me.

I glance at them and look at her.

"They explain that I talked to you about the surgery and the risks."

"And who will perform the surgery?" I say. "Will it be you or some-one else at the practice?"

"Me," she says, smiling. "It will definitely be me."

I nod and sign as if I am getting my driver's license renewed at the DMV instead of making a contract with a doctor who has just prom-ised to cut my body open within the month.

CHAPTER 3

On the weekends, when my mother is not shopping for clothes and furnishings, she is cleaning our house and telling stories. They are all stories of her childhood. She was one of twelve children, if you count the girl who died trapped between a wall and a bed when she was still a toddler.

My mother moves about the house fluffing pillows, showering tables and dressers in lemon furniture polish, and talking. I follow her from room to room. Her stories are about a gang of children, running in a dusty yard, jumping ditches—but also always on the edge of danger, drowning, or being eaten alive by a mad dog. There is never enough to eat or wear, even though her parents work so much that they rarely appear in her stories.

These are the stories that fill the silences in our house. Unlike the graveside recitations of what my father's family looked like, my mother's accounts of her family are real stories with beginnings, middles, and endings. She does not mention the color of anyone's hair, or how tall they were, unless that detail is part of the action of the story. Her stories are stand-ins for all the stories that my father does not tell about his family. They have only one story that matters, the story of their deaths, and no one, especially not my father, can bear to tell that story.

I have all my mother's stories memorized because she tells each one again and again: the story of the neighbor boy who shot her between the eyes with a BB gun as she stood on her porch. "He could have put my eye out," she says in a dry voice while wiping the coffee table. Another is about her attempt to rescue a cat from a tree. She tries to coax the cat down, but it uses her face as a landing strip, shredding her skin into a bloody mess that took months to heal.

In my favorite story, her teenage brother, Bill, is playing horseshoes with their much younger brother. When Bill loses, she laughs and yells, "Look at old big Bill losing to a little boy!" She glances around the yard, expecting others to join in, but they are all looking in Bill's direction. She follows their eyes. Bill is coming toward her with an ax. She runs into the house, and on this day her father, who was ordinarily off working on the railroad, is inside reading a newspaper. She jumps over his crossed legs screaming for help. Her father looks up to find Bill waving an ax over his head. He yells for Bill to stop, and Bill hands over the ax.

I listen terrified, but my mother laughs hard throughout the story.

I laugh at the end because I love the idea of this world so dense with children who were free to tease and play, run and fight, live or die. I want to be there with them laughing at terror, my feet bare against red dirt.

I try to re-create her world on paper, writing stories in the style of Laura Ingalls Wilder. As I fill a notebook, I replace my lonely childhood with hers. Instead of a sister and brother who are thirteen and eleven years older and busy becoming adults, I live there in a house full of too many children, where there is no space to be alone. The words make her world spring up around me like it is more real than my real life of pretend and make-believe.

When I am more than halfway done, I tell my mother that I am writing a book about her life.

"About what?" she says without looking away from the foyer mirror she is cleaning.

"It's about you when you were little," I say.

She stops wiping and turns to look at me. She leans in close and speaks in a devil's whisper, "You don't write a book about me. Do you hear me? You don't ever write about me."

Spit wets my face and my insides shift as my body moves from pride to shame. I step back, but she moves forward, her voice rising with each step. "That's my business. Not yours. I don't want you telling anything about me. You hear?"

I run to my room, grab the notebook, and stick it in a bureau drawer. I cannot throw out all my hard work, but I also know that I cannot visit the world in the notebook anymore. My mother is right. The stories are not mine. They are her stories that she tells to herself. I just happen to be there when she is telling them.

I vow never to steal stories again. But that night I do it in my sleep. I dream that I am San. Not me, but the other one, the little girl who died in the accident. I reach into a drawer in my dresser, and when I look up at the mirror in front of me, I see big wet eyes and skin tinted green like the only photograph of her that I have ever seen. I touch my face, her face, and see my hand also tinted green. Behind me, my tombstone sits on my canopy bed.

I decide that the surgery to remove cysts from my ovaries will be my story to share or withhold. I will not tell my parents until after it is over. I want to spare my father days of believing that I will die and spare myself from my mother's nonchalance.

But I have never had surgery before. I do not know that "routine procedures" are rarely just ordinary stories with beginnings, middles, and endings. There is a before: a problem, a pain, a deficiency, a thing defined as wrong. The surgery itself, the main event for the patient, is too shrouded in drugs and surgical cloth to be processed into memory, let alone story. Stories written on the body have no resolutions. Then there is an after just as varied as death or life in a body held together by stitches and glue.

I am lying in a room where a nurse has prepared me for surgery by placing an IV in my arm when Dr. Z. comes in and asks why I have written codeine under allergies on all my forms. I tell her the story of my twelve-year-old self, a little girl doubled over on the floor, screaming and begging for help, while her mother stands over her asking if she is pregnant because she cannot make sense of her daughter's pain in any other way. The girl screams an angry no. The mother wrings her hands and says she does not know what to do. *Do you want to go to the emergency room?* she asks. But the pain pins the girl's body. *I can't,* she says. *I can't.* She stays on the ground, her forehead bumping against the carpet as she rocks back and forth. Her mother circles her, asking what her daughter wants her to do. Finally, the girl's belly can take no more. She vomits with such force that the contents of her belly fly across the room as if she is a dragon breathing fire. Relief passes through her body. Her mother runs to get towels and rug cleaner.

Dr. Z. says there is no such thing as an allergy to codeine. "You might have had a sensitivity as a child," she says, "but that was years ago." She will call in a prescription for Tylenol with codeine to help with the pain once I'm home.

She leaves and an anesthesiologist whose smiling face I will not remember replaces her. She asks a few questions about my weight, height, and whether I've been under anesthesia before. Then she injects a milky white substance into my IV that silences me and my body.

My paternal grandfather, Daddy Bluitt, who lives with us in the summers and takes care of me, is the only one I can always depend on to tell one story related to the wreck. He waits until my parents and siblings are at work. Then we watch his favorite shows, *The Price is Right*, *The Young and the Restless*, and later *General Hospital*, with him sitting on the sofa and me sitting cross-legged on the orange-and-brown shag carpet in front of him. When the music comes on just before the commercials break, I turn around to face him like always. I am seven years old and I am waiting for him to share one of the three stories that he likes to tell me about the times he was nearly killed. There was the poisonous spider that bit him, the black cat that climbed onto his chest and tried to suck the breath from his body in the middle of the night, and the wreck. Today, he tells the story about when he was in the hospital on the night after the wreck. He was in the car with the ones who died, but what happened to the car and them is not part of his story.

"I was lying in the hospital bed. Lord, I hurt so bad after I got banged up in the wreck that I'd wake up hollering one minute and be knocked out like somebody hit me the next. So they waited until it was night, you see, before they come in there where I was. They thought I was asleep, but I must have woke up when I heard them talking about what they was gonna do to me."

"Look here." He holds out two palsied index fingers about ten inches from each other. "That needle they came at me with when I was in the bed in the hospital was this long. They was gonna try to stick me while I was asleep. I don't know how, but some kind of way I jumped right up and took off." He smacks his hands together and shoots one arm straight forward in front of him.

I know this story because he tells it so often, but I don't complain because I want him to talk to me about the time before I was born. I try to make the surprised face that Jan makes on *The Brady Bunch*.

"Who was it?"

"The one with the needle was that ol' doctor. Then he had two big goons standing by the door. They grabbed me and brought me back to that bed."

"Good lord," I say and suck my teeth like old ladies do.

"Oh, I raised Cain. I swung at 'em and kept on fighting as best I could. But there wasn't a lot I could do to stop them two scouns. They got me by the arms, see." He holds his elbows out to the side with his arms bent. He squints his eyes and jerks his body from side to side to show me how he tried to fight the men off. The way his body jiggles when he does this makes me want to laugh, but I don't. I know that what he is telling me is important.

"They pushed me down on that bed and flipped me over, like I wasn't nothing but a pancake." He stills his body and expands his big sad eyes so that the pouches beneath them look even bigger.

"That doctor said, 'Hold him still now.' I felt a sting in my back at first. Then it went deep." He arches his spine and throws his head back.

I have to get my last line in fast before *The Young and the Restless* comes back on. "That must have hurt real bad."

"You better believe it did. Hurt so bad I wasn't sure if I was dying or already dead."

Daddy Bluitt eventually dies in St. Louis, where he was living with my father's sister. They send his body to Alabama to be buried next to my grandmother. My aunt and my father's oldest brother and his wife drive to our house from St. Louis in a caravan of their adult children and grandchildren. My father's brother James, an army man we almost never see, flies in from Germany with his wife. The family spread about our house, transforming it from a chilly place where I could hear the fork my father scrambled eggs with tapping on the side of the bowl like a bell, to a place that is warm and loud with voices, asking, telling, coughing, and laughing. No one stays in a hotel. My mother says that when she grew up, Black people could not stay in most hotels. And besides, my parents know how to make room for everyone. Adults get beds, and kids and teenagers sleep on sofas and floor pallets made from the quilts my grandmother and great-grandmother made. My father cooks all day to feed everyone, biscuits and country ham fried in coffee gravy for breakfast, barbecued chicken and ribs in the afternoon. We eat with plates in our laps in any seat we can find.

I am sitting on a love seat eating with a girl cousin when I catch my uncle Conrad staring at me from across the room with wide, pink eyes.

I smile and go back to my food. But he does not look away.

"John T.," he says to my father, who is sitting next to him. "That child. She is just like Maggie Jo." He shakes his head and squints. "I can hardly stand to look at her. My god. Ain't it something?"

My father gives him a soft "Mm-hmm" and shoots me a sad tooth-less smile.

"They talk about you like you aren't even here," my cousin says.

I do not know how to explain to her that for them I am not here. So I just say yeah.

When everyone is done eating, my father pours drinks for all the adults, even my mother, who pretends to sip a glass of wine. She tells me all the time that she does not understand why anyone would want to feel drunk. *I don't want to be out of my mind, feeling like I can't control myself.*

Everyone else is drunk and laughing in no time.

"I thought this was supposed to be sad," my cousin says. "Just look at them. They are acting like this is a party." She asks me to go with her to another room to listen to the mixtapes the teenage cousins brought from St. Louis.

"In a minute," I say. I don't want to miss my chance to look at my uncles and aunt, to search their bodies for something familiar while they are not paying attention to me.

Uncle Conrad has surprised eyes like mine, but his skin is reddish and he is short like Daddy Bluitt's family. He wears a loud print button-down shirt, a large gold necklace, and gold rings on every finger. He has two wives: Aunt Belle, whom he married when she was just four-teen and he was sixteen, and Norah, who, though not a legal wife, goes everywhere with Uncle Conrad and Aunt Belle. I do not know when Norah entered their lives, but I don't think I have ever seen my aunt and uncle without Norah present too. Each time they visit, my mother reminds my father to tell his brother that in our house, Uncle Conrad has to share a room with Belle, his real wife, not Norah, whom we pretend is just Uncle Conrad's friend. Once Uncle Conrad sits his plump body down in a room, he never gets up because the two women wait on him like they have felt the weight of his rings on their skin.

Uncle James resembles my father, tall and light brown, but his face is rounder. He is a career soldier and looks like one, with a clean-shaven face, polished shoes, and crisp button-down shirts. The flashiest thing about him is the cigar he is chewing and his choice of wife, a quick-witted glamorous redhead, whose tall, thin body and light, golden skin make her look like she could be one of us. Aunt Judy, the youngest of my father's siblings, has her mother's eyes and golden skin, but she is short with shapely hips and breasts that seem to all bump into each other as they search for space on her barely five-foot frame.

They tell stories, and even though they are all here because Daddy Bluitt died, all the stories are about their mother, Bernice. *Do you remember that time that Mama kicked that joker's ass?* The jokers are almost always white men who tried to cheat her on the price of cotton or make sideshow acts of her children. *She didn't take no shit off white folks.*

They laugh, but at the edges of each story are the shadows of violence. They are laughing because Bernice didn't die by these men's hands even though they could have killed her and her whole family without fear of punishment.

My cousin begs me again to go with her, but even as I wait for the punch lines and the laughter I know will come from the adults, horror at what could have happened freezes my body.

Remember that time Mama went after Mr. G.?

He had just got some boxing gloves in at his store and he saw us walking by and told me and James to come in and try 'em on. I guess we was about eight and ten. He put 'em on us and told us to spar while him and some other men watched. We bounced around and swung a few times and they just kept egging us on, you know.

When we got home and told Mama what happened, she stood right up and told us to get in the car. She grabbed her shotgun on the way out.

When we pulled up in his yard, he was standing on the porch with a cigar in his mouth. Soon as he saw that gun, he dropped that cigar and ran inside. That fool coulda burnt his own porch down.

Mama got out of the car with her gun and was on that porch in three steps with all them petticoats she used to wear to hide how skinny she was flying behind her. He started yelling then. "Now you go on home, Bernice, before you get into trouble."

Mama walked to the edge of the porch like she was about to leave and fired that gun straight in the air.

Ol' Mr. G.'s voice was high as that gal's right there. He says, "Bernice, I was just showing them . . . Now you know I didn't mean—"

Mama said, "Why don't you come on out of there and tell me again what you was meaning?"

He just kept yelling, "Bernice, please!"

She walked down the stairs and circled that house.

He started wheezing so loud we could hear him. Started having an asthma attack or something.

Mama went back up to the door. And told him he better listen.

"If you ever mess with these boys again, I'll be back here and next time you won't hear me coming. You hear me?"

We couldn't hear him, but he must have said okay 'cause she got back in the car and we went home.

She didn't take no shit off white folks at all.

Everyone is laughing because we know that this is not how stories of Black people who step out of line usually end. Those Black people become waterlogged bodies rising in muddy rivers and bloated faces in magazines and documentaries about the civil rights movement. Bernice escaped that fate. She created a story that no white man wanted to tell: a skinny Black woman holding him hostage in his own house while he wheezed like a sick baby.

My father and his brother do not talk about what it was like to sit in that car while their mother wielded a gun on a white man's property, or whether they stayed up late wondering if white men would arrive in the night. Their laughter is a celebration of the fact that she was willing to die for the sake of dignity and self-respect. They laugh hard like the little boys they once were, and I try to laugh a little with them.

When I wake up after the surgery, Reginald is sitting beside me looking like he's the one who has been operated on. The sides of his mouth are turned down and his eyebrows are high.

"Are you okay?" he says.

I nod. "How about you?"

"I'm fine," he says. But he is not fine. This is not the story either of us has planned.

"What did the doctor say?"

"They got everything. There were cysts on both sides."

"Was anything cancerous?"

"No, no. Everything went well. But the doctor says you have endometriosis, and it has probably done some damage. We're going to have to go straight to IVF, taking your eggs out and trying to inseminate them and put them back, instead of just giving you drugs and inserting sperm."

"So, no cancer?" I say.

He nods.

Relief that I am not dying relaxes my neck, despite the ache that is rising in my torn belly.

He cocks his head at me. "Did you know you had endometriosis?"

"I remember a doctor telling me I had that when I was a teenager, but he never said anything about damage. In fact, he gave me birth control because he thought I'd get pregnant, and I wasn't even sexually active yet."

Reginald frowns in a way that tells me he knows that the doctor was a white man who thought every Black girl was sexually active.

Soon I am at home in my bed. I cannot stop vomiting. The pain from the incisions in my abdomen is too excruciating for me to sit up on my own. Reginald tilts my body forward with one hand and holds a wastebasket in front of me so that I will not drown in my own vomit.

"Why the hell did she give this drug to you?" he asks.

I gag and swallow burning bile. "Call her."

He props my body up with a pillow and places the trash can on my lap before he goes to retrieve his phone. I hear him yelling about what is happening to my body from just outside the door.

He steps back into our bedroom and his eyes widen at the sight of me gagging and clinging to the plastic wastebasket like I am adrift and it is a flotation device.

"She's calling in a prescription for Percocet. But are you going to be okay while I go get it?"

I nod even though I am not sure.

He bounds down the steps and comes back twenty minutes later with two blue pills and a glass of water.

I swallow the pills and wait for relief.

I drift off, but when I wake up, I feel like I am still drifting. My face feels cool and my arms float next to my body. I turn my head, and it is as if I am still facing forward watching my head turn slowly to the right. I shift my body and let my feet hang off the edge of the bed before I stand up to go to the bathroom. I am dizzy, but not in the amusement-park-spinning-teacup-ride way. It is bearable dizziness that makes me feel like I am moving inside a cloud, soft and foggy. I am a ghost only half in this world, and the rest of me is somewhere else, watching. I float down the hallway and back. I begin to dream, even before I lie back on the bed.

In my dream, I am airborne, but I am not so much flying as I have been shot through the air like a spiraling bullet. Just as I feel myself slowing, my body slams to the ground. I am on the side of a road and people are gathering around me. They claim that I am dead, but I can see them, shaking sad faces at me. I don't move until my father's dead sister, Maggie Jo, is standing next to me. Then I get up and lean into her bony hips. She picks me up and holds me tight in her arms. She calls my name, her dead child's name. But when I look at her face, my grandmother looks back with huge eyes. Her mouth is a tight line that does not speak. She points at something long and hard that rises into the sky. Her voice tells me not to look down, but her mouth remains as still as a photograph. I keep my head forward as we walk along the road, with bits of glass and metal crunching under our feet.

· · ·

I call my parents two days after the surgery. My mother answers. When she asks how I am doing I tell her that I had surgery to remove cysts.

"Most women have to have that at some point," she says. "I think your cousin Beatrice had something like that too. Oh, and Nell, she had that. You remember her, don't you? Used to be married to Norris? You remember him—the one that ran off that time."

I don't remember any of them, but I say yes because if I do not, she will tell their stories to make me know them.

"That was one of the reasons why I had the hysterectomy after you," she says.

"So you had cysts too?"

"Well, I don't really remember if it was that, but it was female problems, you know. A lot of women have that."

I ask to speak to my father. She puts me on hold, but I hear her say, "San had surgery," just before he answers the phone.

"San?" he says. "Surgery? What's going on?"

"I'm fine. I just had some cysts removed from my ovaries. It's all over now." The two holes in my abdomen burn as if they know that I am not telling the whole truth.

"All right," he says. "I'm glad you doing fine. Hey, your mama wants to talk to you. You take care now, baby. Love you."

"San," my mother says, "you there?"

"Yeah, Mom."

"Let me tell you what Rita said to me at church about what I had on. I was wearing a royal-blue suit. You won't believe what I got it for.

It was on sale at Dillard's and they had marked it down from a hundred eighty dollars to ninety, and then they marked it down again by thirty percent. It wouldn't have made sense to leave it there at that price."

She finishes the story of the suit by recounting the words of the people who remarked on her beauty when she wore it.

At my post-op check, I lie on a table in the dark and watch the black-and-white screen. This time, I know what I am looking at. White shadows collect around my ovaries on both sides, forming a constellation.

Dr. Z.'s eyes widen. And in a whisper to herself, she says, "Cysts. After just one cycle."

I am too devastated to speak.

She shakes her head and sighs.

"So what does this mean?" I say. "I can't keep having surgery."

"No. No. Of course not," she mumbles.

She withdraws the probe and turns on the lights.

"Apparently, this is normal for you. We'll have to proceed with the cysts and just monitor them."

I should say to her, *So this means that I just had unnecessary surgery.* That she should have monitored me longer, rather than cutting me open. But a sob catches in my throat as I realize that there is no undoing this part of my body's story. There is only an after.

CHAPTER 4

Terri is lying on the floor of my bedroom with her legs spread wide. She moans and rolls her head from side to side. Leah holds Terri's hand and screams at me and Bunny to help her. Bunny throws a blanket over Terri's legs while I go to my toy box to find a doll for Terri to give birth to. I pull out a bald-headed brown baby that I never play with and hand it to Leah. She puts the baby under the blanket that drapes Terri and pretends to pull the baby out from between Terri's legs. She hands the baby back to me and I wrap it in an old shawl and make crying noises.

When we are done birthing the baby, we go to the kitchen. My sister pours red Kool-Aid into plastic cups and gives each of us Oreo cookies.

My mother is sitting on the sofa reading a newspaper.

"What were y'all doing back there?" she says. I want to lie, but if I do, I will have to explain why to my friends. I do not want them to feel like they are bad kids. I know I am bad, but I wish I didn't know.

"Terri was having a baby," I blurt out.

My mother looks up from her paper for the first time since we walked into the room. "What?" she says, the word sounding more like a dare than a question.

Terri starts telling my mother about when her mother had her little sister a few months ago. She holds her belly and groans like her mother.

My mother cuts her off before she reenacts the whole birth.

My sister giggles and covers her mouth.

If it had been just Bunny, my mother would send her home. Bunny lives in a half-finished house on the other side of the block. Her father is *no good, always drunk, and riding a motorcycle, with women.* Her mother supports four children by working *a man's job* in a factory. But Terri's mother is educated, a teacher. My mother cannot send Terri home.

So she tries to laugh, but all that comes out is a hiccup.

"What made y'all play that game?" she says.

Terri and Leah shrug like someone asked them if they liked circles. They focus on licking the inside of the cookies. They cannot hear the anger that hums between my mother's short breaths because their mothers talk to them about things like how babies get born.

But Bunny knows. She wraps her cookies in a napkin and says that she has to go. Terri and Leah decide to follow her out the door.

As soon as the door closes behind them, my mother is standing in front of me.

"That's not a game for you all to be playing," she says. "Grown married women have babies. Not little girls. Do you understand?"

I want to say that we are nine years old and just pretending, but that wouldn't make any difference. Pretending to have a baby is the same as pretending to have sex—the boyfriend-girlfriend game— which we also play but know never to tell our parents.

"If they start playing that game again, you tell them I said you can't play that. You understand?"

I nod and go to my room.

• • •

Five months after becoming an infertility patient, Dr. Z. hands me a prescription. "Birth control. We use it to regulate your system before we start fertility drugs."

I have already read about this on the internet. Birth control is the first step of in vitro fertilization. The pills turn off the reproductive system by telling the body that it is already pregnant.

I have taken thousands of birth control pills. But this time the irony will be sharp and painful: my body is so alien to other women's that I need birth control to get pregnant.

Birth control," Dr. B. says. He scribbles on a prescription pad and hands the piece of paper to my mother.

I am fourteen years old, sitting fully dressed on a table covered in paper in his office.

My mother stands across from him, leaning slightly on a countertop. She clutches the strap of her big copper-and-gold-colored handbag in one hand and takes the prescription with the other.

"It will help regulate her period, and it should also make the periods lighter too so she doesn't have as much cramping."

My mother wrinkles her brow and bobs her head fast like she understands. But there is a question trapped behind her mask.

"I wrote the prescription so insurance would cover it. If it's just for birth control, they won't pay. But if it's for pain, they will." He turns to me. "If you ever need to get the prescription elsewhere, you'll need to tell the doctor to write it for pain. Okay?"

"Somewhere else?" my mother says.

"Well, some people just go to these little clinics for birth control, not realizing what it's going to cost them. The girls stop taking it and get pregnant like that." He snaps his finger.

"But she is—"

Dr. B. holds up a hand to stop her. "I know that she's intact now, but given her age, she probably won't be for much longer. It's probably best to be prepared. And the pill will stop her misery every month too."

My mind trips and falls over the word "intact." It sounds like a word to describe a new roll of toilet paper, sealed but soon to be torn into a ragged edge. I track backward and forward to the word "pill" before I realize I am the intact thing that must be torn apart soon. I float right out of my body like it is dead. When I look down, it is still there, sitting between my mother and the doctor like the tip of a triangle. I have the urge to tell it to move, to stop blending into the paper-covered table like it is glued there, but I know there is no longer anyone inside to talk to.

The doctor walks to the door.

I am a Brownie. There are just four of us in my troop, even though Mrs. Cooley has invited all the girls in the third-grade class to join. None of the other girls want to be seen leaving school with her daughter, Polly, who has a speech impediment that makes her sound like her two yellow-stained front teeth are her lips. Polly is always picked last for games in PE. I am picked second to last. My name and Polly's are the two worst insults doled out by the white boys who wear *Dukes of*

Hazzard T-shirts with pictures of the General Lee car that bears a Confederate flag on it. *Cassandra is your girlfriend. Well, you go with Polly.* Polly tells her tormentors off as if she knows that she will be important one day and they will all live in trailer parks. *You are fo fupid.* I hunker down, knowing that if I call them stupid, they will call me "nigger."

After school, I climb into Mrs. Cooley's station wagon with Polly and two girls from their church. The girls pull their heads into their jackets like turtles into their shells. We head to the community center, where we sit around a table painting ceramic puppies a strange salmon color. When we are done, Mrs. Cooley asks us to leave the puppies on the craft table to dry. We will get them back next week. It is time to go. The two girls from Polly's church run out the door so fast that I do not see which cars they get in. I follow Mrs. Cooley outside, but there is no one waiting to pick me up. She asks me if I need a ride, but I tell her someone is probably on the way to get me. Polly climbs into their car and yells for her mother to hurry up. Mrs. Cooley looks across the street at a raggedy house with cars in the front yard. A Black man stands in the driveway working on one of them. She looks back at me, shrugs, and gets in her car.

I walk to the playground and sit down on a swing, trying hard to look like I am not an eight-year-old girl completely alone on a playground. I look back at the community center door like I am waiting for someone inside to come out and take me home. I have seen faces like mine on the news every night under a caption that says "Atlanta Child Murders." The newscasters say my birthday every night because that was the date the first child went missing. They found him days later, dead, along with another dead boy, in an empty lot. Eventually, the list of dead children's names was too long for the newscasters to say, so they just showed rows of school pictures. The person who did it is still out there killing Black kids. No one knows who or why. All we know is that they can.

I watch the cars that pass, looking for my sister's yellow Pinto or my mother's green Thunderbird, but they do not come. I have been forgotten. The sun starts to go down and I wonder if I should hide in the bushes so as not to draw attention to myself, but I also worry that whoever is supposed to pick me up will not see me hiding there and will keep going, thinking that I have already been picked up. I am afraid to try to walk the mile or so home by myself—afraid of who might snatch me off my feet and leave me dead in an empty lot. I do not want to be a nameless black-and-white school picture on the news.

A girl comes out of the house across the street where the Black man is working on the car, and she waves at me. She crosses the street, and I recognize her because I have seen her school picture lying on my brother's desk. This is the girl that my parents are always whispering about. She is the sixteen-year-old mother of my brother's baby. But I have never met her or the baby. I am not even supposed to know that the baby exists.

"What are you doing over here by yourself?" she says.

I tell her about the Brownie meeting and how I am waiting on a ride.

"I'm a friend of your brother's. My name is Shelia. Come on. I can walk you home." She smiles at me, and we walk to my house in the dark.

She asks me questions about school and Brownies and whether I want to play volleyball or basketball when I get to junior high school.

"I hope Nate wasn't the one who was supposed to pick you up. He's always in enough trouble without this too," she says with a half smile.

I smile back and shake my head no.

I put my hand in hers when we cross a four-lane road. Then we walk up and down steep hills until we turn onto my street.

I wonder how she knows where I live.

She walks me to the door of my house and turns to go.

"Wait," I say.

"It's okay," she says. "I can smell dinner cooking. Someone's in there."

"But you can't go all the way home by yourself in the dark."

She laughs the laugh of an old woman—a throaty, child-if-only-you-knew laugh.

The door opens before I can convince her not to go home alone. It's my mother, who stares at me for a moment and looks back inside the house like I am the twin of the real San who is already somewhere inside.

"No one picked me up," I say. "Shelia walked me home."

My mother looks up at Shelia and offers a quick thank-you, like Shelia has delivered a stack of junk mail. Then my mother leans her head toward the kitchen and yells to my father that my sister forgot to pick me up. "Anything could have happened to San," she mumbles to herself.

I walk around my mother to step inside the house, expecting her to invite Shelia to come in behind me, but she closes the door and walks into the kitchen.

"I don't know what Annette was thinking, forgetting to pick up San like that. And with all this stuff on the news too."

I run back to the door and yell after Shelia, "Thank you!" But it does not feel like enough. I want to say sorry, but I am too embarrassed, for me and for her, to call attention to the fact that my parents do not offer to drive her home like they would have done for my teen-age cousins or the daughters of their friends.

"You're welcome," Shelia says over her shoulder without turning around. She walks down our driveway into the dark street alone.

I am seven years old, watching television in the den on a Saturday, when I hear my parents whispering in the hallway. They have been doing this for days in the dining room, the mudroom, the foyer, standing with their faces closer together than I have ever seen them. My father thinks I cannot hear them, but I can make out every word. My mother says all the time that I can hear everything that happens in our one-level house, no matter where I am inside it. She is right. Sound moves through our house getting bigger instead of smaller like we are inside a drinking glass. Because neither of my parents has good hearing, their whispers, a cross between hisses and shouts, are even easier to hear.

"We don't even know if it's his. Her family probably told her who to put it on. They think we got some money," my mother says.

"Well, if it is his, we have to provide for it," my father says.

"She ain't nothing but a child herself. You remember when I told her mama to keep Nate from coming over there? She said she couldn't stop him, like it's not even her house. Of course she could stop him. She didn't want to," my mother says.

"Well, we can get a test through the state."

"You know what the state is gonna say. They'll say anything to make it so they don't have to pay. I tried to tell you and you just let him go on and do what he wanted."

"What's that got to do with anything now?" my father says.

"We can't have her coming around here with a baby in front of San. We don't want San thinking it's fine to just get pregnant at fifteen and have a baby at sixteen."

"Naw. She can't come around. San is too young to understand," my father says.

I get up from the floor and walk into the hallway where they are. My parents stop talking and look at me over their shoulders.

"Hey, Sugar Doll," my father says. His voice is loud and saccharine like he is talking to a two-year-old whose face is covered in strawberry jam.

I say hi and he steps aside to let me by. My mother walks toward the den and he follows her.

They are supposed to warn me not to bother my sister, who is in her room studying for college. But they are so busy trying to get away from me that they forget.

I want to be in a room with someone who will not leave me alone. I knock on my sister's door and walk into the dim cool of thick blue carpet and linens. My sister is sitting at her desk with just the desk lamp on and a stack of flash cards in her hand. She waits for me to tell her what I want.

I want to ask about the baby my brother is having. When will it be born? Will I ever get to see it? Will this make my brother a daddy like my father, or will he still be a senior in high school? Who will take care of it? But I am afraid to ask my sister about the baby because I am not supposed to know about this baby or where any babies come from. If I ask, she might worry about me and tell my parents, and they will look at me with sad eyes and ask how I know about where babies come from. They will say *who told you this*, and they will blame my friend

Bunny, who is poor, and who my mother says is growing up too fast because she lives in a house with a no-good daddy and teenage brothers who bring fast girls around. But Bunny is not the reason I know things that I am not supposed to know.

I have seen my mother grit her teeth at *fast* Black girls and their mothers who let their daughters run around with boys. *That girl will be pregnant before you know it.* But my mother has also told me that I was an accident. If I was a mistake, that meant some babies were on purpose, and men and women had to do something to get those babies. I watched *Dallas* with my mother and sister and I know that Bobby made Pam pregnant when they kissed and woke up in bed together. I know what happened to Kizzy on *Roots*, that she had a white man's baby because he made her do what Pam and Bobby did. But I do not want my father to know that I am this girl who knows things about women and men who make babies. So I pretend to be his Sugar Doll, a girl who believes that a white man would climb into a chimney to deliver an Atari video game made by elves to an Alabama Black girl with knees the color of burnt newspaper. The Sugar Doll would never care where babies come from because she is so filled with lies that there is no room for the truth.

"Where is Nate?" I ask my sister, even though I know she does not know where our brother is any more than my parents do.

"Who knows?" she says. "He might be at Shelia's house or riding around with his friends. Anywhere but here, I guess." She turns back to her desk. "We'll probably see him in the morning when Mom wakes him up. Then he'll take off again."

Even though my brother is still in high school, he drives away every day in a maroon Pontiac Firebird that looks just like a Camaro. Every morning, my mother wakes him with questions, warnings, and threats.

I tried to tell you to stay away from over there. You keep running around you gonna end up with something itchy all over you down there. And it will fall off. You just watch. My brother sleeps through some of this, and then rouses himself, telling my mother to please leave him alone. But she does not leave him alone. She stands outside his door while he dresses. *Do you even know if it's yours?* But he just opens the door and walks fast to his car.

When he is gone, my mother wanders the hallway talking to herself, punctuating her words with angry head nods. *I tried to tell John to talk to him. Told him Nate shouldn't be running around like that. But men think that's fine. Heard him telling Calvin the other day, "Nate likes to go out," like that's something to be proud of.*

"Can I stay in here with you?" I ask.

My sister nods. "But you have to be quiet. I'm not done yet."

"Okay. I'll be right back." I run to the den where my parents are still talking. My mother looks at me like I am chasing her. My father smiles at a girl who is safe, so protected that she does not know what is going on in this house.

From the bookcase, I grab a volume of the *World Book Encyclopedia* that my parents bought from a door-to-door salesman. I run back to my sister's room. I pull back her bedspread and fold it over because if my mother were to catch me sitting on top of the shiny blue-and-white lace bedspread that makes my sister's bed look like a cake, my sister and I would both be in trouble. I sit down cross-legged on her bed with the letter *D* and flip to the "Dog" entry. I read about how dogs descended from wolves, and I stare at the wildly different breeds, reading the name of each one as if I have not already memorized them. Between the covers of this green-and-cream binding, I find the knowable world. The book's weight on my lap and the seeming endlessness of information soothes me and propels me to seek more at once. I am amazed that no one ever stops me and says *no, don't read that one*, or *don't look at those pictures*. The books may as well be invisible. I read and read, almost forgetting about all the things that I am not supposed to know.

I am thirteen years old, helping my mother tidy our house, when she mentions my nephew to me for the first time.

"Your brother's son is coming over in a little bit. He's about five years old. I hope he's not bad." My mother moves from one sofa cushion to the other clearing newspapers and straightening pillows.

I stop dusting the side table and look at her, but she does not look up. I am too discombobulated to pretend to be surprised.

"Why now?" I say. "Why is he coming now?"

She flips a seat cushion over and pounds it with her fist, then smooths her hand over the fabric. "You were too young to understand then. You're old enough now."

I sit down on the edge of my father's lounge chair. He is outside and I can hear the drone of his lawn mower moving closer.

"What's his name?"

"You know what? I don't really know. I think she named him after Nate. We'll probably call him Lil' Nate to keep from getting confused."

I slide from the arm to the seat of the lounge chair, letting the firmness of the seat cushion steady me. I am an aunt to a child I have never met and whose name I do not know. My brother has never mentioned his child to me, and I have not asked, even though they live together, my brother, his girlfriend, and the boy, in a little white house just a few blocks away. I do not know exactly when he moved into the other house because most of his clothes are still here in our house. One morning, his bedroom door was open with the bunk beds made and they stayed that way. He picks up his clothes piecemeal and sometimes he brings them back to launder them. I have never been to the house where they live, and I don't think my mother has either, even though she drives by sometimes to look for his car when she wants to know where he is.

My brother stops by our house sometimes on his way to or from work. If my father is watching a game on television, my brother comments on which teams are doing well or doing poorly and why. But few words pass between them. When he sees me, my brother smiles and calls me "bird head." I smile back and call him "fat head." Sometimes I punch his arm and he pretends to be hurt. I do not know what else to say to him and he has nothing else to say to me. Then he grabs an apple and eats it on his way out. He never stays more than a few minutes and less when my mother is around. As soon as my mother spots him, she tells him he needs to marry Shelia if they are going to live together. But she does not mention his son. And now, out of nowhere, my mother says the boy is coming to our house.

"I hope he's not bad and tearing up everything," my mother says. "Nate was like that. Would have been even worse if we had let him."

I try to picture my brother in the little house with Shelia sitting next to him, smiling at a faceless boy. But they all feel imaginary, like a family in a Sears catalog, real people, but frozen in a place where I have never been.

"Go clean up my bathroom for me," my mother says. "I like the way you clean the tray on the counter. You always get it so shiny. I'll finish dusting in here."

I stand up and realize that I am still holding a rag and a can of furniture polish. I put them on the table and head to the bathroom connected to my parents' bedroom. When I enter, I stare at my own reflection in the large mirror. I wonder if the boy will look like us.

I am almost finished when the doorbell rings. I run to the door but stop short of opening it to wait for my mother. She walks toward me into the foyer with purpose, but in no hurry. When she opens the door, Shelia is standing on our front porch holding the hand of a skinny brown boy.

"This is Dudey," she says, pronouncing the name "Dude-y."

"I thought he was named after Nate?" my mother says.

"He is," Shelia says, "but we call him Dudey because he acted so much like a little man when he was really little. You know, like a dude?"

My mother frowns. Though she disdained the sentimentality of naming boys after their fathers—insisting that the tradition was silly and impractical—she was also not a fan of nicknames like Junior or Sweet Roll. Diminutives were embarrassing, and one day they'd be attached to a grown man.

"Come on in," she says to the boy. He turns to his mother, but his feet do not move.

Shelia nods and lets go of his hand. "It's okay," she says. "I'll be back in a little while." She turns to go.

"Hi, Dudey," I say and reach for the boy's hand. He follows me inside and my mother closes the door. "Do you want to play with some toys?"

Dudey looks at me wide-eyed and back at the door. My mother walks around to face him and stares.

"I am your grandma," my mother says.

Dudey stares at her with raised eyebrows.

"He doesn't look like Nate to me. Does he look like Nate to you?" my mother says to me.

I tug on Dudey's hand. "Let's go find some toys. Okay?"

He walks with me, but his eyes dart back at my mother as if to say, *You don't look anything like my grandmother either.*

I am fourteen years old and sitting in a car line waiting to be dropped off by my mother when Tasha, just one year older than me, walks alone in front of our car heading into the high school. She is beautiful, her belly round and floating so high that it seems as if she might take flight, her sneakers just skimming the top of the car.

"She is going to be stuck with that baby for the rest of her life," my mother says. Tasha looks back at us with a shy smile. My mother flashes a grin and says through her teeth, "Poor thing looks sick—look at her ankles swelling. I remember that feeling. I was sick as a dog with you."

We pull up to the door, and just as I am about to get out, she says, "You realize you can't be hanging around with her now, right?"

I roll my eyes. I have never seen Tasha hanging out with anyone. Even the poorest girls, the ones who lived in the projects and rubbed Vaseline onto their limbs, avoided Tasha with her permanently sad face. She has the look of a forty-year-old whose last dime was eaten by a cigarette vending machine. No one speculates about who the baby's father is because no one could imagine a boy having a good time with her. Her baby will be her only friend.

"Roll your eyes if you want to. But you mark my words. Her hanging-out days are over," my mother says.

• • •

I stand in the high school hallway where all the other Black kids wait for the homeroom bell to ring. I am with the Black girls like me, the ones who bring packed lunches filled with brand-name Oreos and whose mothers wear three-quarter-length mink coats to church when the temperature drops below seventy. We wear clothes that our mothers purchased at the mall, and we try to always wear at least one item that the white girls with money wear—Guess jeans or Esprit shirts bought on clearance—mixed with cheaper, but acceptable, department store brands. Once, when a white girl named Kelly wore the same sweater as me, the white kids teased her all day, saying that she had a Black twin. By lunchtime she was near tears, moaning that she couldn't wait to throw the sweater away. I never saw her wear the sweater again. But I continued to wear mine. I did not want to accept that I had devalued the sweater just by being a Black girl wearing it. But every time Kelly spotted me in it, her blue eyes would tremble at the memory of being called a Black girl's twin and she would duck like I'd rapped her on the head with a ruler.

Everyone is standing in the hallways hanging out while we wait for the homeroom bell to ring. My friends and I stand in the Black hallway, where all the Black kids gather. On the other end of this hallway are the poor white kids, the ones whose parents could live in the projects but instead stay in broken-down houses and trailers because they think it is more shameful to live with Black people. The rich white kids stand in the white hallway, which is perpendicular to the Black hallway, their backs to ours with the corner of the walls separating us from them. Directly across from us are the other Black girls, the ones our mothers have warned us never to be. These girls drifted through these hallways before, in the bellies of their mothers. They wear secondhand sweatshirts and no-name acid-washed jeans. Boys are sprinkled in their group—some hold hands with girls, while others hover, demanding hugs and trying to tease smiles out of them. But the girls keep their eyes trained on us like we are assassins dressed in Benetton tights.

We should keep our eyes on these other Black girls because they hate us. But instead we forget that they are there because they do not have anything that we want. We are focused on one another, talking in a language of high-pitched squeaks that announce our femininity. We covet one girl's tiny Gucci purse that her aunt bought in Italy, a place neither we nor any of our parents have ever been. We discuss which cars to take to the basketball game on Friday and which cute boys from the other high school will be there. Then we complain that we cannot wait to get away from this godforsaken town where there is nothing to do but go to ball games.

On the other side of the narrow hallway, the other Black girls talk about us in deeper voices. They call us names to make us see them: "wannabes," like the light-skinned girls in Spike Lee's movie *School Daze*, even though some of us are dark and some of them are light. If that does not work, they will take two long steps across the hallway and strike one of us. Then they will smile and wait for us to prove that we are equally capable of violence.

Our group looks at one another and mouths, "Jigaboos," the term for dark-skinned girls in *School Daze*. The movie was supposed to make us realize that Black people should unite, but it only taught us new terms for the divisions between us. A girl whose short hair is a Jheri curl on top and an afro underneath shoots a look that says, *I will beat one of your asses today.*

But Antinea walks in before anyone can smack any of us in the face. She is pretty, even in a worn flannel men's button-down shirt and boys' jeans cinched below her belly. The girls who are already mothers surround her. One takes her books and carries them for her without asking. Another wraps an arm around her shoulder. The rest ask her how she is feeling and if she needs anything.

We lean against the wall, watching a scene that should be beautiful, a circle of young mothers supporting one soon to be among their ranks. But our shame at the sight of these girls will not allow us to see them through anything but white eyes, the same lens that our mothers use. We see them as Black girls: too fast, too fertile, multiplying because that is all Black people know how to do—make more Black people. We have seen the white girls who stare at these other Black girls' bellies when they think no one is looking, disgust twisting their lips into grubs. And we know they can see no difference between us and these other Black girls. They are waiting for our bellies to grow too.

The bell rings. The girl with her arm around Antinea rolls her eyes at us as they walk to Antinea's locker. "Act like they ain't never been pregnant," she says in a loud voice. "You know all of them just kill their babies with them abortions."

This is supposed to be an insult, but we smile at one another because we do not care. If any of us get pregnant, this is exactly what we will do, and we are proud of this fact. Otherwise, we would be them.

The Summa Club gathers at my house to try to fix our mistake. At seventeen years old, I am one of the founding members of the club. There are other girls' clubs at school—one for the daughters of the wealthiest doctors, lawyers, and business owners, and another for the daughters of managers of factories, and still another for the daughters of regular workers. But Black girls are not allowed in any of these clubs. So we started our own. We buy expensive jerseys just like theirs and have car wash fundraisers just like theirs. We cannot afford to host the lavish ballroom cotillions called Lead Outs that the two wealthiest white-girl clubs have. But we throw parties with way better DJs than theirs, who sound like somebody's drunk uncle switching out his old disco records.

Now the Summa Club members sit on the thick green carpet of my mother's living room to decide whom we will vote into the club and whom we will reject. Everyone is staring at the floor or their hands.

"We should never have had open applications," I say. "That's how we got into this mess."

"But how could we know a girl with a baby would apply?" Renee says.

Portia looks up at the ceiling. "I thought she'd quit for sure. I mean we did awful things to them. Made them carry our books, not talk for whole days, and wear stupid pacifiers. Why would somebody with a baby want to be in a club enough to do all of that anyway?"

"Yeah. Why isn't she joining the Cherished Club? That's where all the other girls with babies are," Cynthia says with a smirk.

A week after we showed up at school in our white Summa Club jerseys with pink lettering, the other Black girls who liked to stare at us in the hallways before school started a club of their own called Cherished. But unlike our club and the white-girls' clubs we modeled ours on, the Cherished Club has boys in addition to girls. They'd all marched into the hallway before school wearing bright white sweatshirts with screen-printed red letters with the club name on the front and each member's nickname on the back. By the following week, the bright white shirts had blended with the red lettering and the hallways seemed filled with a dingy pink fog.

Jasmine rolls her eyes and lets out a loud sigh. "It's not fair to reject Priscilla. She did everything she was supposed to. And now we're going to say she can't be in the club because she has a baby? And what about her sister Courtney? Are we going to reject her too because she has a sister with a baby?"

Jasmine is right. Priscilla and Courtney faced every humiliation we'd thrown at them while calling us the silly honorifics we'd chosen for ourselves, like "Big Sister Most High Almighty," and they'd managed to do it all with good-natured smiles, while other girls had quit.

"Fair is neither here nor there," Cynthia says. "It doesn't matter if it's not fair to reject Priscilla. It's just what has to happen."

"This is what all the kids in the Cherished Club have been saying about us—that we were just stringing Priscilla along and she was a fool to think we'd let her in," Jasmine says. "But Priscilla hasn't done anything more than half the girls in this room have done."

"But she has living proof of what she did," Cynthia says. "Nobody in our group has that."

Two of the junior girls cover their faces with their hands, and one cries openly. "I just feel so bad for her," the one who is crying says. "She made one mistake."

"He's a person," Jasmine yells. "He is not a mistake. He is not proof of something. He's a baby person."

The room goes quiet as we stare at Jasmine, processing the ways in which she is different from us. Even though her father is like ours, a successful factory worker who lives in a big house with his wife, a teacher, Jasmine lives in a tiny house with her mother and her sister, who has a different father. Jasmine's mother is known for one thing: she is loud in a way that makes the rest of our mothers ashamed to be Black. Jasmine teeters between two worlds of Black people. She is here with us now because she is what all the Black girls like us want to be: fair-skinned, pretty, smart, and a cheerleader with a cute boyfriend whose mother buys him brand-name clothes from the mall.

"He is almost a year old," Jasmine says. "His name is Desmond." She is trying to bring us into another world, where right and wrong can exist outside of the rules of respectability. But hearing the baby's name makes him too real and my stomach turns with disgust as I imagine cries in a cramped room that smells of Vaseline and baby shit.

I want to tell myself that Priscilla cannot join our club because of what my mother says, that girls with babies have to live wholly different lives from Black girls like us. But I cannot separate Priscilla's poverty, her neat but cheap clothes and long, over-greased black hair, from the fact that she has a baby. I trip over a tangle of thoughts: Priscilla is poor. Poor Black girls have babies because nobody expects them to do anything else. Babies make poor Black girls poorer. I do not want to be Priscilla. I wish that Priscilla did not exist because when white people look at me at school or at the mall, they see Priscilla, a teenage Black girl with a baby, because there can only be one kind of Black girl.

Neither I nor anyone talks about the fact that if we could press a button that would fade Priscilla—all the Priscillas—from our lives, we would. Never mind the marvel of their mothers, these women who can still imagine their daughters as members of social clubs and cheerleading squads. We would watch the last curves of the Priscillas and their mothers' bodies disappear and tell ourselves a new fairy tale: that they would reemerge in a better place, where all the teenage mothers would live happily ever after, out of our sight. And we would never mention the children they left behind, because to most of us, the babies of teenagers are not yet people as much as they are obstacles, cautionary anecdotes that remind us of who we do not want to be. But there is no button, and we cannot admit how much we want Priscilla to go away because to do so would mean having to unpack all of our hurt: all the times that white teachers, principals, and strangers at the mall curled their lips in disgust at us because they thought we were a Priscilla.

"Look," I say. "The bottom line is that if we let her in, the club ends. How many girls' moms have said they can't be in a club with a girl with a baby?" All the girls but Jasmine raise their hands.

"We aren't going to be a club anymore if we let her in." I pause to let that sink in. "Of course it's not fair," I say, looking at Jasmine. "But the choice is not about Priscilla or whether her baby should exist, or who had sex and who didn't. This vote is about whether we want to continue as a club."

We vote on everyone else first. We vote unanimously yes on Courtney, Priscilla's sister. Everyone but Jasmine votes no on Priscilla.

"What's the point in letting Courtney in? She isn't going to join a club that rejected her own sister," Jasmine says.

We know Jasmine is right, but this is the only way we can think of to say to them, *It is not you, but the baby. It's not us, but our mothers.* They are the problem. So easy to blame our mothers without acknowledging that we have already become like them.

We make a plan to slip letters into all the applicants' lockers, scattering paper bits of joy and hate as we have seen the white girls do. Because their lockers are in different hallways, Courtney will assume that they have both gotten in, until she sees her sister's face, streaming with tears. The girls from the Cherished Club will suck their teeth at both of them and say, *We told you about them, but you wouldn't listen.*

I am a teenager, sitting in the den with my parents, when I ask my father if he rode horses on the farm where he grew up. My mother laughs and I know that they are about to play the dozens.

She smiles at my father and says, "Horses? Humph. They were so poor that they'd have eaten a mule if they had one." She and my father laugh hard.

"You know what?" my father says. "Your mama and them lived in a raggedy house so full of holes that they didn't have to go outside to feed the chickens. They just called them and fed them through the floor."

I laugh with them, hiding the uneasiness that rises a bit in me each time I remember what we are laughing about.

My father is still chuckling at his own joke as he heads outside to work in his garden.

When the door closes behind him, my mother says, "You know your daddy's people weren't really as poor as we were. They couldn't buy no land or nothing 'cause whites wouldn't allow that, but they had cars and their own farm equipment. We didn't have a car even though we lived in town."

I stay quiet while she continues, talking half to me and half to herself.

"There was just so many of us. My folks could barely make it with twelve kids to take care of. I asked Mama one time why she had so many. And she said she didn't have nothing she could use to keep from having them. I said they always had rubbers, Mama. And she said, *I told you that I didn't have nothing I could use.*"

"But Daddy's mama only had five kids," I say.

"And I have never figured out how. We didn't know them back then, but if we had, they would have been one of the smallest families we knew, and definitely the smallest farming family. How did a woman barely thirty years old just stop having kids before the pill? It's a mystery."

I picture the skinny wide-eyed woman with a hard line for a mouth I have seen in a black-and-white photo. Could she have known something that the others did not?

I am not thinking of the pain that made me feel like I was imploding every month before I started taking the pill when I ask, "Do you think something was wrong with her?"

"Well, I never thought much about something being wrong with her, but you know what? Her sisters, Aunt Duke and Aunt Dave—well, they was really your grandma Bernice's first cousins, you know, but they was raised in the same house like sisters—the two of them didn't have no children at all."

I am driving home from the fertility clinic when I see her swinging her hips back and forth like the sidewalk is her own personal runway. She wears a gold puffer jacket with matching high-top sneakers, and her hair is slicked into a shiny fake ponytail that hangs down her back. A sliver of a beautiful brown belly, round and ready to burst, peeps out from between her jacket and the blue jeans that glide over the curves of her chubby teenage body. She is too far away for me to smell her, but

I know that she smells both clinical and sweet, like Vaseline and melon body wash.

I slow down to let her cross and envy and disgust wash over me. I try to shake them both off, but they stick to me like childhood shame.

I should be used to seeing pregnant girls and teenage mothers in this city, where crowded public housing and neighborhoods of romantic Victorians buttress one another. Just blocks from my two-and-a-half-story house is a home for teenage mothers, Black girls who walk to the bus stop each day hunched over raggedy umbrella strollers, bracing themselves against a heavy wind that no one but them can feel.

Soon this gorgeous girl might join them, but for now, her shoulders stand high, letting her breasts lead the way. I know it is wrong to think that because she is young and poor she is somehow less deserving of a child than I am. I know that no one is "owed" a child and that this baby will be okay, just as mine would be okay if I could just get pregnant.

But as I watch her cross the street with her own baby fat still around her neck, I want to strangle this glorious, shiny girl. To force her body to stop its magic. Tell it to stop proving that we are all bodies with or without the powerful forces of estrogen and progesterone and reproductive organs.

She catches sight of me watching and peers into my car without coming over. Then she tosses her head back, a New Jersey gesture that means *What the fuck do you want?*

I drive away still trying to answer her question. I want what she has, and yet I do not want to be her. If given the choice to be a poor pregnant teenager or an infertile middle-class professional, I would choose infertility. So what the fuck do I want?

CHAPTER 5

I enter an office filled with women whose eyes are trained on books, magazines, tablets, and phones. Some of the women are infertile. Others are egg donors or surrogates. They are all hiding in plain sight. Somewhere else, they are lawyers, supermarket clerks, veterinarians, students, and factory workers. Some are already moms. But here, they divorce themselves from that other life, applying all their ambition to a sole purpose: to blend into the coarse floral fabric of a waiting room sofa.

I take a seat next to them and try to disappear.

A man walks in wearing a baseball cap. He puts a paper bag on the reception counter and waits patiently for the receptionist to acknowledge him. She smiles at him, and he nods like he has handed her a cookie instead of a cup of sperm concealed in a brown paper bag. He is seasoned, unlike the newbie men who are waiting to make their sperm deposits here at the office. A receptionist takes them one by one into a room with porn magazines and a TV that plays porn on low volume all day. When the men come back from this room, we clock their flushed faces and unwashed hands before we look away.

I recognize a woman who sits across from me. She works at a clothing store nearby. I almost say hello, but she cuts me off with her eyes.

I catch on and pretend to be absorbed in what I am reading. I am used to secrets.

. . .

I am nine years old, sitting on the floor of the den, flipping through a photo album. I stop at the old photograph of my paternal grandmother, Bernice. I angle her face toward mine, trying to see the thin reflection of my own face over hers, hoping to see what everyone else does. But as I tilt the album, another photograph slips out from behind it—a black-and-white photo of a teenage girl. Her face is round and pretty and framed by short curls that lie flat on her skin.

"Who is this?" I ask my mother, who is sitting nearby on the sofa.

She sticks her head out above a newspaper and looks at the picture upside down.

"That's John's first wife," she says and ducks her head behind the paper again.

"John who?"

"Your father."

"Daddy had another wife?"

"She was killed in the wreck," she says without looking up from her paper.

I study the round contours of the woman's plump face, her small eyes and smooth skin, trying to make myself know her because my mother has said "your father's first wife" like I am supposed to know.

"What was her name?" I ask.

"Willodene."

I repeat her name, first aloud, and then in my head. But I have never heard this name before. Panic rises inside me, and I feel like I cannot find the edges of myself. Like my mother might say at any moment, "You know, she's your real mother," without ever looking up from her paper. I want to scream, *What else is there? What else don't I know?*

"What was her last name? I mean before she got married?" I say.

"Wilhite. You remember Mr. and Mrs. Wilhite, who we used to visit sometimes?"

I picture two kind brown faces grinning at me when I was four or five years old. The couple led me and my parents into a giant shed filled with yellow baby chicks. Their constant cheeping bounced off the metal walls, making the room weep like it too had lost its mother. While the man talked and showed my parents around, the woman scooped up a chick and gestured for me to do the same. I picked up a wobbly chick and caressed its downy softness. Just as she warned me that it might poop on my hand, it did. And we both laughed as if we did not notice that among the chicks, there were also a few dead ones looking like dirty toys that someone forgot to stuff. When it was time to walk out, my parents followed the man to the door. I wanted to go with them, but I was surrounded by chicks. My stomach curled at the thought of stepping on a chick, of my foot on the plump flesh that would push back just before the crack of thin bones. My parents walked out, but the woman was watching me—had kept her eyes on me the whole time I was there. She reached for my hand. As I walked out with her, the chicks moved aside. Still, I tiptoed, looking down at a moving cloud of yellow and white, already knowing that the novelty of this moment meant that even in memory it would never feel real.

"The Wilhites that used to raise chickens for Kentucky Fried Chicken?" I say.

"Yeah. That's them."

I look at the picture again. I don't look like the pretty girl, but my sister does with her round face and perfect teeth. She could belong to this woman. If she did, it would explain the question that dogged us every time we stepped out of the house together: Why do we look so different? My brother and I are all noses and eyes with skinny sticklike limbs, uneven skin, and sandy hair. But Annette is beautiful, with perfectly smooth yellow skin, brown eyes that are large without being too large, lips that are full but still thin enough to make lipstick stains on her teeth that line up as straight as a chorus line. Her body is all curves, turning and dipping, like soft-serve ice cream, and mine is all angles with elbows so sharp that a neighbor once called them dangerous. Despite the thirteen years between us, people compare my body to hers aloud when we are together as if we cannot see our differences. Neighbors, church ladies, and nosy salesclerks at the mall stare at us with raised eyebrows or scrunched-up noses, like we put salt in their Kool-Aid. They chuckle and shake their heads like we are a puzzle they cannot solve. I never looked at my sister, whom I love, without also wondering why the connection between us was not written on our bodies. How could my sister look so different? Surely this is a question that has an answer, something that I can investigate on my own. Someone is hiding something. I make a plan to find out what.

My life splits into two: a visible life as a professor and an invisible life as an infertility patient.

My Visible Life: I go to work and lecture and lead discussions with students about art and literature. I sit in meetings with my colleagues and try to care about their disagreements. Every day, I work on writing a scholarly book that I believe is about art, but it is really about violence, pain, and grief.

My Invisible Life: Reginald and I sit side by side while the nurse, Sherri, sits behind a desk, removing vials and needles from a plastic bag.

"I know it looks intimidating at first," she says. "But you'll be giving yourself shots like a pro soon."

I raise my eyebrows at this suggestion. What if I do not want to be a professional infertility patient?

Sherri pulls out what looks like a blue pen and a clear little cartridge. She opens the pen, which is hollow, and slides a cartridge inside.

"This is your Follistim pen," she says. "It's really easy. Once you put the cartridge in, you just dial the dose written on your patient instructions and you're ready to go." She twists the end of the pen and it makes a clicking sound.

"This is a subcutaneous shot. That means you just stick it in your stomach."

"The stomach?" I say. "Like a rabies shot?"

She throws her head back and laughs wildly through sagging cheeks. "It's really not as bad as all that. Now, if you dial it wrong, you just do this." She presses a bright red fingernail against the end of the pen, but nothing happens.

"That's weird," she says, pressing harder.

"Hmm. Guess it's not working." She smacks the pen against her desk, and when abuse doesn't reset the medical device, she glares at it and shrugs.

"Oh well, I think you get the point. If you ever have problems with the pen, we can get you another one."

I look over at Reginald, who is staring at the stack of plastic bags on Sherri's desk. There are three more sets of needles, syringes, and vials.

A series of shots will stimulate my ovaries, while another set will prevent me from releasing eggs too soon. A single injection will stimulate the maturation and release of the eggs at the right time. And, yet another course of shots will support the implantation of an embryo. This last one, the progesterone shot, is the most intimidating of all. The needle is huge and has to be inserted into a muscular part of my ass.

"Does the needle really need to be that long?" Reginald asks, pointing to it.

Sherri wraps her short, thick fingers around the syringe and holds it up. "Yeah, it's important that this one be long because the progesterone is in an oil, and the oil has to get deep into the muscle to be absorbed. Otherwise, it just sits in hard lumps under the surface of the skin. This is the hardest shot just because of where it goes. It's nearly impossible to do it yourself, though some women have to. It's better for your spouse to do it. Reginald, you have to practice inserting this one today before we can prescribe the drugs. Are you ready?"

She gestures for me to stand up and turn around, and I realize that he will be practicing on me. She tells me to hold my dress up with one hand and lean on a small bookshelf.

"Now hold the needle like a dart," she says to Reginald.

I glance back at his face. Muscles bulge out of his forehead as he breaks into an instant sweat.

"You ready?" he says.

I nod and brace myself.

"No, wait," the nurse says, pointing at me. "You need to take your weight off the leg he's going to put the needle in."

I lean on my right leg and put my left foot as far behind me as I can.

"Yes," she says. "Just like that. Now shoot her like you're throwing a dart. Quick."

Before I can say anything about being compared to a dartboard, a sharp pain stings me.

"Are you okay?" Reginald says. I nod and let go of my dress and begin to breathe again.

"Well, it's not that bad at first," she says, clearly disappointed by my silence. "But as the shots build up over time and you get sore, they will hurt more and more."

She looks down at my hips and shakes her head. "You're really not that big. So there won't be a ton of places to give you the shots either."

I wait for her to offer a solution, but she does not.

"So you're just going to tell me I need a bigger ass? That's it?" I say.

She laughs hard and slaps my shoulder. "You are a funny one."

I fill a syringe and air bubbles that I believe are going to kill me appear. I have heard stories about drug users pumping air into their veins and accidentally killing themselves. I do not know if these stories are true. But the idea is enough to make me more afraid of dying from the shot than I am of pain.

It never occurs to me that since my shots are subcutaneous, not intravenous, the chances of accidentally whacking myself are close to nil. I hold the syringe up and thump it hard until the air bubble floats to the top. Then I depress the syringe gently, trying to release the air instead of the drug.

"Honey, can you look at this?" I say.

Reginald leans over my shoulder. "I still see air in there," he says. He looks as afraid of death by an air bubble as I am.

"Let me see." He takes the syringe and thumps and presses on the bottom.

A long arc of clear liquid shoots out of the syringe into the air above our heads. We are a medical comedy sketch.

"Give me that!" I say. "Do you know how much this shit cost?"

"Well, you can't go around injecting yourself full of air," he says.

I start over. I inject sterilized water from one vial into a vial of powder and begin shaking it like I'd seen the nurse do. Then I pull the liquid into the syringe, but more damn killer bubbles appear.

Reginald looks at me with alarm in his eyes.

I bang on the syringe again, pinch the fat on my stomach, and hold my breath. "Fuck it. If I die from the bubbles, just tell everyone that I was a heroin addict. 'She died from infertility shots' sounds so much more pathetic."

I wait until everyone is out of the house. My mother is in the yard, trying to tell my father, over the din of the lawn mower, that he is cutting the grass too short. My brother is at work at the grocery store. My sister, Annette, is washing her car. I walk into my parents' bedroom and reach under their bed. I pull out a brown leather briefcase, an anniversary present my father received from his job even though, as a factory worker, he has no use for it other than storing papers at home. I press two little buttons and the case pops open. I shuffle through life insurance papers, mortgage documents, and every other piece of paper that my parents deemed important enough to keep. Finally, I find my sister's birth certificate. I scan the page, searching for names. I see my father's name first and then my mother's, each with the word "Negro" printed next to it. This can't be right. That's not possible.

I look at the year of my sister's birth, looking for some discrepancy that would indicate that the document is hiding a secret. But I have no other dates to compare it to. I don't know what year the accident happened or even the year my parents got married. Whenever I ask about their anniversary my father says that it is on my birthday and that's why they don't celebrate it.

I run my hand across the State of Alabama seal. The paper has to be true. No one could change a birth certificate. Could they? I stare at the boxes on the paper, wondering if they could be rewritten as easily as the words on the backs of cereal boxes. Of course not. The certificate came from the state.

But I cannot shake the idea that the paper is a lie. There had to be a reason that my sister and I have had to endure being a walking version of the *Sesame Street* game One of These Things Is Not Like the Other. I set the certificate aside and rummage through the briefcase, but all I find is my own birth certificate sandwiched between insurance policies.

I hear footsteps in the hallway. In my head I say, *God damn it*, in the way my father does when he spills flour on the kitchen floor. I close the briefcase and push it back under the bed. The exhilarating feeling that I am about to know something hidden sinks and transforms into something more like the feeling of finding mold between the last two slices of bread. But I am not done investigating.

In my Invisible Life, I begin the day at the fertility clinic; at first every other day and eventually every day at 7 a.m., I write my name on a slip of paper and hand it to a receptionist. Then I sit and wait for a nurse to call my name.

I walk into the blood-draw room, where rows of women sit in little chairs with armrests across the front. The women are dressed for work, but they all have one sleeve rolled up or they've removed their blazer to reveal a camisole and bare arms underneath. Nurses dressed in candy-colored scrubs glide back and forth on stools with wheels to gather fresh needles and vials from a countertop on the opposite side of the room. When they are ready, they poke butterfly needles into their patient's waiting arm and smile when dark red blood moves through a tube and spills like wine into a clear vial. They talk about the weather, jewelry parties, and how they will celebrate their birthdays. They do not talk about needles, blood, bodies, or their children.

Everything is smooth and choreographed, like the opening scenes of a sci-fi movie set in the suburbs. A nurse in pink Dora the Explorer scrubs waves me over, and I too am part of this movie. I walk in, smile, and take my seat. She glides across the room on her stool to gather her things and glides back while I roll up my sleeve and rest my arm on the cushion.

When she returns and looks at my arm, her smile fades. "Oh dear," she says. "Your veins—they are just so small." She taps my arm and turns it. "I wonder if . . . well . . . I don't know if . . . hmm," she says.

Dora Scrubs sucks in her breath and pokes the needle into my arm. We wait for the blood to run through the tube, but nothing comes out. She removes the needle and asks if I am okay, but she is too loud. Everyone in the movie stops to look at us. We have been demoted to audience members who have forgotten to turn off their cell phones. She tries again, this time with all eyes on her. The room is silent as everyone waits for the vial to fill, but nothing comes out of my body. She begins to fumble through needles nearby, and eyes widen all over the room. I sit there aware that my body is strange in yet another way and that it has just told its secret to everyone.

The nurse next to us says in a soft voice, "Just get Sherri."

Dora Scrubs goes to the door, picks up a phone from the wall, and mumbles something unintelligible into it.

When she returns she asks me to wait in a chair in the corner. I move, and Dora Scrubs waves over a patient standing in the doorway. The movie resumes without me, without my body that refuses to play its part.

When Sherri arrives, the nurses all point in my direction at the same time. She greets me with a smile and tightens the tourniquet on my arm. She puts a needle in and all the nurses turn to look. Nothing comes out. And though some version of this moment happens almost every time I come to the blood-draw room, even I stare at the empty tube and begin to wonder what I am.

"Try this. Hang your arm straight down by your side," Sherri says. I let my arm hang and blood flies through the tube. The nurses let out tiny sighs of relief and turn back to their patients. Sherri smiles like she has put a genie back in the bottle.

She turns to the nurse next to her and asks if she needs new sheets. There is a bedding sale at the mall.

In time, I learn to relish the sterile smell of alcohol pads, the gleam of thin needles, and the sharp sting of pain as I pierce my body. The things that make me feel real.

At night, I prepare the shot. I am in control. My body has no concrete limitations. I can penetrate it, drug it, change something as essential as the smell of it, just by taking these little shots. I can force eggs inside me to ripen with just the prick of a needle. I make my body sweat constantly. The odor I make myself excrete is both musky like a feral cat and metallic like a burning beer can. I touch the dampness of my pits with my fingers and smell them.

For the first time, I understand the feeling that drives people with anorexia to starve themselves, the deep fulfillment of control over one's own body.

There is just one shot that I cannot easily do myself—the one to my own ass. I prep the needle and point my husband to a spot that has not already been stabbed.

When he goes out of town, I consider asking a friend. But instead, I practice twisting my body enough to inject a shot into my own butt. I feel my way blindly and jab hard and fast. It works, and I am hooked.

When my husband returns, he wants to resume giving me the shot. He needs something to do in this process. But I can no longer wait for someone else to puncture me like a balloon. I will not hold myself down and wait for medical violence to split me while talking about whether it will snow on Friday. At home, I am my own nurse, doctor, husband. I am my own secret.

I am ten by the time I get up the nerve to ask her. I go outside, where Annette is washing her little yellow car, the Pinto that she inherited from my mother. A wave of nausea passes through me. But finally, I manage to get out, "Are you?"

She stares like I am someone important about to say something necessary.

I stumble through, "Are you her daughter? Daddy's first wife's daughter?"

She cocks her head to the side, and for the first time, it occurs to me that maybe she doesn't know that she is another woman's child.

She throws back her head and laughs for a long time. When she stops to catch her breath she says, "Where did you get that silly idea?"

My heart is beating in my throat. I have betrayed her. I am sorry that I have hurt my sister, who does TV-mom things with me, like make picnics and candied apples, and lets me use her makeup to give my friends makeovers. She tells people that she is the one raising me. But she is better than a mother precisely because she is not one. She is not weighed down by the responsibilities of bills and balancing checkbooks.

She is still giggling as she washes the top of the car. But she does not say anything else to me.

I try to laugh with her. Then I pick up a sponge and begin scrubbing a tire.

I am in bed at night when my mother walks into my room without turning on the light. She lays her body down on top of the shiny pink bedspread so that it stays between my body and hers.

"Aunt Sadie, Uncle Morgan's wife. You didn't know her. She died before you were born. She told me to do it."

I do not understand what she is talking about, but I know not to ask questions when someone is talking in the dark.

"Aunt Sadie just kept on telling me to do it. She was a mean woman. Everybody knew Uncle Morgan just married her 'cause she was a teacher and had money coming in. Back then, teaching up at the colored school was the only kind of decent-paying job a Black woman could get. Uncle Morgan was good-looking—could have married any-body, but he loved money. Everybody knew Auntie was mean. Mean to her own son because he was dark-skinned."

My mother wrings her hands so hard that I can hear her dry skin rubbing like flint and steel.

"I was engaged to a man before your daddy. And Aunt Sadie just kept telling me to go on and do it. After that, he stopped coming around, and then I had Annette. Your daddy adopted Annette after we got married."

"What about the man?" I say.

"He's dead."

The outline of her face emerges as my eyes adjust. She is lying on her back, staring at the ceiling.

"Mama was real mad at Auntie for a long time for doing me like that." Her head rises still, like a mask, as she gets up and floats toward the door.

"Don't say nothing to your sister or your brother about this."

"Does she know?" I say.

"Yeah. She knows. But we don't talk about it. Your daddy is her fa-ther now. So ain't nothing to talk about."

I ask her if my brother knows. But she walks out and closes the door behind her without answering.

I lie in bed all night replaying my mother's words—*And then I had Annette. And then I had Annette. And then I had Annette*—and mak-ing new sentences to connect the missing pieces of my mother's story: Annette's father is not mine. He is someone else, someone I do not know. My mother was engaged to this man. Her aunt told her she should have sex with the man. My mother got pregnant and the man left her with a baby, my sister. My father married my mother, who already had a baby. He adopted that baby. My sister is my biological half sister. But not in the way that I thought.

I want to sleep, but pain keeps me awake. I hurt like someone has hollowed me out, emptied me and refused to give the pieces of me back. This is what it feels like when you land on the wrong truth. I cry, softly at first, and then hard, moaning into a pillow. I feel foolish because it should make no difference. In my theory, my sister was the daughter of my father's dead wife, Willodene, a woman I never knew. And now she is the daughter of my mother's dead lover, a man I never knew.

Still, I mourn my version of the story because in it Annette is a connection to the past, an answer to questions that can never be asked. *What happened to your family, Daddy? When did it happen? Who did you lose? How did you go on?*

My mother's secret takes my sister further away from our family. She is not an answer but a new question. *Who was your father? Do you have other brothers and sisters? Where are they, and do you want to know them?* She is no longer just my sister. She belongs to someone else too. And though our loss is still hers, she has a profound loss that is all her own.

She is a secret. She is our secret. And a secret is just another word for a lie.

I am at the grocery store when I catch a checkout clerk staring at my arms. I have thrown on an old T-shirt on this unseasonably warm day, thinking that no one will notice anything out of the ordinary about my body. My body, Black and young-enough-looking, is good at keeping secrets. Even the receptionists at the fertility clinic cannot process the idea that my body is both Black and infertile. They regularly direct me to a sign-in list for egg donors, twentysomethings who, for a fee, allow doctors to harvest their eggs and give them to infertile women.

When the clerk spots the bloody game of connect-the-dots on my arms, with one spot still red from an early morning blood draw, a thin shudder passes through her dark brown neck. She curls glittery pink lips into a wince and looks into my face. I am too startled to answer her narrowed eyes. She tosses her long dark weave over her shoulder and returns to her work scanning each item. But her eyes dart back and forth between the groceries and the marks on my body as she tries to make sense of me—an apparent heroin addict buying Greek yogurt and organic baby spinach. By the time she hands me the receipt she is sucking her teeth and rolling her eyes. I thank her in a voice too happy for the supermarket. She makes "You're welcome" sound like a curse, spitting the words so that they hang in the air in a comic-book word bubble.

I smile, feeling seen even if I have been mistaken for someone else.

I walk out of the store, pushing my cart with my arms facing as far outward as I can turn them. I greet strangers, daring them to see me too, but they smile back and look right through me, their eyes filling in the gaps in my skin. I am invisible again.

CHAPTER 6

I am six years old, lying on my stomach on the floor of the den. I am supposed to be watching television when I hear my sister's soft voice, the one she uses when she is afraid of how my mother will respond, coming from the kitchen.

"Ma, Daddy is an alcoholic."

I turn around just as my mother lets out a sharp laugh. My sister wipes a rag in slow circles on the counter.

"We've been reading and talking about this a lot in my classes. Daddy has all the symptoms—he's knocked out every day."

Now my mother is not laughing. "John only has a drink or a beer or two once a day. He goes to work every day—never misses. That's not an alcoholic."

"Ma, that's just because one drink or a beer is all it takes to knock him out. The result is the same as when other people drink five or six drinks. He needs help."

My mother waves angry soapy hands over the sink. "You think 'cause you read something at college that you can say John's a drunk? Drunks drink all day. And they don't go to work every day sober to pay for college. I could show you some real drunks and maybe then you'll realize the difference."

"It's depression, Ma. He's just thinking about them, his family that died. The alcohol is making it worse though."

My mother scrubs dishes that are already clean. "So he's got depression now too? Girl, you don't know anything about that."

My mother puts the last dish in the washer. She wrings out a towel and hangs it inside the cabinet. She tells my sister to finish cleaning the kitchen and she walks away.

My sister shrugs and goes to get the broom from the corner. I sit down at the kitchen bar facing her as she sweeps.

"Is that on the cards in your room?"

"What?" she says.

"Those cards you study. Is 'alcoholic' on there?"

"Yeah," she says.

Each card has a word written in red on the front—a disease or a condition—and on the back is the definition. She is always either making the cards or reading them. My sister is smart. She knows what an alcoholic is.

"What is help? You said he needs it."

She shakes her head and sighs.

"Does someone come and pour it all out?" I picture a man dressed in a plumber's uniform taking all the whiskey bottles from the cabinet that holds the Windex and Mop & Glo.

"Can't we do that ourselves?" I say.

She puts the broom away and leads me to my bedroom. She waits while I put on my pajamas and then turns to go.

"I know where we can hide it all," I say.

She looks at me with a sad smile and tells me to go to sleep.

I sit on the paper-covered table undressed from the waist down, waiting for her. There are the usual magazines scattered about, but I can't bear to read them. I am busy thinking about whatever processes are happening or not happening in my body. I run one hand over my face, which is covered in strange bumps, and another over my swollen abdomen, both palpable signs of the drugs' powers. At my last visit hardly anything was happening inside me. The doctor had reassured me that some women's eggs grow slowly at first and catch up later. Today, I would find out if this was true for me.

A knock on the door and the doctor enters. I recline and put my legs in the stirrups on cue.

"How are you feeling?"

"My belly feels achy, swollen," I say.

"Par for the course with infertility drugs," she says.

"My skin too?" I point to the acne on my chin.

"Oh yeah. Skin can go crazy on these drugs. But it's just temporary."

She hands me a pen and a small clipboard with a sheet of paper that has two columns. One column says "Left Ovary" at the top, the other, "Right Ovary." Underneath each heading are numbers from one through twenty.

"Just circle numbers for each side as I call them. If I call a number on one side more than once, just write the number two or whatever next to the one you circled. Okay?"

I nod, even though I can't help thinking that with all this high-tech equipment around, surely there is a more reliable method than manually circling numbers while a handheld probe moves inside me.

"Each number represents one follicle. The number itself is the size of the follicle in millimeters. Let's take a look and see what we have." She flips the lights off and slides a slick probe inside me. We both turn to look at the screen next to her.

She moves the probe back and forth with one hand and slides a mouse with her other hand to measure little pouches on my ovaries.

"Okay, left side. Twelve, nine, eleven. Right side. Fourteen, seven." I circle each number and let out a sigh, relieved that there are five follicles. The drugs are working.

She removes the probe and flips on the lights. Her face tells me that I am not supposed to be relieved.

"You're not responding to the drugs," she says. "We're going to have to cancel this cycle."

"But you counted five eggs, right?"

"Well, no. Follicles aren't necessarily eggs. We hope that there is an egg in every one, but sometimes there isn't. When you take that into account, you might have three, maybe four eggs in there. It's hard to tell."

"But if there are eggs, why not retrieve them?"

"You need at least six eggs to go forward. Otherwise, IVF really isn't worth it. Chances are without at least that many it's not going to work. Not every egg is going to fertilize, and of the ones that do, not all of them will mature into an embryo. It's really a game of odds, so the more eggs you retrieve, the better your chances of getting a viable embryo."

I am stunned by how quickly we have gone from relying on science to playing an odds game.

"But what if this is all I produce?"

"Well, let's don't get ahead of ourselves. This cycle isn't going to be wasted. We'll cancel the IVF—no egg retrieval. But we can do an IUI instead—insert your husband's sperm and see what happens."

"But didn't you say that IUI wouldn't be likely to work for us? That's why the insurance company allowed us to skip IUI treatment altogether, right?"

She sighs and shrugs. "Yes, but it's our best option at this point. The chances are low, but there is still a chance. That's why we can't rule anything out."

"So if we can't rule anything out, why aren't we going ahead with IVF?"

"Your insurance will only give you four chances at IVF because egg retrieval is expensive. They give you unlimited IUIs because insemination is cheap by comparison."

"So does the insurance company say I can't do IVF unless I have six eggs?"

"Well, no. We just don't think it's worth it with so few."

She retreats from the room abruptly with a wave of her hand and leaves me to get dressed.

I meet my therapist, Kristy, at her new office. She sits on an oversize love seat and invites me to sit on its twin opposite her.

She smiles and stretches out her hands to direct my attention to the room. I smile back and look around at the dizzying maroon and gold floral patterns that cover the sofas, the rug, and wallpaper.

Her cleanly washed face and the faded jeans she'd been wearing since junior high school appear ridiculous in this room that seems to demand lipstick and pantyhose. Her old basement office was spare and slightly unfinished, much like her. She is gangly, with dirty blonde hair that seems permanently damp.

Her inability to seem cool endears her to me even though she is not my first choice for a therapist. All my previous therapists were Black women, but since moving to this area, I've had difficulty finding Black women who practice talk therapy. The few I located work primarily through agencies that serve children and families who are unable to pay for private therapy. A friend had recommended Kristy.

"So, what's on your mind today?"

I start where we left off last time. "Trying to have a baby is the hardest thing I've ever done. It's almost not something you do, but more like something that does you."

She nods and leans forward, with one bony hand on her chin.

"It's like my body is ill, except I'm not sick. I am in the same body I was in all along, but now I know that something is wrong with it."

"You know, I had a friend who desperately wanted to get pregnant and when she finally did, she had a special needs child. It's been so hard on her." She leans back in her chair, nodding slowly as if she has said something so profound that it requires contemplation.

My stomach tightens into an angry knot. "Are you suggesting that she loves her child less than she would a child without disabilities?"

"No . . . well . . . what I mean is that sometimes what we want and what we need aren't necessarily the same things. It's too late for her to do anything about her choice, but if my friend had it to do all over again . . ."

"Wait. Are you saying that I'm better off without a baby because at my age it might have special needs?"

"No . . . I am trying to explain that life with a child might not make you happy, even if it is what you want."

"Happy? When did I ever say anything about happiness? I am not giving myself shots and going to a fertility clinic daily to achieve happiness. That would be crazy."

She cocks her head and blinks at me as if I am the suspicious package that airport announcements warn passengers to report. "Well, what do you want from having a child?"

"It's something more like . . ." I search for a word to communicate something that is not a word but a feeling. The closest I can come is "fulfillment."

She furrows her brow. "I don't know if I understand the distinction you're making, but let's go with 'fulfillment.' How is a baby waking you at two a.m. going to lead to fulfillment? Aren't there other, better ways?"

I am seeking help in the wrong place. But I keep talking as if words can make her understand.

"No, I'm not talking about personal fulfillment. It's something bigger. It's not about happy endings. It's more like beginnings, or continuation, or both." I start to say more and stop myself. Though I have told her about my father, his grief, our grief, I do not want to reopen this history to someone for whom a friend's child is nothing more than an anecdote. And even if I wanted to explain, to name the connection between my lost family and my desire to make a new one, it would be like stripping feeling down to an X-ray. Words seem to convey only the bones of the thing in a way that is pat and convenient, as partial truths usually are. Such a description would not explain that I wake up each morning with a hard pit of longing in my belly and that I can also feel in it a soft center made of the past. When I try to translate this feeling suspended between an urge and a wish, I describe something pathological: girl born into a whirlwind of grief thrusts herself toward a future that is equally out of her control and probably another source of profound grief. Western ideas about pathology are too neat, too simplistic to capture what I am, a link between the past and the future. Even my name is a caution sign, at once a triangle that points to something already broken and a yellow invitation to proceed slowly. I think of a novel about a girl whose mother, grandmother, and great-grandmother tell her that she has to "make generations," have babies who would become women and pass on the stories of the abuses their enslaved ancestors suffered. Their testimony would serve as evidence of their family's survival. But the girl couldn't have children and had to make music instead. How could this white woman understand all that when I wasn't even sure if I could? What did I really know to pass on anyway? So instead, I ask her if she has ever wanted a child.

"No. I made a decision a long time ago that that's not the life I want for myself."

Though I have said the same thing, something about her slow pronunciation of the word "decision" tells me that her words are not a performance of unconventionality or an attempt to convince herself that a life without children could be satisfying. She means what she says because unlike me she does not care what anyone thinks.

She glances at the small clock on the coffee table between us. "We need to talk about ways to address your anxiety and give you more clarity and perspective. Have you heard of EFT?"

I shake my head.

"It stands for emotional freedom techniques. It helps you reduce anxiety by tapping on body parts. Watch me."

She closes her eyes and hammers the side of one of her hands with two fingers as if she is having a mini seizure. "Even though I have this feeling of anxiety—you can insert any feeling here—I deeply and completely accept myself. Even though I have this feeling of anxiety, I deeply and completely accept myself."

She opens her eyes. "Okay, now you try. Remember, you can insert any feeling."

I close my eyes and poke the side of my hand with two fingers.

"Harder," she says. "Okay, now repeat after me. Even though I have this feeling of anxiety, I deeply and completely accept myself."

I repeat her words and open my eyes, but hers are closed, and she is poking her forehead.

"Now you are supposed to continue tapping on different pressure points while repeating the mantra. Watch me." She bangs on the sides of her head, making her way down her face, and finishes by pounding her chest fast like a cartoon chimp.

When she is done, she opens her eyes. "So how would you rate your anxiety now?"

"I think it just went up." I do not say that it went up because I need to find a new therapist.

She laughs. "Practice it at home. After it becomes more automatic it works."

I should explain to her that I am not joking but instead I reach into my bag for my wallet.

As I leave, I see a woman sitting in the waiting room. If she were a Black woman, I would give her a look that said, *Girl, don't waste your money here.* But she is a petite young white woman with salon blonde hair. She looks like she could be someone seeking personal happiness. I am sure she is not like me, seeking legacies known and unknown.

At home in front of my computer, I discover that I have a new name: Poor Responder to IVF. The name sounds like a rummage sale boombox gone bad with corroded batteries. But the words "poor responder" can sound an alarm in a fertility clinic. Because each clinic has to report the number of treatment cycles, egg retrievals, and embryo transfers that result in a live birth to the Centers for Disease Control and Prevention, clinics that treat poor responders risk diminishing their success rates. The CDC publishes the data on the internet, and patients rely on it to choose a clinic. If doctors discover that a patient is a poor responder and as such is unlikely to produce enough eggs to result in a live birth, doctors can cancel the cycle. Then the poor responder no longer has to be counted in the most critical data category: egg retrievals resulting in live births. The poor responder does not disappear completely from the record because each practice also has to report the number of cycles started and canceled before eggs were retrieved. But she is also not very visible. In a statement published along with the IVF success rates, the CDC acknowledges that "a high percentage of cancellations tends to lower the percentage of cycles resulting in live births but may increase the percentage of retrievals resulting in live births and the percentage of transfers resulting in live births." For patients looking to do IVF, the most critical indicator of a practice's success is the number of egg retrievals resulting in live births, not cycles resulting in live births, because treatment cycles can be canceled for any reason by doctors—but also by patients due to the emotional and/or financial costs of treatment. By canceling cycles that don't look promising, clinics can erase poor responders from that data point.

We poor responders are present and yet not entirely seen, like a dust bunny that peeks from under a rug, or a gray hair that catches a bit of sunlight despite a dark layer of temporary hair dye. But once doctors see us, they cannot unsee us. It's only on paper that they can stick us under a piece of correction tape.

We lurk on discussion boards telling stories that no one wants to hear:

I was billed for everything leading up to IVF, but the doctor
still refused to retrieve eggs because I only had 6 follicles.

After two failures, they refuse to continue treating me.

They turned me away because I had a miscarriage last time.

I am overweight, and they refused to treat me.

Tomorrow, I will get erased again. I will lie down on another table
covered in white paper and put my feet in stirrups. Dr. Z. will enter
and insert a tube filled with sperm into my body, and say good luck,
though we both will know that this procedure is a ruse with less than
a 2 percent chance of working. There is a reason why the CDC does
not track IUI success rates. When the doctor is done, she will direct
me to lie there for thirty minutes, and she will leave.

Reginald will sit beside me reading a book aloud in his tenderest
voice. But my mind will wander to my first meeting with Dr. Z., when
she said, "Let's get you pregnant," with such certainty, even after she
saw the cysts on my ovaries. When she looked at my body, its thinness,
its disguise of youthfulness, its Blackness, she assumed that I would
be a slam dunk case.

I find Isabel's house in a neighborhood of million-dollar midcentury
homes. I approach a side entrance, as she'd directed me to over the
phone, and knock. A tiny, pale elderly woman with equally pale hair
opens the door. She looks at me and then around me as if she is expecting someone else.

"I'm Cassandra. I scheduled an appointment."

"Oh. I didn't realize."

"Is this the wrong door?"

"No. No. Come in and have a seat."

We sit down in a dim office filled with dingy antique midcentury furniture. A layer of mildew almost as thick as the dust on the table hangs in the air.

A friend who has had more therapy than anyone I know recommended Dr. P., citing her as one of the best therapists she'd seen. But I feel my difference here as if I have been cut out of a picture and placed in this room so shabby that it could only be acceptable among the white rich.

I compliment the architecture and she waves a hand as if to say, *This old thing.*

"So, what brings you here?"

"I've been struggling to get pregnant, and I'm getting treatment, but emotionally, I find it hard to address my own feelings of failure."

She nods and looks down at an open notebook in her lap.

"It's already been a trying process, and I haven't even completed an IVF cycle yet. The coping part has been harder than the treatment itself."

She looks up from her notebook with her eyebrows lifted. "Have you considered that given your age . . ." She glances down at the notebook.

"I'm thirty-seven," I say. "I started trying almost a year ago without medical help. Then I went to an infertility doctor about five months ago. After a lot of tests, monitoring, and also a surgery to remove cysts, I've only just started injecting fertility drugs. After all that, my doctor canceled my IVF procedure because I wasn't producing a lot of eggs. It was devastating."

She nods and writes for a minute before looking up at me. "Have you considered that it is quite possible that you won't ever get pregnant?"

Her words strike me somewhere between the throat and chest. Heat rises into my face, and my hands close into fists as my body enters fight mode.

"My diagnostic tests suggest that it's possible for me to get pregnant."

"But what if it is not possible? Not everyone can have children. You don't have the control you're pretending to have. Have you always felt like you were controlling everything?"

I pause for a moment because my chest feels like it is on fire and I am trying not to react to her combative tone.

"I have struggled with anxiety. And there's a family history of anxiety and depression. So yes, I realize that I don't have control over everything, and I also struggle with the desire to control things. To my mind, that's sort of the definition of anxiety."

She looks down at her notebook again. "You're a professor."

I nod.

"Very ambitious," she says into her chest.

"I suppose. I am very focused, determined."

"How old were you when you finished your PhD?"

"Twenty-eight."

She frowns and writes something in her notebook.

"It sounds like you are very driven to get what you want." Her tone, previously ambivalent, shifts as if she is recording a movie trailer. I have seen this movie about a Black woman fighting her way out of the ghetto, trying to learn to read, or get her kid out of foster care, while a benevolent white person, the real hero of the film, proves that all Black people need is the generous tutelage of a white person.

"You have to understand that I didn't have a lot of other options. I had to finish my degree while I had funding, or I would have had to go back to Alabama and work at Walmart."

She winces at the word "Walmart" as if I have said "butt plug."

"I'm sure you've worked very hard to be here. And now that you've been unable to get pregnant, it's very hard to accept that you don't have control. But you don't have to have a child. How do you imagine your life without a child?"

"I don't have to imagine it. I'm already living it," I say.

"No, you're not. You're projecting a future that includes a child, and that is causing you a lot of stress. What would happen if you chose to give up that"—she hesitates and looks up at the ceiling, searching for a word—"idea of yourself."

"I am seeking infertility treatment right now. Obviously, I'm not ready to give up on the idea that I can have a biological child."

Her eyes widen, but still, she cannot see me. I am an idea, a concept—a foolish barren woman wandering about in the Bible trying to cut a deal with anyone who can procure a child. I am defined by emptiness like the "museum without statues," in the Sylvia Plath poem. I am a desperate and deluded wife in *The Handmaid's Tale*. I am an experience that she has never had nor will she ever have. And her imagination cannot bridge this gap, even if she wanted to.

I stare at her tiny body that I am sure once harbored a child whom she would refuse to imagine her life without.

"You can choose to give up the desire."

"And, what—then I'll be happy?"

She tilts her head and raises her eyebrows as if to say, *You are learning, Grasshopper.*

"Your aggression has probably benefited you in your life, but it won't serve you in trying to get pregnant."

"My aggression?"

She nods, and I am Tyler Perry's Madea with a cigarette in one hand and a gun in the other. I am the sassy best friend who can roll her eyes and her neck at the same time. I am Mammy, and Florence, and Cookie Lyon all rolled into one. I am angry, and I want too much— more than my tiny share.

At the exact minute that the session is to end, she waves her hand to shut me up and asks if I will return at the same time next week.

"You realize that I do not take insurance, right? You'll have to get reimbursed for these sessions." The corners of her mouth are heavy with condescension.

"I know that. But it's not the reason I won't be returning."

She raises her eyebrows.

I reach into my bag for my wallet. But she waves her small hand again. I take this gesture as her acknowledgment that this was not therapy, and I gather my things to go. I let myself out.

Two weeks later, a scrawled itemized bill for $250 with a stamped addressed envelope appears in my mail.

I begin a second cycle of treatment, starting with birth control and egg-stimulating drugs. But this time, I inject myself with nearly twice the dose of medications that I took before. My body begins to bleed, but I am not supposed to have a period. I am supposed to be developing eggs. I call the practice and they tell me to come in right away. When I arrive, a nurse takes me to an examining room and covers the table with an absorbent pad. As soon as I am undressed and situated on the table, I hear a quiet knock. Dr. D., a small white man who is part owner in the practice, comes in with a nurse following behind him. He greets me, and I nod and put my feet in the stirrups.

He inserts a probe and they both stare at the screen next to my head. He squints and frowns, tilting his head left and right like a confused cocker spaniel.

"What's happening?" I say.

He makes a wordless sound and pauses. "You're bleeding, but you're not shedding follicles. They are still there." He points to the fuzzy images on the screen. "It's like your body is confused."

"What would cause that? I thought everything was being regulated by the drugs."

He pulls the probe out and shakes his head like he is trying to get water out of his ear.

"When you get home, just take the HCG drug you have in the refrigerator."

"What will it do?"

"It will make your body shed the follicles. Then we can start the treatment over again when you get a normal period. I'll send new scripts for more meds."

"So this treatment cycle is canceled?"

He nods, and as he walks to the door, the nurse opens it and slips out.

"Is there any reason to be concerned about my body's reactions to the drugs? You said it's confused?"

He shakes his head no without looking at me. "This kind of stuff just happens sometimes." And he is gone.

The phantom bleeding stops and two weeks later my real period comes. This means that I can start a third IVF cycle. Again, I inject myself with high doses of drugs intended to make me produce multiple eggs instead of the single egg that women usually produce each month without drugs. I go to the practice regularly to get blood draws and vaginal ultrasounds that monitor my progress.

The drugs transform my body. I begin to smell again like metal dipped in acid. My breasts and abdomen swell until they are sore with their own weight. I am tired and teary.

With each monitoring appointment, there are just four follicles. I need six to proceed with IVF, but more don't seem to want to develop.

Reginald comes with me to the last monitoring appointment, where I already know what the doctor will say.

As I lie on the table, he hovers in the corner next to me while the doctor moves a probe inside me and stares at a screen. She shakes her head and removes the probe.

I am still on my back with my feet in stirrups when she says, "We are going to have to cancel the egg retrieval."

Something breaks inside me and tears stream down the sides of my face and into my ears before I can get up. I cannot muster any more protest than this.

Reginald reaches for my hand, and Dr. Z. heads toward the door. She is saying something about scheduling the insemination. But Reginald stops her with questions that I am too crumpled and too female to ask: Why is the magic number six? What if we don't reach that number? Is there anything else you can do to try to get more eggs? His tone is even and firm.

Dr. Z. stops with her hand on the door and looks at him with startled eyes and a parted mouth like an invisible hand is holding a knife to her throat. I squeeze Reginald's hand to warn him that she cannot see him now. He is a phantom, a masked mugger on a TV drama, a mug shot of a rapist-murderer on the news. He keeps talking, and I squeeze harder to say, *Be careful—if she uses the word "intimidation," you will be dragged from this place*. But he keeps talking, pleading, because he cannot see the boogeyman he has become. In the Black middle-class world of Houston where he grew up, with its Black doctors, dentists, lawyers, and politicians, he rarely had to negotiate white fears. When he is at his most sincere, he loses his "second sight," W.E.B. Du Bois's word for Black people's ability to see themselves through white eyes, a burden and yet also the thing that allows us to survive white supremacy.

Dr. Z. squeezes the doorknob so hard that her hand turns pink. I pull my feet from the stirrups and sit up as if my body is not weighed down with fluid and grief. I force words to come out of me not just because I too am seeking answers, but also because I feel like I must stop his words, interrupt the Black phantom reflected in the doctor's eyes. If there is to be a problem, it is better, though not ideal, that it be me, a woman talking in a voice that sounds like marbles pouring into a glass. I think of something my mother told me. *Black men have to sometimes let their women stand in front of them because a white man would kill a Black man for just looking wrong*. She spoke of a time when a white man came to her mother's door and asked for her husband. My grandmother lied and told the man that her husband was not home. The white man asked again and pulled back his coat to show her his handgun. She told the man that if he didn't get off her porch, she would make him eat that pearly-handled pistol. The man left. It didn't mean that white men never killed a Black woman for disrespect or less, but that sometimes Black women took a dangerous gamble that could have resulted in being beaten, raped, or killed to protect a husband or son from sure death. My father's mother took that gamble every time she negotiated a cotton price or demanded payment or general respect from a white man. She knew she could have died, but she must have believed she had a better shot at staying alive than her husband.

Now it is my turn to get in the way, before this woman's fear births a Mandingo fantasy. "What about other drug protocols? I read something recently about low stimulation plans, where doctors have had success getting more follicles with fewer drugs."

She sighs and the look of fear on her face turns to frustration. "I don't think that's going to work for you. There just isn't enough research on that method. We'll switch to insemination now, and we can talk more about this if it doesn't work. There's always a chance it could, even if it is a slim one."

She steps out of the room, but Reginald follows her. The last thing I can hear him say is an exasperated, "Can I please talk to you?"

I get dressed as fast as I can and walk into the hallway, but they are gone, and I'm not sure which way they went. By the time I get to her office, he is walking toward me, smiling.

"They are going to do the egg retrieval," he says.

"What?"

"She is going to discuss it with the other doctors at the practice. She said she'll tell them what I said, and she thinks they'll listen. If they can agree, she's going to do the egg retrieval."

"What did you say to her?"

"I just told her this could be our only chance."

"But she already knows that," I say.

He smiles and shrugs. "We're still in this round. Can you hang in there?"

Weeks later Reginald will recount our IVF experience to a friend whose wife has just begun infertility treatment: "Man, I learned that you have got to go to every appointment because these doctors will pull all kinds of bullshit on a woman."

I see Rhonda in a hard-to-find office park. Her office is small with white walls and gray-speckled tile like you'd find in a medical facility or a school. She has an ear-length mushroom haircut that makes it look like she travels back to the seventies to get her hair done.

She does not smile, even when she greets me.

I sit down opposite her, and she asks me why I'm here.

I explain that I am struggling with infertility, and I have read that she specializes in chronic illness. I am hoping that her skills might transfer to my situation since I cannot find a therapist who specializes in infertility.

She nods and asks questions about my infertility, my history with therapy, and my family history.

I fill in as much of my backstory as I can, trying to explain the connection between the generational grief that I inherited from my father and my grief for a never-born child.

"This infertility treatment process sounds very hard," she says.

"It feels like the hardest thing that I've done, but I'm also ashamed to even think that, let alone say it. So many Black people have been through worse for me to be here. And I'm whining about having access to expensive treatments that aren't working. That makes me feel selfish, foolish."

She presses her lips together and nods again.

I tell her about how frustrated I am with the practice, their refusal to retrieve eggs, and my feelings of dependence on a doctor whom I can't convince to help me.

I stare at her bookshelf while I wait for her to say something. All the books are about coping with disease: books on chronic illness and family therapy, cognitive behavioral therapy and psychotherapy for cancer patients, group therapy for breast cancer patients and their families.

"Sounds very difficult."

I nod and wait for her to say more, but she does not.

"Can you tell me a little bit about how you imagine my therapy proceeding?" I say.

"How would you like it to proceed?" Her voice is calm, genuine.

"I'm interested in coping techniques, ways that I can relieve the stress and deal with the parts of this process that are out of my control."

"This is all very new to me. All my clients are terminally ill cancer patients or they are losing a family member to cancer. You are healthy." Her eyes scan my body as if she is checking to make sure that all the parts are there.

"That depends on the definition of healthy, doesn't it? To a reproductive endocrinologist, I am not healthy."

"Yes, but that's not the same as having cancer."

"Of course not. I didn't mean that. What I'm trying to say is that in this process of infertility treatment, I am being defined as sick and I feel like I'm internalizing that idea—accepting the idea that my body is deficient."

She frowns. "There are some connections to my work, yes, but what you're looking for is not quite grief therapy. I mean, you are still trying to get pregnant. And I'm just not sure if . . ." She rambles on listing the pros and mostly cons of her treating me as if she is talking herself out of buying a new coffee maker. I cannot follow her train of thought fully, but I catch up to her meaning when she ends with this: "I didn't have any problems getting pregnant or any losses or anything, so I don't know much about what that's like."

For a moment, I want to argue with her, to tell her that perhaps what I am going through is not as different as she thinks from the grief someone might suffer losing their identity, or a loved one, to illness, but I realize how ridiculous arguing with someone who does not want to treat me would be. She does not know how to help me. And if I cannot make her understand the duality of my body that is both healthy and sick, how would I ever make her understand the twoness of my grief, how I grieve the dead and someone yet to be conceived at the same time?

I reach into my bag to get the co-pay. When I hand it to her, she says one last time, "This whole thing sounds very hard."

I am at home when the nurse calls to tell me the precise time that I am to give myself a shot that will cause my eggs to go through the last stage of development. The time, she explains, is based on the time of my egg retrieval procedure in the morning. She warns me that the timing must be precise—too soon and I could release eggs before the doctor retrieves them, too late and the eggs won't mature and be viable for fertilization.

The drug is a hormone called human chorionic gonadotropin (HCG). Months before, when I put the vial in my refrigerator, I noticed the word "human," Googled it, and discovered that the drug is collected from the urine of pregnant women. Now, as the nurse says "HCG" and warns me about timing, I think of the word "human" and the fact that I am to consume this human thing. I am in the darkest of the old European fairy tales, the one where the wolf offers Little Red Riding Hood meat and wine, and she unknowingly consumes her grandmother's flesh and blood.

My anxiety rises as I watch the clock all evening. Finally I walk to the refrigerator fifteen minutes prior to the designated time to prepare the shot. I scan the shelves of the refrigerator, but I do not see the human thing. I pull out everything inside until the refrigerator is empty.

I scream: "It's not here! My god, it's not here!"

Reginald approaches from behind me. "Are you sure? Did you take it upstairs?"

"No! I only have to take it once and it has to be refrigerated."

His eyes scan the jars and bowls that I pulled from the fridge.

My stomach sinks until I feel like I am going to collapse. I hang on to the kitchen counter with both hands.

"When did you last see it, and did you have any reason to do anything at all with it?"

"No! I just told you . . ."

"But you checked the medications when they arrived. I remember you organizing them. So it was here."

"Yes. That's right. It was—oh my god! Dr. D. told me to take it weeks ago. When the last cycle got canceled, he told me to take it to shed the eggs. He never prescribed me more. I didn't realize it was the same drug until just now. Oh my god, this is our only shot and it's gone!" I sob.

"Stay with me now. Let's just call them. Is there an emergency number?"

I run to find my purse and Reginald follows me. I find the card in my wallet, and he pulls out his phone and dials. "We'll get this sorted out."

I try to stop crying, but the hormones that are coursing through me seem to be spewing out of my eyes, my nose, my mouth as the feeling of loss sinks in.

Reginald paces to the living room and I follow him.

"Hello. My wife is a patient at the practice and we're having a problem with a drug. Yes, this number is fine." He hangs up and tells me a doctor will call back.

"I am so sorry. I should have double-checked. But I didn't understand that the medicine he told me to take was the one I would need tonight."

"It's not your fault. You aren't the IVF doctor. You've never done this before. How could you know?"

The phone rings and Reginald answers. I lean in close and hear Dr. D.'s voice on the other end. Reginald explains the situation and asks Dr. D. how we could get the medication.

"Is it too late?" I say. "Can I still take it?"

"Well, yes, I suppose. You'd just need to call in and let us know what time you took it so we could reschedule the retrieval, but I'm not sure how you can get the drug. We might need to scrap this one."

"We'll get the drug," Reginald says. "Just tell us our best options. Is it something a twenty-four-hour pharmacy would have?"

Dr. D. answers in a voice so high-pitched that it sounds like a recording sped up. "I don't know. I mean, I don't think so. But I guess it's possible. You could call around, I suppose. But you'd need to hurry, I guess."

"What about specialty pharmacies?" I say.

"They're probably all closed now. I think it's just too late in the evening. I mean, that's what I think, but I suppose you could call. I don't really know for sure, but—"

"Can you at least tell us what time would be too late to take the drug?" I say.

"I don't know . . . I just—well, you can take it anytime tonight. You'd have to call in the morning and tell us what time you took it. But I don't know how you're going to get it tonight."

"If we find someone, can you—"

"Good luck," Dr. D. says and hangs up.

"He is useless!" Reginald says. "What is the matter with that man?"

I run upstairs and come back with my laptop and phone. The two of us call every twenty-four-hour pharmacy near us. None have the drug.

Just as we are about to give up, I remember that the pharmacy that sent the drugs was an hour or so away. I find the website and locate an after-hours number. I call. And in a few minutes, a woman named Erica calls me back.

"I'm sorry about the noise in the background," she says. "Our family is having a party for my mother-in-law."

I apologize for the interruption, and I explain what I need and why. She gives me directions to her house. I smile and nod at Reginald. When he screams, "Thank god!" she laughs.

We arrive at her house an hour later, at 10 p.m.

Reginald stays in the car while I scamper to the door of an enormous stone house. A smiling petite blonde woman meets me at the door.

"Come on in," she says, extending one arm as if I am there for cocktails. "Where's your husband?"

I tell her that we don't want to disturb her any more than we have to. I do not say that the minute we entered her neighborhood in the dark, we knew that his Black male body could cause alarm, and that two Black bodies would only make it worse. Given everything that had already gone wrong that night, we did not want to add the police to the story.

"I really thought your poor husband was going to explode on the phone. He must have been so scared. Poor man."

She stands there for a moment smiling and staring at me while I shift from left to right wondering what else I need to say to get the drug.

"I have everything ready for you. You'll just need to sign the papers on the table in the kitchen. And you can wash your hands and take the shot right there too."

I start to shake my head in an *Oh, I couldn't possibly impose* sort of way, and she waves me off.

"I know how it is. Both my kids were conceived with IVF."

I walk into her kitchen where I sign the paperwork and wash my hands. She's even set out a clean towel, a sterile needle, alcohol pads, and a sharps container for me. I raise my top and give myself a quick shot to the belly.

"Thank you so much. We are so grateful."

"Wait just a minute, before you go. I want to show you something. Come over here."

I think of Reginald in the car, hoping that no one has spotted him and called the police. But I follow her over to a small glass tank in her living room.

"Look inside. Do you see it?"

I peer inside, trying to spot a frog or lizard, but I cannot see anything.

"Look inside that miniature tree log thing."

I get closer and two round, intelligent eyes look back at me from a small furry face.

"What is it?" I whisper.

"It's a sugar glider. We just got it yesterday so he's still a little scared. But isn't he magical?"

The creature crawls out. It looks like it is made from the spare parts of other animals—the knowing eyes of a primate, the ears of a mouse, the fur of a squirrel, and claws like a bird. On his sides flesh drapes like an old woman's shawl. He looks like something mythical, something that an ancient people made up to explain the existence of the inexplicable.

"I wanted you to see him because I thought you could use some magic tonight."

I thank her, and the sugar glider cocks his head and disappears again into the log.

CHAPTER 7

I am supposed to be conducting scholarly research when I begin instead Googling words to describe what I am to my father: "doppelgänger," "stand-in," "rebirth," "proxy," "second chance." I land on the term "replacement child" and a world of pathology fills my screen.

Coined by Barbara and Albert Cain in the 1960s, "replacement child" refers to a child conceived as a replacement for one who died. Sitting at my desk, I lean toward my computer as if I am looking for myself in a photo of a crowd. A replacement child grows up in the shadow of a dead child. The parents' grief for the dead child becomes part of the replacement. I lean back, realizing that I have been holding my breath. Is this what I am? My parents did not lose a child prior to my birth, and I was born twelve years after the wreck. But I am a replacement for too many dead to count: my father's sister and her almost four-year-old child whose name I bear, his nineteen-year-old bride and the children they dreamed of but never had, and his mother, who had recently moved in with him. Replacements experience intense identification with the dead child, and this condition is exacerbated by their parents, who unconsciously impose the identity of the dead child on the living one, even calling the living child by the dead child's name, whether by mistake or because the living child was named after the dead one. I say the words aloud: "Replacement child." This term is the closest I will come to a name for what I am. It explains why grief seemed to have a place setting at my family's table, why my name has been on a tombstone since before I was born, why old men and women looked at me like I had come to haunt them. Something was unfinished, and I was here not to finish it, but to continue the work.

At age six, I asked my mother why they named me San. She smiled and looked away with the same expression she got when she talked about scoring while serving in a volleyball game so many times that the PE teacher had told her she had to give someone else a turn.

I had a name picked out for a boy, Corey. But they didn't give girls boy names like that back then. I remembered your daddy talking about San, and I always liked that name. When I told him that I wanted to name you San, he got so happy he ran out of the hospital room to call your aunt Judy and find out what San's whole name was. He wanted you to have her real name, even though we knew we'd call you San for short.

So my parents named me for the dead child twice—both her formal name and her nickname. My mother told the story again and again, sometimes when I asked her, and other times unsolicited. Always, she looked away as if the scene in the hospital were playing out on a screen that only she could see. *Your daddy was so happy.* I loved that there was a story with a happy ending behind my name, and I was the happy ending.

But why would my mother choose a name so distinctly part of my father's previous life? My name was her decision. She had chosen my siblings' names too. As far as I knew, all the names in my family on both sides were chosen by women. Naming was not men's business and my mother often expressed resentment toward women who had allowed men a say in naming their children. Whenever anyone mentioned a boy child named for his father, she complained, *Why would anybody want to have two people in the same house with the same name? Then the boy ends up with everyone calling him Junior, like that's a name.*

But it seemed to have never occurred to her that a child named for a dead one might produce a similar kind of confusion. Hadn't she heard my father saying the dead child's name in his sleep? A friend once told me that if one is to be functional, repression must have a pressure valve—some place where the hurt can be released just a little so that the whole operation doesn't explode. Maybe my name was a pressure valve. To call me "San" was to acknowledge that once upon a time a child died, while in the same breath reassigning the name to the joy of a new baby. A name could memorialize the past, while also insisting that the child's death was indeed past—so much so that her name could be made new again. Had my mother sought a way to acknowledge the dead without waking them?

My father had accepted this memorial, according to my mother, happily. But could he have said no without setting off alarms? If he had, it would have been like admitting that the past is never really over—that even in the moments after birth a dead child was there with us. Or was the excitement my mother saw gratefulness for a way to acknowledge the past without having to investigate its meaning? Perhaps my father needed the release of a pressure valve? His sister had done something like that when she named her daughter Bernice, after their mother who was killed in the wreck. Now they all associated his mother's name with his niece. They even pronounced it differently, "Ber-NIECE" instead of "BUR-nis," as their mother had been called. Maybe reassigning San's name could take away the sting of grief?

My name was a kind of death work, like when I was little and went with my parents to my grandmother's and aunt's graves. Naming turned grief from a feeling into a job that we could do. The job was infinite because even silk flowers would fade and have to be replaced. But this sort of work carved out rituals that acknowledge the past while also containing it. That was what my mother was doing when she recited the details of my ancestors' bodies as we stood over their graves. *San's hair was real red. Wasn't it, John?*

I close my computer and think of my father asleep in his recliner chair, calling my name, the dead child's name. *San, stop. San, are you okay? San?*

Reginald and I arrive at the IVF practice giddy and nervous. A nurse directs us to a closet-size room where Reginald puts on blue coveralls, a hair cap, a face mask, and shoe covers. I undress and put on a thin hospital gown and hair cover.

I smile at the bulbous blue cap on his head. "You look like you have a Jheri curl underneath there."

He pretends to swagger and sings a line from a fictional Jheri curl ad in an old Eddie Murphy movie: "Just let your Soul Glo."

We laugh, but the stress of not knowing what comes next fills our eyes.

The nurse returns and we follow her to a large, chilly room. Pink curtains hang from the ceiling, dividing the space into more than a dozen three-wall rooms that we can glance inside as we walk by. In each one, there is a woman lying on a bed and a man sitting or standing next to her. In one is a South Asian couple, the woman still drowsy from anesthesia, and her husband hunches over her. Next to them is a white working-class couple probably in their late twenties. The husband paces and chatters away on the phone in a North Jersey accent complete with the word "youse." Our neighbors are a young Hasidic Jewish couple sitting in silence.

In New Jersey, any company that has at least fifty employees is required to include IVF coverage in healthcare plans. Thus the waiting rooms often look like a meeting of the United Nations. I once asked a friend who received infertility treatments in New York if she was ever stunned by the diversity of people she saw getting treatment—assuming it was the same everywhere. But she said, "No—it's just me and the entire Junior League every time."

Despite what appears to be a diversity of people, we are the only Black people in this busy room of patients and practitioners. I am not surprised because I have read that even though Black women suffer from infertility more than white women, they are less likely to get treatment.

I enter my pink stall and take my place on the bed in this sci-fi version of a 1950s maternity ward where fabric and whispers take the place of privacy. I become one of a silent we, a community that refuses to commune. We sit or lie on display with our faces scrubbed clean of makeup and our heads topped by blue bulbous caps. Instead of babies, our arms circle the tension that will dog us for the next two weeks while we wait to find out if we are pregnant. As each couple enters, they peer in at us, anxious to see who sits in the next stall. If we meet their gazes at all, we do so briefly, retreating into our pink shrouds, grateful that we are all strangers and hopeful that we will stay that way.

A nurse tips into my stall. "I'm just going to attach the monitor to you and get the IV ready for Dr. R. She's our anesthesiologist."

She tacks sticky nodes to my chest and arms. "The adhesive will come right off later with soap," she says, as if my biggest worry today will be getting the glue off my body.

She turns a knob on the monitor. But it does not come on. "I guess something's not right here." She turns it off and turns it on again. She looks at me as if to make sure that I am indeed still alive. "I'll go get another one," she says.

"She looks annoyed with you for contradicting that machine," Reginald says. "Maybe you should play dead when she gets back."

Just as I roll my eyes at his joke, an older woman in a neat pantsuit and Chanel shoes steps in. "I'm Dr. R.," she says, and reaches for my hand and then Reginald's.

She grins, showing a few overlapping teeth, and lets her eyes move over the outline of my body on the bed and back to my face. "Well, you are beautiful, aren't you? So tall. Just like a model."

I try to smile, but just knowing someone is looking at me as I sit here in a shower cap and no makeup makes me feel uglier.

"I guess that's why I'm here," I say. "To pass it all on." This is supposed to be a joke, but I hear the truth of it as soon as it leaves my lips. I am not here to get a child, but rather a genetic child—one who looks like me, like my ancestors.

Dr. R. laughs and looks at Reginald. "She's funny too, huh?"

She asks me to confirm my weight, height, and allergies and checks off answers on her clipboard.

When she is done, she picks up a vial of milky liquid from a rolling tray and attaches it to my IV. This is the last thing I will remember before I wake up from the surgery.

My great-grandfather, Bunyan Cleere, replaced his whole family. A wife and two children. He was gambling on what should have been an ordinary night in Alabama. But when this night ended, a white man was dead. I don't know exactly why Bunyan killed him, and when I ask my father, he shakes his head and says, "White folks was so mean back then." Later, a cousin will tell me that Bunyan was winning and decided to leave with his money when a white man said, "Nigger, you aren't going anywhere."

Good Negroes learned to keep their heads down, to answer without eye contact, to sidestep gracefully out of white people's paths, and to generally stay out of trouble. This was how a Black person avoided becoming a burnt corpse hanging from the crook of a tree. The Cleeres were bad Negroes. They argued with white folks over cotton prices, peering down at pasty faces that they towered over. Their children sassed white men, and when white folks complained about them to their parents, the Cleeres just smiled and hid their pride behind a shrug.

When I ask my father why his family dared so much, he smiles and laughs a little. *Them niggas was crazy.*

After Bunyan killed the white man, he fled Alabama, leaving behind Lucy, his wife, and two small children: Bernice, my father's mother, and little Bunyan Jr. Bunyan Sr. fled to St. Louis, where he got a job on a large riverboat. But he still had not learned the lesson of what happens when you gamble with white men. He refused to accept that the dice, the table, the cards, the money, all of it belonged to them. He believed he was a player, but instead, as a Black man among white men, he was the game, a toy that they could play with. It was their game, and just twenty-one years before his birth, he could have been put up on that table as property to be lost and won. No one knows exactly what happened in the game, but it ended with Bunyan killing another white man. A group of men gave chase through the riverboat, but before they could capture him, Bunyan jumped into the Mississippi. Miraculously, the river that had led so many enslaved people deeper into slavery and spawned the term "sold down the river" buoyed Bunyan up, delivering him to relative safety.

He surfaced in Oklahoma and started a new life with a new name. He married and had more children. In his absence, his first wife started anew as well, marrying her former husband's brother Collis, a widower with five children. Together Lucy and Collis raised their children as siblings.

I wonder at all of them, Bunyan, Lucy, and Collis, their ability to make new families out of whatever they were given. You flee a lynching. So you marry and have more children. Your wife dies. So you marry the wife your brother left behind. Your husband flees and you marry his brother and raise your children and his. Had they learned this skill of making and remaking families from their parents and grandparents who were born in slavery? Being sold away from one's family to settle someone else's debt or so your mistress could buy a piano was the ultimate test in one's ability to survive precarity. Without the most basic freedoms, including to travel back to see their families, enslaved people had little choice but to become experts in replacing their lost families with new ones cobbled together from undocumented marriages, births, and adoptions of children belonging to dead kin.

But Bunyan was a fugitive, not a slave, and there were rumors that he sneaked back into Alabama to check on his family periodically. Black townspeople told stories of spotting him on country roads at night, headed to the home where his former wife and brother lived with his children. I imagine him, his tall, slender body hidden in the darkness, watching the lit windows of a shotgun house. Inside, his brother caresses his wife, and his children call his brother Daddy. It would have been like stealing a glimpse of a shadow self, the one you could have been, the one that you once were. Then he would return to the new life he had built for himself in Oklahoma. Once there, maybe he would call a name he used to call in Alabama and a child with eyes at once old and new would appear.

I wake up with Reginald sitting next to me. Someone has closed the pink curtains so they surround us on all sides.

"How many eggs?" I say.

"They haven't told us yet. Are you okay?"

I nod, but I am not back in my body.

Dr. Z. slips inside the curtain and asks how I am feeling.

"How many?" I ask.

She holds up one finger, and for a second I think that she is pointing at the ceiling.

"One?"

She nods, still unwilling to say the number aloud. She says she'll be right back and disappears behind the curtain.

"One egg. All this for one egg?"

Reginald puts his hand on mine. "It's still more than we had yester-day," he says.

But I know better. I have read infertility discussion boards teeming with the stories of women who retrieved fifteen eggs and still ended up with nothing. Some eggs don't fertilize. Some fertilize, but their development arrests and they just die.

A nurse pops in and asks how I am feeling. I shake my head at her, knowing that if I start to talk, I will sob.

She tells me that she will bring me a snack soon and asks if I need to go to the bathroom yet. I shake my head again.

She steps out and then pops her head back through the curtain. "It only takes one," she whispers and disappears.

I try to will myself to sleep. But another nurse, one we have not met, enters. I sit up, thinking that something must be wrong. Has the egg died suddenly?

"Don't get up," she says. "I just wanted to see you."

Reginald looks at me as if to ask, *Do you know her?*

"They were all talking about how beautiful you are. And you are. Both of you."

Her eyes shift to Reginald and back to me. "You're like a model couple or something. I would have thought you were a donor, but they . . ." She lets her sentence trail off and looks over her shoulder to see if anyone has heard her.

I lie back on the pillow and eke out a weak "thank you" to make her and her words that surprise me with hurt go away. But she remains, standing and staring. I glare back, assessing her body the same way that she assesses mine. My eyes scan her wide hips, thick waist, and low, heavy breasts that tip her slightly forward as if she is about to attack. Her face is round and plain, except for spots of acne on her cheeks. She is neither offensive nor attractive by conventional standards. But I am sure that she is fertile or at least believes she is or she would not be standing here talking about something as foolish as beauty.

Reginald shoots her a look that says, *Get out of here before you make my wife cry.*

"Umm, can I get you anything?" she asks.

"Fertility," I say. "I think I would rather be fertile than beautiful."

Her eyes widen, and she darts through the curtain, the words "good luck" trailing behind her.

Reginald looks at the spot where she was standing. "How stupid . . ."

I look down at my swollen belly and feel warm blood trickling from my body onto a pad on the bed. "I certainly do not feel beautiful," I say.

"You just had surgery. What was she thinking?" He fusses about the nurse and considers aloud whom he will report her to. But he is also angry at more than the nurse, and so am I.

I lie back down, wanting to be better than her, to care about things bigger than bodies. But on this bed, I am a body trying to make another body. I leak a Rorschach blot made of brown blood and phlegm because I want to make that biological essence that answers to dead names. I want the magic of legacy that lives in bodies, not merely resemblance, but that place where likeness crosses over into something uncanny, the mystery of kinship that even science struggles to comprehend. As strange as it had felt as a child to see how my body had bent the backs of old ladies worried that I had been in this world before, what I remember now is brown faces wanting to make sure that it was safe to love me.

My aunt and grandmother were strange-looking in the same ways that I am—taller than most, skinnier than most, with eyes, lips, and noses bigger than most. By today's standards, they would have been considered beautiful. But in their own time, when curvy figures were more desirable, they wouldn't have been called anything but skinny. The only picture I have seen of my aunt Maggie shows her at age four, with eyes so large that she looks as peculiar as I did as a child. In the two photographs I have seen of my grandmother, she looks back at the camera so sternly that the very idea of beauty seems inconsequential. I can see my face in hers, the round eyes, the crooked nose, the high cheekbones, and the full lips. But the weariness at the corners of her mouth frightens me. How could beauty matter when you are a Black woman living in the South long before the civil rights movement? Beauty would not give her the right to buy land, earn fair wages, attend equitable schools, or vote. She still picked cotton alongside the beautiful, the ordinary, and the ugly from before the sun rose until it went down.

What did beauty matter if the very same flesh is vulnerable to all manner of violation?

I am ten years old and looking through a photo album when I see the newspaper clipping of my baby picture. My mother sees me staring at it and she laughs.

"When your uncle Bunyan saw that picture in the birth announcements in the paper, he came by here and said, 'Who is this ugly baby?' You remember that, John?"

My father looks from behind his newspaper and presses his lips together into a tight smile.

Uncle Bunyan is named after my great-grandfather who killed white men, but Uncle Bunyan could not be more different. He is my paternal grandmother's brother. He is a small, elegant man, so afraid to be alone in his own house that he comes to spend the night with us whenever his wife leaves town. My father says it is because he is afraid of ghosts.

"Your sister got so mad at him for calling you ugly," my mother says. "She stomped out of here and didn't say a word to Bunyan for a long time."

"But I was ugly," I say, staring at the photo.

"No, you weren't!" my mother says. "You were real cute with big ol' eyes. Bunyan didn't like the picture because it made your skin look dark. The real picture we sent to the newspaper was in color, but they printed all the baby pictures in black-and-white. He thought you looked too dark to look like them, the Cleeres. That's what he was mad about."

"He didn't know any better than to say something like that. Him and Aunt Della didn't have any kids of their own," my father says.

I picture Aunt Della, a pecan-colored woman who wears wigs that seem to always be tilted to the side and ill-fitting dentures that make her mouth protrude. A teenage cousin joked that Aunt Della looked like the female ape from the *Planet of the Apes* movie, and though everyone told my cousin that she was terrible for saying it, they could not help laughing at the joke. Uncle Bunyan cared about looks, but he also cared about money, and Aunt Della was a teacher who earned more money than Black women who were cleaning houses and picking cotton. I wonder how Uncle Bunyan would have felt if he had children who looked like her instead of him. Would he have called them ugly too, or would his mind have tricked him into seeing himself in them?

I turn to the color photo of the same baby picture that is in the newspaper clip. The baby's skin is light brown, not dark, and she is ugly, with a mature wrinkled brow and eyes too large even for her fat face. She leans forward slightly as if she is about to fly at me and sink her toothless gums into my flesh.

On the third day after the retrieval, we arrive at the IVF practice to have the fertilized egg transferred to my body.

A nurse directs us to a large, sunny room styled like a daytime talk show set. Big, comfortable chairs face each other.

A young woman with a low brown ponytail and a soft smile approaches me and Reginald and introduces herself as Dr. V., the embryologist. She is the one who fertilized my egg with Reginald's sperm.

We all sit down and Dr. V. hands me a small folder. I look up at her wondering if this is some method for imparting bad news without having to say it aloud.

She smiles a wide, brilliant smile. "You can open it. It's a picture of your embryo."

I flip the folder open and there it is. A cluster of lumps. I have seen similar pictures on the internet, but I am still not sure what I am looking at, and judging from the confused expression on Reginald's face, he isn't either.

Dr. V. leans forward and uses her finger to point to each lump. "Each of these circular growths is a cell. Your embryo has eight cells. That's really good for this stage."

I stare at the picture of the lumpy cells, trying to imagine it as an ugly little pop-eyed baby. This is how hope sneaks back into my body.

Dr. V. grins at me, clearly proud of her work. "Are you ready for your transfer?"

I look at Reginald and he grins too. "Yes," I say. "We are ready."

I am thirty-four years old. I take my father to the doctor. After he goes to the examination room, I sit in a waiting room alone. I realize that I left my phone in the car, and I head to the door. A large woman comes toward me. She is carrying a cane but standing upright. She puts her face too close to mine.

"I know who you are," she says. "You John T.'s daughter. Ain't you?"

"Yes, ma'am," I say.

"I was his sister Maggie Jo's best friend. We used to sleep over at each other's houses." She smiles a little, but her eyes that never leave mine are not smiling. "You are just like her. You know that? Just like her."

Though as a child I had been spooked by these old ladies who looked at my body and saw the women they used to love, now I recognize these elder women as surrogates for my dead ancestors. When they looked at me in awe and fed me from chipped candy dishes, they gave me tokens of what it meant to be special, important, not for a talent or ability, but just for existing in my form. What more powerful gift was there to any child, but especially to a little Black girl in Alabama?

Even after all these years, I have never figured out what to say to these women who tell me I look like Maggie. I cannot agree with them, because I have never seen Maggie. "Thank you" would sound ridiculous, even though I am thankful for these strange moments of belonging that I have done nothing to earn. But I cannot shake the feeling that there is something I am supposed to say—something I can give her in exchange for the feeling of kinship she radiates toward me. I want to play a part in a script that someone has forgotten to give me. I try to smile, but I say nothing. I am six years old again, shifting my weight from one spindly leg to the other while a soft wrinkled face comes closer to mine. I feel the sting of a scab pulled back too fast and her longing for her friend that oozes out of it. She wants more than the genetic coincidence that I am. Her love surrounds me, soft, thick, and warm like undercooked dough. And in this moment, I see her, the girl who spent the night with her best friend, and I realize that I love this girl too.

CHAPTER 8

Before I was born, my mother lived in a dead woman's house, slept in a dead woman's bed, ate at a dead woman's table, and drank from a dead woman's cups.

In 1961, she married my father, then a twenty-six-year-old widower. She was twenty-three years old and already pregnant with my brother, who would be born three months later.

My mother moved into the house that my father had shared with his wife and parents. She bought new things for the house, but nothing could rid it of ghosts. My father had gotten rid of nothing but clothes. The rest of the dead women's things were everywhere. Their quilts tumbled out of closets. Cups stained by their lipstick sat in the cupboard, while a broom still thick with the dust they swept stood nearby.

The baby boy in my mother's belly was supposed to change things, make everything new. But those hopes were dashed when the baby ended up being delivered by the same doctor who had told my father that his first wife was dead.

The couple struggled to find a new house to rent, but few owners were willing to rent to Black people. They saved and bought a plot of land in one of the few neighborhoods where they were allowed to buy. There they built a new house that was supposed to be theirs alone. But when the time came to move in, they brought the old things with them. They packed up plates, quilts, whiskey, and sundry other things. My mother put the old glasses in her new cupboard, including one so jagged that it once tore open the lip of a guest. She hid the photos in boxes and put the quilts in the attic. My father needed the whiskey to live, so she left it in a cabinet next to the bleach and ammonia, as if these chemicals could strip the alcohol of its power. Then she went about filling the rest of the home with things she deemed beautiful and luxurious, hoping their novelty and value might overshadow the power of the past.

In the end, the house was too small for a living family and a dead one.

So they built another house across the street. Sitting on a hill overlooking the old one, the new house was bigger and better, with wall-to-wall carpet, a formal dining room with a chandelier, a den for everyday living, and an elegant living room that no one used. The Black people they knew admired the house and so did my parents. But in no time, the dust of the past settled on this new house too.

I am ten years old lying on the carpet of our den, watching television. Behind me, my father snores with an empty glass next to him. My mother, who is sitting on the sofa, puts her newspaper down and approaches him. She whispers his name and waits to see if he will wake up. He stays as still as a corpse. She calls him again, this time louder. He startles, opens his eyes, and mumbles something, but then his eyelids close again. This is how he sleeps when he has been drinking, talking with eyes that open as if he can see us, but he cannot. Half of him, the unconscious body, is here with us. His mind is somewhere else, navigating a world made of second chances, where San, the dead girl, is still alive and he can save her, and if he can save her, he can save them all, the family who died. No one in my family talks about how scary my father is in his sleep. Instead, my mother and I make a game of what we can do to him as he dozes. My mother can tap on the crown of his head, and I can braid and decorate his hair with bows, and we can all laugh at how silly he looks. This is easier than looking into his bloodshot eyes wondering if he sees me or the dead girl looking back at him. I half expect him to call her name, my name, now. But he turns his head to the side and his mouth goes slack. My mother laughs and walks to the garage, where she hides all the household goods that she buys. The trunk of her car is like a magician's hat, mysteriously containing a never-ending parade of vases, fake flower arrangements, paintings, side tables, and curtains.

She returns carrying a package so large that I cannot see her face as she walks past my father, toward their bedroom.

A few minutes later she calls my name in a loud whisper. "Come see?" she says.

I follow her to her room, where she points at a maroon bedspread trimmed in a silky gold rope with matching pillow shams.

"Isn't it beautiful?" she says.

I nod, unwilling to tell her that the new bedspread, with its gold tassels and antique print, looks like the old one, except for one difference: the shiny pleated maroon border on this new one looks like the liner inside a casket.

"I been watching this one on sale since last summer. First, it was fifteen percent off, then twenty-five percent, but I got a coupon for an additional twenty-five percent. Can you believe that? I got it half off." She sits down on a chair and smiles at her work.

I walk back to the den where my father is sleeping and sit down on the floor in front of the TV. A few minutes later, my mother comes to wake him again. She yells his name and knocks on his head like it is a door until he opens his red eyes with surprise.

"You need to get in the bed, John," she says.

He stands up and walks, his body stiff as a cartoon caveman. He heads toward their bedroom where he crawls under the new bedspread that he does not know is new and falls asleep.

The next morning is Saturday, and my father wakes and yells my mother's name. She cannot hear him because she is in the garage digging through the trunk.

I get out of bed and run halfway to him, but turn back for the garage when I realize that he is awake and angry. He has probably figured out that the bedspread is new. I go to the door that leads to the garage, just as my mother walks in carrying a painting.

"Daddy is calling you," I say.

"I hear him," she says as she walks into our dining room and hides the painting behind the door. She dusts her hands off and walks toward the bedroom. I follow her down the hallway while my father continues to call her name.

She opens the door to their bedroom but does not close it behind her, leaving me standing in the open doorway as she walks in. My father is waving his hand at a lamp on the nightstand.

"What is this?" he says. "I told you not to buy nothing else. We just can't—" He hesitates and looks at me and back at my mother. "You know what I told you about my job, and you just keep on buying new stuff."

"That lamp?" she says. "It's not new. It's been there for six months."

My father stares at the lamp as if it has spoken some gibberish from the planet of the lamps and shakes his head. "You telling a story. You just bought this lamp."

My mother lets out a genuine laugh and rolls her eyes. "It's been there for six months and you didn't even notice it." She is telling the truth. I can remember when she carted the lamp into the house and plugged it in.

She turns to walk out, still laughing. "It was on sale, back then, like it would matter now anyway."

My father runs his hand along the brass-colored stem of the lamp as if touching it will tell him when and how it arrived at this spot in his house.

I almost tell him that the bedspread that covers him and the throw pillows next to him are the things that are new and that if he looks in his wife's trunk, he'll find new bath rugs, brass goblets, and a small plant stand all waiting for their turn to sneak into the house. But if I tell him, we could no longer make a joke of his drunken sleep. I will have to talk about the things that we do not talk about—the times when he opens his eyes and seems to look at me, but he is really looking through me like I am a magnifying glass. How the stillness of his eyes scares me because he looks like he is neither dead nor alive. We'll have to admit that the whiskey is a doorway to another girl named San, and that when he is with her, he is yelling at her to stop whatever she is doing that might make her die. I am afraid that if I wake him, me and this other San will collide, that for a moment between a dream and real time, I will become the one who is about to die. What difference does a bedspread make to someone who is trying to stop death in his dreams?

With the embryo inside me, I walk through my house, sure that this two-story home with spare modern furniture has turned itself into an abortion factory. I am carrying an embryo in my body, but that embryo has not implanted in my womb and could pass from my body at any moment. Each stairstep makes me into an old woman, clinging to the rail for fear of falling. When I lean forward to get on my low platform bed, I feel my abdominal muscles squeezing the embryo out of my body like toothpaste from a tube. The shower threatens to spray water so hot that it will boil my offspring before breakfast. The bathroom whispers all the tales I have heard of young mothers whose babies surprised them by slipping from their wombs into toilets. If a whole baby could be accidently pushed out of a womb, how could a tiny embryo stay put? Every time I shit, I wonder if my embryo has been baptized in bacteria and flushed away.

None of this makes sense. If new life required all this caution, there would be no babies. When I am out in the world, I return to reason, my mind on ideas, work, and the mundane. But when I come back to my house and I am myself without witnesses, the house's walls saturated with rich, dark paint that I chose because it was comforting now seem to envelop and suffocate me, and I creep through the rooms as if I am trying to hide from a god.

On the ninth day after the embryo was transferred to my body, I go to the IVF clinic for a pregnancy blood test. When I arrive at the fertility clinic, I sign in with the same slips of paper I have used for all the previous blood tests. But this time, instead of checking a box next to "monitoring," I check "pregnancy test" and hand the paper to the receptionist. I sit down wanting something else to be different, to match the excitement and fear that sits at the base of my throat. But when the nurse calls my name, she leads me to the same chairs I've been sitting in for weeks. Today my dark blood races out of my body at the first chance, zipping through a thin tube and into a vial. As she drops the vial in a pile of others, the nurse says in a soft voice without looking at me, "Good luck."

Eight hours later, I am walking on my toes between the bathroom and my bed when my phone rings. I answer and a voice says, "I'm sorry. Your pregnancy test was negative."

I thank her, in that way one thanks a funeral director for making arrangements—polite but absent. Grief slices through me, intense and unexpected, and my body freezes against a wall.

When I can breathe again, I call Reginald to tell him that I am not pregnant. He tells me how sorry he is. And I tell him I am too, but I say it as if this is all my fault, my body's fault.

"I'll come home as soon as I can," he says.

I nod as if he can see me and my guilt and hang up.

I go to my bedroom and climb into my bed while light streams in through the windows. I shroud myself in my bedspread and wail like something is eating my entrails. A dreamless sleep takes over my body until Reginald's footsteps wake me.

He sits on the edge of the bed and tells me again how sorry he is. I think of that phrase, "Sorry for your loss," and realize that no one existed for me to lose. One day there were tiny cells dividing and another day—I don't even know exactly when—they stopped.

Reginald is trying to talk about what we have been through, about how hard all of this has been. As he searches for words for what has happened to us, he lands on "miscarriage."

I sit up in bed and cut him off as if some mean spirit will hear this and wish miscarriage on us too. "This was not a miscarriage. You have to be pregnant to have a miscarriage. We were never pregnant."

He cocks his head and stares away from me at the wall.

A strange poem plays on repeat in my head:

I did not have a baby. I had an embryo.
I did not lose a baby. I lost an embryo.
I cannot grieve a baby, because all I had was an embryo.

I tell him about a cousin who miscarried many times when she was still in her twenties. I had overheard my mother say that the problem had something to do with the shape of my cousin's womb. Each time her belly grew round and high, someone would have to rush her to a hospital. Once, as a little girl at a family get-together, I had ridden along on one of these hospital trips. I sat in a waiting room with my mother and her sisters while a doctor explained to my aunt that my cousin would be okay, but the baby had died. We waited for hours while my cousin pushed a dead baby into the world. Technically, this was a stillbirth, but everyone I knew called losses like this one "miscarriage," a word that hides the fact that dead babies demand the strength of their mothers' birth canals to enter the world, just like living babies do.

"Miscarriage" was not the word for what I experienced, but neither could it describe what my cousin had been through. Her loss was given the wrong name, and mine had no name at all.

Reginald squints as he searches for a better word for losing someone who never existed. For him, loss must have a name because names separate experiences from the people who have them. A name could make our vague loss singular, something that happened in real time, with a beginning and an end.

He lets out a soft puff of air and presses his lips together. But his eyes dart about as if the right word might be written somewhere on the walls of our bedroom. To me, the walls seem to have grown even darker with the sticky syrup of our grief.

I lean my head back on the pillow. I do not need a word for what I am feeling because I know it is not a thing separate from me. The grief of losing that which I have never known feels like coming home, devastating and familiar as the stink of Old Forester whiskey.

I am seven years old and sick with the flu. I lie on a sofa in the den with the TV blaring even though I am not watching it.

My mother climbs down from the attic carrying a quilt. She stands over me and spreads the quilt in the air. The rich smell of cedar hits me before the quilt lands on my body. Blues, peaches, and maroons cover me in star patterns, each one soft, precise, and mathematical.

"Your daddy's mama made all these quilts we got," my mother says. "All these little pieces are scraps left over from their clothes that she sewed."

I already know this because she tells me every time she brings quilts from the attic, where they are hidden.

Years later when I am in my early twenties, I will ask my mother to save these quilts for me. I will tell her about an art exhibit of quilts made by Black women in Alabama, and how important it is to preserve my grandmother's quilts. She agrees that the quilts should be mine since neither of my siblings has any interest in them.

But as I lie under the quilt at age seven, it is not yet an object to ask for because it is not separate from me. While my mother disappears into her room, the quilt's heaviness sinks into me. I sweat and shiver, drifting and waking to the colors of my grandmother's clothes.

• • •

I am eight when I find the photograph of a little Black girl in a small brass frame hidden in the bottom of a side table drawer. I ask my father who she is. At first, he says that she is my cousin San, and then he blinks hard and shakes his head. "Naw, that's her mama, my sister, Maggie Jo. Both of them died in the wreck."

I stare at the slightly bucktoothed, smiling three-year-old wearing a hair bow that is too big for her head. Her cheeks have been tinted pink by a heavy-handed photographer, and she leans forward as if she is about to leap toward me. Her eyes are like mine, except that they show more joy than I can ever remember feeling. I prop up the photo on the end table. But in a few days, it goes missing again. I look in the drawer of the table, and there I find Maggie Jo facedown, pressed against the bottom of the drawer under stacks of junk mail and receipts. I return her to the table, and she stays there for a week before she disappears again, and I put her back again. Someone (probably my mother) and I go back and forth like this for weeks, with Maggie Jo getting buried in the drawer and me resurrecting her.

The last time I notice that the girl is missing from the table, I open the drawer and dig to the bottom, but she is really gone. This time, for good.

I spend the days after the nurse called to tell me I am not pregnant in bed. On the third day, I bleed and ache as if passing clotted blood is my only job. I lie in my bed trying to read to forget my body. But grief, as powerful as floodwater, overtakes me and I surrender. I'd drown, except I imagine I can hear my father's voice calling me home. I want to tell him a truth that is also a lie: that I am experiencing a loss, not of a person, but the idea of someone who would be connected to our bodies by blood. And just the thought of telling him such a thing makes me ashamed of myself for even briefly letting my grief overlap with his. I remind myself that I am not in that place where his dreams took place, where time turns backward and dangles a chance to save a loved one who is already dead. But the rolling waters of his loss and mine have already mixed and I have no way to completely separate them. Perhaps his loss was always also mine. I feel the pink walls of my childhood bedroom close over me like an envelope. Like my name, I am a haunted thing.

Desire takes root in a twisted spot in my belly, replacing grief with a question that can be answered. What hellish catastrophe was hidden behind that phrase, "the wreck"? What exactly happened to our family who died, and to the ones who grieved them? And just as I commit to the unearthing, I realize that I don't even know how or where to dig. In my head, I flip through the past, but it is a book of mostly blank pages. I know almost nothing—not even when or where the wreck happened.

My fingers dial my father before I know how to say what I want from him. In my mind, he walks to the old corded, mustard-yellow phone of my childhood and answers.

"Hey, baby." The soft joy in his voice startles me back to the present. I am in a bed bleeding. My father is almost a thousand miles away in Alabama. I can hear the fuzzy sound of the cordless phone that replaced the phone of my childhood as it brushes against his ear, feel him smiling at a new world he made from ruins. And I cannot snatch him back to his hellish dreams, nor am I ready to bear witness to his pain. In the brief silence, I feel the thick wall of foliage that has always separated and supported us, allowing us to live in the present despite a past that proved catastrophe could always happen. I do not want to pry holes in that wall.

I collect myself, and instead of asking him to relive the worst day of his life, I ask him for a quilt.

"What quilts are you talking about?" he says.

"You know, the ones your mom made. The ones we always had."

"I don't think we ever had any of those," he says. "My sister Judy took all of them way back when. Let me get your mama. You can ask her what you're thinking of."

My mother gets on the phone. "The quilts?" she says. "We never had those."

"The ones you kept in the attic. You used to get them out when I was sick."

"Naw," she says. "You must have been thinking of something else. You had a little baby blanket that my mama made, but no quilts."

I keep talking as if I can make her remember until I realize that she does not want to remember.

So I ask for the only other thing I can think of, photographs of my father's mother, sister, and niece. She tells me that she has seen just one photograph of my aunt as an adult, and she doesn't have a copy. But she agrees to send me whatever she can find.

Days later, the photos, printed on thick construction paper, arrive in a brown envelope. One is a photograph of my grandmother that I have seen many times. She looks square at the camera with big sad eyes, and her hair is pulled back tight into two braids that sit on her shoulders in loops. Her face is resolute like she is working her way through a cotton field. On another sheet of paper is a photo of my aunt

Maggie's daughters, San, who died, and Liza, who survived. My mother has written their names above them in the wrong order and drawn arrows to indicate which is which. But I can tell them apart because Liza is older, around six, and San looks about three. Liza sits upright, while San looks too tired for this world as she leans her head on her sister's shoulder.

On the last page is the green-tinted photo of the little pop-eyed girl who kept disappearing from my parents' end table. Above the photo, my mother has written my father's sister's name, Maggie Jo.

I prop each photo on my dresser, next to a row of infertility drugs. The relics of death and the thin promise of new life.

I wake up to these photos for one week before I call my father again. I will not wait for him to call me "baby." I will sit with the softest question I can think of under my tongue, letting it spring out as soon as he speaks.

"Hello?"

"Daddy, can I ask you a question about the wreck?"

For a moment, I think that the call has dropped. But just as I am about to ask him if he is still there, he speaks.

"Yeah, baby?"

"When did the wreck happen? "

"Oh, I guess that was 1960 or so." He sings that first word, like he is talking about the prospects of a mediocre high school football team, surprising me and making me wonder if the questions I have waited my whole life to ask mean something different to him, something further away in time than it seemed to be in my childhood. Or was his tone an affect intended to hide a quick jolt of unexpected pain? What I remember is the thick grief of a wound that never healed. But is that what the past was to him?

"I believe it was June twenty-fifth, or around there somewhere, because Mama died right after July Fourth, and she lived nine days or so after, I think."

"But I thought that they had all died in the wreck."

"Naw. It didn't happen like that. Mama lived the longest. I believe she died on July fifth. Doctors thought she'd make it. Said all of 'em who was still alive would make it, but they didn't."

"And the others, how long after did they live?"

He lets out a heavy breath. "My wife and San—they were dead by the time I got to the hospital." He says "my wife" as if he had been calling her this in his head for my entire life. The words carve out a canyon between us, not because they are said with the tenderness of lost love, but because they are not. He names her with a matter-of-fact tone that forces me to see him in a kitchen making coffee next to someone I have never met. He is someone else, someone before me, my mother, and my siblings.

"And the others? How long did they live?"

"My brother-in-law, Maggie's husband, Robert Ray, died at the hospital before I got there too. They took Maggie Jo into surgery, but she died in the afternoon that same day."

"You said the doctors told you that they would all make it?"

"Yeah, they told me Mama and Maggie would make it, but Daddy and Liza were the only ones who did."

"Why would they tell you that?"

"Them doctors didn't know nothing back then."

"Where was your dad?"

"He was already in a coma. Liza was sitting up though."

"So what happened, Daddy? How did the wreck happen?"

"The newspaper. It was all in the newspaper. I guess you could get the paper. I don't know how you could get it though."

His voice peters out like the end of an echo.

Talking on the phone, becoming voices that travel on radio waves, should have been easier than staring into the lines of each other's faces. But instead, being connected by nothing but sound amplified our words into sonic booms that shocked our bodies, making my belly hurt and taking my father's breath away.

We say goodbye and hang up.

I sit on the edge of the bed, feeling like someone has changed my birthday. I am not a body, but a flood of spinning ideas and questions: the accident was not a single thing in time, but a thing that had gone on and on, not just psychologically, but the event itself, with some dying instantly, others later at the hospital, another living for days, and two who had struggled on. And my father had watched it all. Why did doctors tell him with certainty that his family would survive? Had they really not known, or had they lied to him on purpose? And if I cannot process all of this now all these years later, how did my father process it then? Had he processed it, or merely accepted it? And what was the difference?

I do the only thing that my academic training has taught me to do. I pick up my laptop and search, but there are no digitized newspapers from the tiny town where it all happened. I settle for the thinnest straws of history, context rather than story. I type "doctors lying to patients." It takes me a few minutes to refine the search, but eventually I discover the phrase "benevolent deception," a term used to describe the practice of withholding a poor prognosis. Common well into the mid-twentieth century, "benevolent deception" was supposed to protect a patient whose demise might be hastened by the knowledge that they were going to die. In some cases, family members were told the truth, and in others, they weren't. Doctors believed that, in the end, they knew best whether the truth would best serve the patient's interest. It was a practice so cowardly, so cruel, that I couldn't see it in any light as "benevolent." If anything, withholding the truth extended more benevolence to the doctor than the patient, conveniently allowing them to avoid the burden of delivering bad news. And if doctors felt it was their right to withhold information from white patients, what did this mean for Black patients, often considered by whites to be too ignorant and unintelligent to understand medical science? At best it meant that doctors probably rarely bothered to communicate with them, at worst it meant that doctors could leverage their power to withhold information and treatment and make Black patients into the subjects of medical experimentation.

That's just what happened in the Tuskegee experiments that took place from 1932 to 1972. In Alabama, doctors had withheld both diagnosis and treatment from hundreds of Black men with syphilis while pretending to treat the men for something they called "bad blood." The men, unbeknownst to them, were test subjects in a study of the long-term effects of syphilis. This deception was hardly "benevolent." I wonder if this paternalistic power is what my father encountered at an Alabama hospital in 1960. Were the doctors as incompetent as my father believed them to be? Or had they withheld what they knew, that my father's family was dying one by one all around him?

I go to the Alabama death records website and type in the names of each of my relatives and the date range of their deaths. I put in a credit card and click purchase like I am buying a sweater instead of five death certificates.

• • •

I arrive home from work and Reginald hands me a thick envelope from the Alabama Center for Health Statistics.

We sit down on the sofa, and I unwrap a stack of papers, each one as pink as the inside of a baby's mouth. At the top of each page is an accidental poem, "THE FRONT OF THIS DOCUMENT IS PINK— THE BACK OF THIS DOCUMENT IS BLUE AND HAS AN AR- TIFICIAL WATERMARK—HOLD AT AN ANGLE TO VIEW."

The rest of the page is made up of two layers of writing: a background that repeats "State of Alabama Center for Health Statistics" in small white type, and a top layer of black outlined boxes, each with small black type indicating what is to go in each box: place of death, name of deceased, informant, attending doctor, place of injury, burial, cem- etery, and more. Each space is filled with handwriting from another time, loopy *p*'s that curve into themselves, *J*'s that look like butterflies turned on their side.

I spread the pages out on our coffee table to see if the administrator has been able to find all five certificates despite the scant information I had provided. They are all there, each pink paper folded in thirds, in on itself, as if trying to keep a vulnerable underbelly from view. I flip through each page taking in the top-line information—the headlines of the death certificates.

Bernice Jackson [my father's mother].
Died July 5, 1960. Time of death—blank.

Willodean [sic] Jackson [my father's wife], 19 years old.
Died June 25, 1960. Time of death—blank.

Maggie Jo Ray [my father's sister], 23 years old.
Died June 25, 1960. Time of death—3:30 p.m.

Robert Ray [Maggie's husband], 29 years old.
Died June 25, 1960. Time of death—blank.

Sandra Ray [Maggie's daughter], 3 years old.
Died June 25, 1960. DOA [dead on arrival].

This last one I double-check to make sure her parents are listed correctly because as far as I know her name was Cassandra, not Sandra.

I do not realize that I am shaking until I feel Reginald's arm circling me.

"Oh my god. They were all so young. Your dad? How old was he again?"

"I guess about twenty-five. I don't know how he managed to stay alive himself after losing so much."

I turn to my grandmother's name and glance over the lacy handwriting in search of her cause of death. But as I make my way down the page my eyes light on "Occupation: Domestic."

"She wasn't a domestic," I say. "She never worked a day in anyone's home. She was a farmer." This was one of the few things I was sure of about my grandmother. Her volatile temper would have made working in white people's houses a more dangerous occupation than it already was for Black people.

Reginald shakes his head. He put his finger on the large lacy C for "colored," directly above the occupation box.

"They saw she was Black and just decided she had to be some white woman's maid," he says.

"That must be what happened. Jesus." My body turns hot as humiliation and resentment descend on me.

I scan the page until I arrive at my grandmother's cause of death: "Pulmonary embolism . . . Antecedent causes internal injuries, fractures, and lacerations." She had survived a violent car crash, lived ten days with internal injuries, broken bones scattered inside her face, arms, and legs, only to succumb to a blood clot that had made its way to her lungs.

"My dad doesn't even know this is what killed her. The doctors didn't even bother to tell him."

Reginald picks up Maggie's death certificate and points to the occupation box, which also says "Domestic." I understand what he's getting at. This was a world where those with the power to determine the record could not imagine a Black woman having an occupation other than maid to a white woman, and where the idea of inquiring about a Black woman's work would have seemed as absurd as probing the occupation of a mule.

"They probably couldn't have been bothered to tell a Black man anything back then," he says.

"No, I guess not."

"Why do some of them list the hometown as North Chicago?"

I stare at the certificates and realize that Maggie, her husband, and child are all listed as residents of North Chicago. Hers has "Tuscumbia, Alabama" listed first, but it has been marked out and replaced with "Illinois."

"I don't know. I thought they all lived in Alabama. I'll have to ask my dad if they had moved away by then."

"You don't think they were visiting or something?"

My breath catches in my throat at the thought of a family visit that ended with five dead family members, two widowers, and an orphaned child. It was too much to consider.

Reginald closes his eyes and rubs his mouth with his hand. There is nothing left to say.

I stack the papers, fold them, and put them back in the envelope. I take them upstairs and place them on the nightstand next to my bed, where they will lie as bright and still as an old patchwork quilt.

CHAPTER 9

While we wait for the follow-up appointment with Dr. Z. to figure out our next steps, I do research on the latest IVF protocols. The information I find excites but does not satisfy me—only a baby could do that. I keep looking because it is easier than sitting helpless in the void of not knowing. Searching implies that the problem that is my body has a solution I can discover on my own. I read article after article with the same intensity that I read the encyclopedia as a child. But now my mind is like a gambler's, running just ahead of the present, high on possibility and the illusion of power. I search until the information seems to circle back on itself, words like "experimental," "double-blind," "inconclusive" forming a loop. Every bit of information I find is promising and yet none of it can make any real promises.

I have run out of search terms, but still I sit with my fingers curved over the keyboard, not wanting to admit that in a world where doctors can extract, fertilize, and implant human eggs, Western medicine still cannot guarantee me a baby.

Unwilling to sit with this thought, I turn to my other obsession: the wreck. I have always been a sleuth, a snoop, an inquirer reassured by the idea that determined pursuit could reveal buried truths. The internet provides me with a tool for endless probing. I search key terms and names and find nothing about the wreck. But I keep looking for a few minutes more in case there is some avenue of information I have missed. The tiniest possibility that I could find answers to questions that are more like hunger pains than words keeps me searching for something that cannot be found on the internet. I open a database of newspapers, but it accesses only major city newspapers—papers that would never have taken note of a wreck in Alabama. I scan to see if there are other databases of small local newspapers, but there are none.

In the list of databases, my eyes rest on a reference resource from Oxford University Press. I click, ready to sink into a space where information flows as effortlessly as sweet tea in Alabama. The illusion of easy answers comforts me when I am drowning in questions. I type the word that rises in me when I am alone with my desire to have a baby. And there it is on the screen, variations of the word "belief." Obscured behind that window are a half-dozen others that detail fertility studies, all of which demonstrate that Western medicine is still trying to figure out where babies come from. Could there be some mysterious thing at the heart of reproduction that science cannot name—let alone harness? Some elusive life force that demands the spiritual more than the animal? That idea is embedded in every piece of casual advice people give about infertility: "Stop thinking about it and it will happen." "There's a little bit of magic." "It only takes one."

Even if I were to accept the existence of an unknowable power, I am not sure what that acceptance would require of me. Praying, manifesting, committing to something other than my own persistent will? I have no map for any of it. When catastrophe turns your family into a fill-in-the-blank test that you could never pass, belief also gets lost in the blank spaces.

I return to the concrete definitions that fill my screen and pore over them as if they are a manual for a new life.

Believe—accept (something) as true . . . : *Christians believe that Jesus rose from the dead.*

—have faith, esp. religious faith: *there are those on the fringes of the Church who do not really believe.*

Will to believe—In his 1897 article entitled "The Will to Believe," William James said that, under certain specified conditions, we have a right to let our passional nature decide which of two alternative hypotheses to adopt. These are that the matter cannot be settled on intellectual grounds, and that the choice between them is *living* (we find each credible), *forced* (we must act in the light of one or the other), and *momentous* (really important). Examples are the choice between theism and atheism or free will and determinism.

Make-believe—the action of pretending or imagining that things are better than they really are: *she's living in a world of make-believe.*

Disbelieve—[to] be unable to believe . . . [to] have no religious faith: *to disbelieve is as much an act of faith as belief.*

Cassandra—(as noun, *a Cassandra*) a prophet of disaster, especially one who is disregarded.

My body goes still when I see my name, and the definitions begin to blur. I am realizing there is no way to explain belief without also explaining disbelief. And I, like this other Cassandra, exist in that uncomfortable overlap.

• • •

My father is cooking and I am eight years old, sitting on the kitchen countertop nearby. He is singing a song. I try to hum along, but even though it sounds familiar, I do not know the tune.

"Where did you learn that song?" I say.

"At church, I guess," he says. He dips a pork chop into flour and drops it in a skillet.

"I've never heard them sing that song at church."

"I meant the church I went to when I was a kid."

"Y'all went to church?"

"Mm-hmm," he says.

"All the time?"

"Sometimes. But them folks down there was so crazy. Just about every time we went, somebody stuck a shotgun through the window and told somebody to come outside."

"For what?" I say.

"To fight about something. Could have been anything."

"Did they do it? Go outside when somebody told them to?"

He laughs. "Most did. But one time some old man asked for the preacher and that so-and-so jumped out a window on the opposite side and ran."

The story is funny and not funny to me at the same time. I try to imagine someone sticking a rifle through a window at the church we attend, what it would be like for the mundane to be interrupted by something so out of place that it would seem like a dream you know is a dream even while you are having it.

"Were you scared?" I ask.

He stops and thinks for a moment. "Naw, I don't reckon I was," he says.

"But didn't you worry someone might shoot you or your family?"

"Them niggas mighta been crazy, but they wasn't crazy enough to mess with my mama. They didn't know what she might do to them and didn't want to find out." He dips more chops into the flour with his long, thin fingers and then drops them one at a time into hot grease.

When he is done, he hums some more and walks over to where I am sitting. He kneels, and I lift my feet so he can open the cabinet behind them. I try to catch the tune and hum along as he pulls out a bottle of whiskey and pours himself a drink.

Dr. Z. greets us with a warm smile when I arrive in her office. She sits down behind her desk, and Reginald and I sit opposite her. In my lap, I have a green folder with all the research I collected on IVF protocols for women who have struggled to produce eggs.

She folds her hands and looks in my direction but seems to focus on a spot over my head. "When a woman is a poor responder to IVF medications, there isn't much else we can do. In some cases, the ovaries may be damaged," she says.

"Poor responder?" Reginald says.

I have not shared this label with him because I do not need any more names for my brokenness.

"Her body is not responding to the drugs," Dr. Z. says.

"But we've only completed one IVF cycle," I say. "What about other types of stimulation cycles? We never did a long drug cycle. Could that help?" I say, quoting my research.

Dr. Z. folds her lips in and presses them together into a tight line like someone is trying to force her mouth open with a spoon.

"We really don't believe a biological child is likely for you," she says.

"But what about the egg you retrieved? It was a good egg. It turned into an embryo. Doesn't that mean I have good eggs in there?"

"We're not saying that it can't happen. Just that it is not statistically likely. We believe it's time for you to start considering other options."

"What other options?" Reginald says.

Dr. Z. lets out a puff of air and reaches into her desk drawer. "We believe your best options for a child are donor eggs or adoption." She places two pamphlets on her desk and pushes them toward us.

"Donor eggs would allow you to carry a child, but you'd be using another woman's eggs and Reginald's sperm. But if carrying a child is not important to you, we could put you in touch with adoption resources."

"But what if we want to continue IVF with my eggs?" I say.

"You would have to do that at another practice. We don't believe that's a good option for you."

"You're refusing us care?" I say.

"No," she says. "There's just no point in continuing IVF with your eggs. You could try IUI, but the chances are less than five percent that it would work."

"IUI?" Reginald says.

"We did that once before, remember? The procedure where they insert sperm into the uterus." I say.

Dr. Z. flips through a folder on her desk. "Yes, that's right, you did one IUI when your first IVF was canceled."

"But my tubes are blunted. Doesn't that mean that IUI couldn't work for us? Isn't that why you recommended we go straight to IVF in the first place?"

"Well, yes. But we can never completely rule something out. That's why we give percentages rather than saying yes or no."

"So you can't rule out a successful IVF for me either?"

"Well, no, but we don't believe that's the best route for you. Why don't you take some time to consider the other options?" She folds her hands and pushes her chair back in a way that signals to us that we are supposed to leave.

I want to say okay. To pretend that I am above caring about biology. To prove that I have the intellectual capacity to understand the unimportance of my genes, my biological self. But my body matters to me. To my mind, my body contains a legacy that can be had no other way. I do not know how to explain this to the doctor. How do I say that I am a memory for someone I have never met? That an old woman who loved my dead aunt will one day weep and love again at the mere sight of my daughter, and that this experience is how my girl will learn that grief and belonging can be one? I want to say that my own face looks back at me from another time on my dresser. That my tall, stringy brown body matters because of all the ones who died before I was born.

I look over at the bookshelf that holds a picture of a little girl who, except for her freckles and reddish hair, looks almost exactly like Dr. Z. Then I look back at the doctor.

"Did you consider adoption?"

She does not answer.

We leave.

I sit on my bed at night and try to believe in things that I cannot see. I have already asked a friend who prays to do this for me, but it seems wrong to ask for prayers without also praying myself. Yet when I try, I conjure the wrong god, cling to the wrong superstitions. I imagine a god who punishes hope. One who will surprise you with catastrophic loss the second you forget that you and everyone you love might die. It is not that I cannot make myself believe in a god, but rather that I cannot trust one. This is the god whose name my parents never spoke because what was the point in pretending to know a god who didn't seem to know you—who would let bad things happen, or worse, make them happen to you. When I squeeze my eyes shut, I am that little girl sitting on the front pew at church as the preacher tells the story of Eve, who wanted too much, and of an all-powerful god, who saw her desire and punished her with suffering. What did it matter that suffering was supposed to come through the bearing of children? If a god could give children as punishment, then couldn't it also take them away? I hide my desires, for fear that god will curse me with barrenness. Never mind that I am already barren.

I stare at the West African fertility doll on my dresser. A colleague who was moving out of her office found it rolling around on the floor underneath her desk. She recognized what it was and barreled around the corner, stopping at the first open door. "This is not mine," she declared, pointing it at me like a gun. "Do you want this thing or know anybody who wants it? Because I certainly don't." I smiled the smile of someone who has no idea yet that she's infertile and took the doll with its poky, black arms and large, flat head. As my colleague fled back to her office, I examined the wooden doll, searching for anything that might indicate whom it belonged to. But it had no tags to indicate whether it was from West Africa or the clearance shelf at Marshalls. Surely the person who bothered to bring it into the office must have known what it was. I picture various women colleagues sitting in that dim windowless office with the doll standing on the desk looking back at them as unsuspecting students made their way in and out. Or had she hidden it there under the desk in the first place, searching for magic when nothing else had worked? Maybe she forgot about it, or abandoned it after she got pregnant or because she didn't. The thick layer of dust on it made it impossible to determine if it had come into the building a year before or twenty years before. Either way, I would never find out whom the doll belonged to because there was no way I was going to roam the hallways holding a fertility doll and asking colleagues, "Hey, is this yours? Did you lose your fertility talisman?"

I took the doll home and put it on my bedroom dresser. Soon I discovered how it got under a desk. If there was the tiniest movement within three feet, the doll would slingshot through the air and bounce across the hardwood floors with a loud clang. Each time the hollow thing attempted suicide by fall, I scrambled to scoop it up, holding the dry, gritty wood like a baby. I would check to make sure all its limbs were still intact, and place it lightly back on the dresser again, in search of the magic spot that would hold it there.

But now I walk over to the dresser and stow the doll in the top drawer, resenting the fact that while I do not believe in it enough to leave it be, I also cannot disbelieve in it enough to throw it out.

I put my grandmother's photo in the doll's place and stare at her until I can no longer stand looking at the stern twin to my own face. I close my eyes and pray to her without words, asking her to convince one of the babies, wherever they are, that it is okay to come to me.

My new fertility doctor believes in alien abductions.

When we meet for the first time, Dr. K. is sitting behind a dark wood desk the size of a compact car. Its legs are twirling columns thicker than my thighs. One wall is covered in huge matching cabinets that reach to the ceiling. All the furnishings in this office look like they belong to a long-dead pope. But the surfaces—the desk, the shelves, and much of the wall-to-wall plush rose-pink carpet—are covered in two- to three-foot-tall stacks of letter-size paper, like a giant copier went rogue, shitting printouts of information all over the room. If cloud storage was a place, this is what it would look like.

Dr. K. pops up from behind the desk and shakes my hand and then Reginald's. He is a tall thin man, the top of his pale head sparsely covered in blond wisps that look sprayed on. When he sits back down behind the desk, he looks as small as the cherubs in the dusty tapestry that hangs behind him.

"So, you've done IVF before, right? How many eggs did you get?"

"One." Shame swallows my face in thick, wet heat.

"Other practices would start telling you it's time for donor eggs or adoption, but that's not what we do here. You see, we're looking for that one good egg. We just don't want to miss it. For all we know, it could show up in your next cycle. So the first thing we want to do is get you on some hormone support and start doing some natural cycles."

"Natural?" Reginald says.

"Well, everyone wants to do IVF when they come in here, but there are other ways to get pregnant, like sex." He giggles. "It's just a matter of catching the right egg."

Reginald smiles like he's been knighted and given the title Sir You Can Get Pregnant Normally.

"But I'm infertile. Right?" I say.

"The truth is that we see patients that can't seem to achieve or maintain pregnancy, and then it just happens, and nobody knows why that particular time was the charm. My philosophy is that since the medical community can't determine why that one egg becomes a baby, we have to give every egg that shows up a shot."

"Are you saying we can't do IVF?"

"No. We aren't that kind of practice that tells patients they can't do IVF because their chances of pregnancy aren't as high as a nineteen-year-old's. We aren't worried about success numbers like those other practices. This is a teaching and learning practice. If you want to do IVF, we can start there."

I let out a breath that I did not realize I have been holding.

"How much stimulation medication did they have you taking?"

"The maximum dose of everything."

"Well, that's where I believe they went wrong."

He jumps out of his chair and zooms around the room, picking up papers from one stack and then another.

"I focus on getting the best eggs instead of the most. Maybe just a couple of eggs, but we will have more of a chance of one of those eggs turning into a baby." He hands each of us a tall stack of papers and sits down again.

"That study on top is about a forty-year-old woman who we were able to bring out of menopause and get pregnant!" His voice gets louder and faster as he talks, like he's announcing a football game. "Now, everybody out there is telling you that you can't get pregnant, right? But you're not even in menopause!"

He waves both his hands above his head as if he wants us to shut up, even though neither of us is saying anything.

"Let me tell you a true story. This guy comes in and wants to know if I can help him find out if aliens really could get human women pregnant."

I smile, waiting for the punch line.

"No, really. You've heard about these alien abductions that lead to pregnancy, right?"

I freeze and Reginald frowns.

"But this guy, he was from the government. There was some research they were doing on alien abduction, and he wanted to know if I could figure out what these aliens were doing. And I told him that if you could get one of these women to let me examine her, maybe I could find out. Now, he couldn't get me a woman to study, but what I'm trying to say is that there's still so much we don't know."

He hops up again, searching through the towers of papers that surround us.

"Well, I can't find it now," he says. "But we had a thirty-nine-year-old woman with hormone problems who had three babies through IVF. You could be just like that."

He pulls a small handheld recorder out of his desk. "I just want to dictate what I'm telling you about your treatment. You'll receive a letter in the mail with everything I've said." He starts talking into the recorder.

Reginald and I look at each other. I point to the stack of papers in my lap. Each one lists Dr. K. as the lead researcher, along with a long list of other doctors on the faculty at a prestigious medical school. All had been published in prestigious journals that confirmed Dr. K.'s international reputation and included stories of women who had come from all over the world to be treated by him when other practices had failed. We smile and nod our approval of the doctor before turning back to him. Dr. K. is still talking into the recorder. He repeats everything he said earlier about my treatment plan. He skips the part about the aliens.

• • •

I am six years old and I have never heard my parents say the word "God." But on most Sundays we go to church. Whenever I ask my mother why, she says because you're supposed to go. I point out that my father and brother don't always go, and she does not go when it's raining. But instead of answering, she tells me to hurry up and get ready.

On this Sunday when my mother tells me to go get dressed for church, I walk in my room and wait for her to close her bedroom door. Then I walk back down the hallway to the den, where my father is watching television.

"Are you going to church today?" I say.

"Yeah, I think I'll go with your mama."

I am disappointed. If he was staying home, I could stay too and watch westerns with him.

I go back to my room and put on a crunchy crinoline slip and a fluffy yellow dress that bounces when I walk. I dance around for a while like I have a partner, keeping my body stiff like the white lady in *The King and I*. When I get back to the den, my father is dressed and sitting in his recliner. I sit down on the sofa and we wait for my mother, who always takes the longest to get dressed. My father bounces his leg as we wait for her to come down the hallway. Sometimes she arrives fully dressed, but most of the time she is wearing a dress and no shoes, or two different earrings. She will ask us if we like the dress or which earrings look best. We will nod at everything, but when she presents us with a choice, my father will wait for me to answer first and then nod at my choice. My mother will scurry back to her bedroom to finish getting ready while my father yells after her that we are already late.

We will wait for her to return. Sometimes she will come back in the finished outfit. Other times, she returns in a different dress altogether and we start all over again. *Ain't nobody going to be at church on time anyway.*

My father complains about CP time. It stands for colored people time, and when Black people say it to other Black people, they laugh and nod. But my father frowns and shakes his head. He says that being late on purpose is sorry and trifling, and getting in the habit of being late gets some Black folks fired from their jobs because white folks won't put up with it.

But CP time is okay as long as everyone is Black, and everyone at our church is Black. One time, I asked my mother why there were no white people at our church and she said, *We have to have our own churches because that's the only way Black folks can be in charge of anything. White folks won't let a Black person tell them what to do.*

Even though we arrive over a half hour late, there are plenty of others waiting for an usher to let them in. When the deacon ends his prayer and the choir begins to sing, everyone makes their way through one of two aisles. And everyone who is sitting turns around to see who has arrived. My father walks fast to a pew in the middle of the church and I chase after him. When I look back, my mother has stopped to talk to a woman in a big hat. My mother smiles at the hat and says something, and the woman laughs and touches my mother's shoulder. My mother moves on to another lady, tiptoeing to keep her snakeskin heels from sinking into the thick red carpet. When she gets close to us, she smiles and pats the woman behind us on the shoulder, calling her "pretty lady," and the woman compliments my mother's dress and tells her that she is the pretty one.

By the time my mother sits down, the song is over. Now there is nothing to do but wait to see who else comes in. The service won't be over until after the preacher talks about God and what he likes and doesn't like people to do. When he starts to get loud, I know he's almost done and we can go home. If he talks past time for the ballgame to start, the men, including my father, will start to leave.

I am hot and my crispy slip digs into the backs of my thighs, making them itchy. Finally, the preacher stands up. He is wearing the same white robe that made me ask my mother a while ago if he was Jesus. She had laughed and said no, that Jesus lived a long time ago. The preacher prays, but when he is done, instead of preaching, he tells all the children to come forward and sit on the front pew. I don't move until my mother nudges me. As I and the other kids walk to the front of the church, the adults giggle softly and coo at us. I hate the preacher for making a show of talking to us, something he could have done without marching us all to the front pew, and I hate the old people who are smiling and pretending to like us as we pass by, even though they usually ignore us unless they are telling us to be quiet.

The preacher walks down from the pulpit and stands close to us. "Who can tell me who the first man and woman were?" he says.

I raise my hand first just like I do at school and he calls on me. "Joseph and Mary," I say. Everyone laughs like I have said something funny. But I am confused because I know that I am right. At school, I am always right.

Then I hear my mother's laugh. I look back and her mouth is open so wide that I can see the shiny metal that connects her dentures. My father is smiling and looking straight ahead as if the child everyone is laughing at is not me.

Another girl raises her hand and says, "Adam and Eve." Then she turns and looks down at my legs like I have ashy knees. The preacher smiles and says yes. Then he tells a story about Adam and Eve in a garden and Eve eating something she wasn't supposed to, and God punishing her and a snake who got her to eat it. I am trying to listen, but I am still embarrassed and sweat is running down the insides of my arms. I want the preacher to shut up so I can go back home.

When the preacher stops talking, he sends us back to our seats. I walk back to my parents and sit down, my stomach flipping like something is chasing me.

When I get home I will ask my parents, "Why didn't you teach me about Adam and Eve?"

My father will shrug without taking his eyes off the television.

My mother will stop polishing her new coffee table for a moment and look at the ceiling. "Just never thought to teach you something like that," she will say before she sprays another coat of furniture polish on the table.

It is Sunday, and my father's sitting on the front lawn, pulling wild onions that have invaded the fancy hybrid grass he planted. I am eleven years old, sitting nearby, trying to master his technique of twisting and snatching out the root.

My mother returns from church in her shiny Cadillac and parks in the driveway. She gets out wearing a white skirt suit and stands at the edge of the yard to prevent her heels from sinking into the grass.

"You need to put some clothes on," she says to my father. "Everybody can see your butt crack. Pull your pants up. The new preacher is coming by."

"For what?" my father says.

"To talk to you."

"About what?"

"I guess about you not going to church."

"I don't give a rat's ass about him. Why'd you tell him to come talk to me?"

"You look a mess out here," she says, and walks into the house. My father turns back to his yard and uses his long fingers to dig out an onion by the root. He tosses it into a pile.

When Rev. F. pulls up an hour later in his shiny black Oldsmobile, my father is on all fours, crawling across the yard in search of missed weeds.

The Reverend waves hello as he gets out of the car. My father grunts, gives a nod, and goes back to his work.

When Rev. F. steps onto the deep carpet of spongy grass, his black dress shoes sink and he teeters. His arms flap like he is trying to fly. He makes his way over to us, glancing at me like I am a bug he wants to squash. When he gets close, he waits a moment for my father to get up and shake his hand. Instead, my father sits down with legs crossed, like Kermit the Frog.

"Missed you at church," the Reverend says.

"You best go on and say what it is you have to say so I can get back to work," my father says.

The Reverend looks at me wide-eyed as if I am the one who told him to fuck off. I stare right back with a twisted mouth that says, *I could have told you this wouldn't go well.*

The Reverend recites a string of incoherent Bible quotes while his feet shift back and forth like they are about to run from the rest of his body.

While the man jabbers, my father crawls back onto all fours, but his jeans have slipped down and the Reverend is left to quote scripture to my father's half-bare ass. My father pulls up a tiny weed and examines the root before adding it to the pile.

The Reverend's voice gets higher and then he stops talking mid-sentence.

My father turns back to him and squats. "Man, you don't know shit about me, else you wouldn't be here. Now git the hell off my property before I help you off it."

The Reverend half runs, half walks to his car without looking back. Once in the car, he gives a nod as if this was an ordinary visit. But my father doesn't bother to look up. As the Reverend pulls away, I give him the stiff wave of a Barbie doll hand, and I smile my twisted smile.

My uncle Conrad and his two wives have come from St. Louis, along with my aunt Judy. They have been fishing on Uncle Conrad's boat all day. My father fries the fish until it is light and crisp. After we eat and drink, they tell stories of their mother, who was the only power they ever put their trust in.

Did John T. ever tell you about that time a white man put his foot on him? They all laugh in a way that says, *Probably, but tell it again anyway.*

We was at the store, and this white man says that's one of Bernice's boys, and he put his foot on my pants. I guess I was about seven years old. I turned around and kicked that old white man dead in his belly. Then I took off running. We went home and I told Mama what happened. She put us in the car and we went back to town.

That fool was still sitting there gabbing in the store when we walked in. He says, "You ain't raising them boys right, Bernice— you gonna get them killed." Mama said, "If you touch any one of my kids again, you better make sure you kill me too." He says, "Now, you know you don't mean that, Bernice." She said, "I'm fine with dying, as long as I know I'm taking you with me." His whole mouth went slack. She turned and walked out. I heard one of them white men say, "You best get out of here before that crazy nigger comes back looking for you again."

My fear of grown white men who hurt Black children pins me where I sit on the floor. When I watched *Roots* on TV with my family, my body froze on the sofa with one foot folded underneath me. The show ended, and still I sat there, my ankle throbbing like my foot had been cut off just as Kunte Kinte's had. My mother had to force me to get up and go to bed. When I finally unfolded the leg, I was relieved to see that my foot was still there. I stood up and half ran and half skipped to my bed, as if letting the foot linger too long on the floor would sever it from my leg. I learned that it was easy for me to slip into another Black person's body when I witnessed their pain. I try not to watch movies about Black people in the past. But sometimes, my mother tells stories about being chased by older white boys when she was too little to know what they might do to her if they caught her, and I freeze again. I tell myself, *You are not there, you are here in a different time.* But I am lying. My friends talk all the time about a rumor that KKK meetings go on just a few blocks from my house. And while I cannot prove it, I have seen grown men wearing their bedsheets about town. Sometimes, I dream of these men coming for my father, of having to stand by while my father is flayed alive. I want to believe that time is a straight line, that I can be separate from the past. But I already know better. Time is more like a roller coaster, flying forward but also looping back in spite of our screams. As I sit, caught in the loop, I wish my grandmother, the skinny woman who was fine with dying, was here so that I could stop being afraid all the time.

My uncle's sharp laughter followed by everyone else's startles me from my trance. They are not laughing because this happened a long time ago. They laugh because it was *not* so long ago, and they knew that their mother would always put her body, thin and sturdy as a winged elm, between them and death.

I arrive at Dr. K.'s practice in the early morning to have my blood drawn. No one sits in the waiting room here. Instead, all the patients walk into a hallway and stand in a single-file line that moves faster than McDonald's. Instead of getting a Quarter Pounder when it's my turn, I give my blood. On the walls are signs reminding everyone that they must have their insurance card ready when they walk in. Most of the women stare at their phones, taking a few steps forward whenever they sense movement in front of them. I stand behind a woman in a skirted business suit and a neat but slightly damp bob. A woman pushing a toddler in a stroller gets in line behind me. As the line moves, she coaches her little girl on how to wait for her quietly in the hallway. No children are allowed in the blood room. Two women at the front of the line look up from their phones and give the kid deadly stares as if she is proof of their biological inadequacies. I give the child a fake smile and reserve my resentment for her mother: How dare you, who already have a child, bring her here to leave a trail of Cheerios among the infertile? The feeling makes no sense. Any of the women in line could have children at home. This child could be the product of infertility treatments and her mother could be here to make a sibling. The child could have been conceived naturally and her mother might have been experiencing what doctors called secondary infertility. The woman could be selling her eggs or becoming a gestational surrogate for another family. None of this is any of my business. No one ever explains how they ended up in this line.

When I get to the front, I stop at a line of red tape on the floor. A woman walks out and a nurse says, "Next." I walk into a large room with sickly cream-yellow linoleum tile and walls lined with cheap gray cabinets. Though the room is large, like it was intended for surgical procedures that require lots of people in the room, there are just two blood-draw chairs set up in opposite corners like boxing-ring stools. A nurse sits next to each one. Neither nurse looks up at me. I walk in the direction that the voice came from and sit down on the chair. The nurse hands me a form and tells me to fill out the top with my insurance information, while another nurse attends to a woman sitting in the other chair. I hand the form back to my nurse and roll up my sleeves. She cleans a spot on my arm, sticks a needle in, and my blood fills the tube on the first try. When I thank her and explain that others have had difficulty drawing my blood, she shrugs and replaces the filled vial with an empty one. A thin gold cross dangles from her neck. But I have a feeling that not even a sneeze would get a "Bless you" out of her. Whatever she believes in, she keeps it literally close to her chest, at a safe distance from this place where failure is so abundant and where faith could be devastating for the believer. When she is done, she bandages my arm and directs me to the ultrasound line. As I walk out of the room, she calls, "Next!"

I get in the ultrasound line at the other end of the hallway. This line is short since patients do not get ultrasounds at every visit. When it is my turn, I walk into a small examining room with a nurse. Doctors do not perform ultrasounds here—just nurses and physician assistants who have been trained to stick probes into vaginas and count follicles all day. The nurse tells me to undress from the waist down and I strip while she prepares a probe. I lie down on a table and put my feet in stirrups. The nurse gently glides a probe into me without a verbal warning. She tells me I have one follicle and rattles off numbers that indicate how thick the lining of my uterus is. She makes no comment about what any of this means. She removes the probe and tells me to expect a call later that day telling me how my drug protocol should proceed. I thank her and get dressed.

I am back in the parking lot just thirty minutes after arriving. My body has been penetrated twice and I feel both invisible, like a factory part, and relieved that I did not have to perform the role of the positive patient. No one had encouraged me to believe or made me feel like getting pregnant required me to believe that I could. No one had said, *It only takes one*. Here, I didn't have to believe in anything.

My egg has chosen Thanksgiving Day to be ready for retrieval. At the practice, I put on a hospital gown and lie down on a cushioned table covered in dark red vinyl. A nurse puts an IV port in my arm while a doctor I will not remember introduces herself and then leaves the room. Dr. K. is old and no longer performs procedures, though he directs the treatment.

A few minutes later a smiling man walks into the room and introduces himself as the anesthesiologist. He is the happiest person I have ever seen in this place. He pulls out a clipboard and asks about my height, weight, allergies, and experiences with anesthesia. When he is done, he prepares the drug and asks what I do. I tell him where I teach, and he turns around grinning. "That's my son's first choice," he says. He wants to know if there is anything I can do to ensure his son is admitted. The answer is no, but I am caught off guard by the fact that a rich anesthesiologist is asking me to get his son admitted to the local state college while I wait for him to knock me out with anesthesia. I mumble something about possibly inquiring about the application and regret it instantly.

He writes down his son's information and says he will have the nurse leave it with my things. "So lucky that I met you," he says.

While he attaches the IV to my arm, I am trying to explain to him that I have no influence over admissions and that his son probably doesn't need any help. My words trail off, and I am floating in a milky bliss, a space without thought, just sublime feeling.

When I wake up, the table I was reclining on has been adjusted so that I am sitting up with my legs spread wide and my feet in low stirrups. There are two nurses, one on either side of me. They are nothing like the nurses that I am used to here. They have soft, sympathetic smiles, and they talk to me like I am a child who has lost her mother. They ask me how I feel and one of them tells me that she can give me "something for the pain." I tell them that I'm okay. The two of them help me up and walk me to a large room divided by curtains into smaller spaces for each patient. Inside one of these makeshift rooms,

Reginald is waiting for me. He helps the nurses place me onto a bed with a disposable pad draped across it. One of the nurses tells me not to worry about the blood. The pad will catch it, she says. But I do not feel any blood. She asks me if I am feeling the pain yet. I close my eyes and concentrate on my body. I feel a dull ache in my back and fatigue like I want to go back into the soft, deep sleep of anesthesia, but I do not feel pain. I tell her no. The nurse says she will be back to check on me.

Reginald reads aloud to me from a book while we wait to hear if the retrieval was successful. I can barely listen because I am trying to feel pain and blood—proof that at least one egg was separated from my body. But all I feel is exhaustion.

When one of the smiling nurses comes back to check on me, I ask her how many. "One," she says. "But remember, though, it only takes one."

I do a double take and realize for the first time that there is a reason why I do not recognize any of these honey-voiced nurses in this part of the practice devoted to egg retrievals. The clinic must hire different nurses to work in this section. They are probably part-time nurses who also work someplace else, where the prospect of success must be greater than here. The hands that helped me onto the bed did not draw blood all day from the wrinkled veins of women they would later dial to report a failure. Instead, these hands helped hold up this strange world where we pretend that curtains are walls, call surgery under general anesthesia "a procedure," and literally count eggs before they are hatched.

I look at the sweet nurse and close my eyes, refusing to acknowledge her clichéd hope and wishing for the nurse who yelled, "Next," like there was no longing left in the world.

• • •

Three days after the retrieval, Reginald and I arrive at the practice to have a four-cell embryo transferred to my uterus. I enter a dark room with Reginald trailing me. I can hear the soft rustle of the yellow tissue caps and gowns. My lower half is wrapped in a thick white sheet that I drag behind me. A nurse wearing a face mask points to the table, and I climb up and lie down. The room is cold, and I shiver while she uses an ultrasound machine to make sure that my bladder is full enough to be transparent on the screen.

A voice counts slowly in the adjacent room, "One, two, three . . ." and another voice lighter and airier repeats the numbers. This is the call-and-response of egg retrieval. The doctors count each one of the eggs so the embryologist knows exactly how many she should receive in the tube. Then the embryologist counts to confirm that she has removed each egg from the tube. Together they count sixteen eggs. When that woman comes out of surgery, there will be good news waiting for her. I picture an average-size middle-aged white woman lying on a cot smiling while holding her aching belly. She is the patient who is supposed to be here, the one the doctors know how to treat, the one whose body they had in mind when they made this place. I am the aberration, the Black woman no one had ever imagined doing anything but cleaning the floors beneath me, and whose body is such an outlier that no one seems to know how to treat it.

I wonder what it must have been like when I was the woman on that table and a doctor said, "One," and nothing more. Did she continue to poke follicles expecting to keep counting, only to find out that there was nothing more to count? Did the embryologist stand there waiting to hear the number two until the doctor said, "That's it—just one"?

A tiny light flickers behind a glass window in the wall. Then dark-ness again. Embryos do not like light. They also cannot stand perfume or scented lotions. The fragrances that we find enticing repulse and kill them—a reminder that they are not meant to be out in the world. They are supposed to be floating in the dark fluffiness of a womb.

I close my tired eyes and disappear into the darkness, a photograph waiting to be developed, dunked in caustic chemicals until someone can finally see me, made whole, reproduced.

When I open my eyes a Black woman with eyes that smile is beam-ing at me in the dark. When she introduces herself as Dr. A. in an accent that sounds ancient, West African, my feet go prickly as I real-ize that she is not a Black girl from Alabama, or Texas, or even Califor-nia or Connecticut. She is someone who grew up in a place where people had names, ethnic groups, languages that made them a people, indelibly connected to Black Americans and yet also profoundly differ-ent. As much as her smile makes me want to linger in it, I remind myself that there is no way to know what she sees when she looks at me—a forgotten cousin whose ancestors were unlucky enough to have been enslaved, or someone whose ancestors failed to maintain and pass on the discipline and work ethic of successful African immi-grants. Dr. A. is not like me, and even if she was, what would it mean here in a cold dark room designed not for people, but for embryos? Dr. O. was like me and that did not stop her from telling me that Black women are not infertile. She had once been a Black girl, with shoes stained with the red clay of Alabama, but somewhere between picking collards and becoming a doctor, she had learned not to see me, and her Blackness hadn't changed that.

Dr. A. places a speculum inside me, twists it open, and turns on an ultrasound machine. She picks up a clear tube from a tray and sticks it inside me.

"This isn't the real thing yet, just a trial run," she says.

I wince at the now-familiar pain of tubes wiggling around in my uterus. When the doctor is satisfied with the trial run, she withdraws the tube. Then she picks up a clipboard and holds it close to her nose. She reads my full name, directing her voice toward the sliding window. A masked woman slides the window open and sticks her head out. Attached to her head is a headband with a tiny, blinding light. This illuminated cyclops repeats our names again in a loud voice. The doctor, perched on a stool with wheels, slides over to the window, grabs the tube, and slides back to her spot between my legs. Again, I feel the warm pain of something going through my cervix the wrong way, and I let my head roll to the side. On a small black-and-white screen, I see the outline of the tube, and then it is gone.

Dr. A. stands up and gives me a toothy grin. "A smooth transfer," she says. Her voice does not match her smile. She sounds robot-like, as if she has trained herself to say this all day whether she means it or not. Would she tell us if the transfer was not smooth? Would she say, *Well, that was terrible—I'm not even sure if I got that thing in there?*

I am supposed to lie here for thirty minutes, but the pressure of my bladder is too much. Dr. A. says she will send a nurse with a bedpan to relieve me. On her way out, she says, "Good luck"—the final admission that the outcome of weeks of pills, shots, medical procedures, and surgery would always be uncertain no matter how smooth any or all of the steps went. This must be how she continues working in a field where there is always more failure than success.

I want to emulate this noncommittal attitude, to separate from my body long enough to wish myself good luck and be done with hope. But instead, I pray—at first to a god, but the words ring hollow like they are coming from a recording playing somewhere inside me. I give up and talk instead to my ancestors, all the women who stood between their children and the white men who could have killed them. I hear my father and my uncles laughing because their mother was so ferocious, so miraculous, that she had been like a god to them. I ask her to see me on this table and grant me a child, who would also be her child. And this is how belief slips back into me—as I picture my grandmother's face.

It is the day of the pregnancy test, but I already know that I am pregnant. I woke this morning with a headache and backache. I read about this symptom the night before on an internet discussion board for pregnancy symptoms. Each time I read women's accounts of their early pregnancy symptoms, I seem to feel that symptom soon after. Yesterday, the yogurt I ate tasted too tart, and my breasts were sore. Two days ago, I felt a twinge on the left side of my lower abdomen, like a rubber band snapping every time I sat down. I feel myself transforming from one person into two.

As I get dressed, I glance at the photos of my grandmother and my aunt, but I do not stop to stare at them anymore. Instead, I get in my car and drive to the clinic, reading signs of my ancestors' presence all around me: a stray fawn, unseasonable wet warmth, like the moment before a tornado. I talk to the women because I believe they have sent the life inside me. I do not say thank you because that is something you reserve for those who are completely separate. To thank them would be like thanking part of myself because they are always with me and I am with them. Instead, I say, "Yes, I know," and I try to see them, slight and ethereal, nodding back from somewhere without walls.

I drive to the clinic and wait in line as I always do, but today is different. I catch myself staring at the other women in line as I realize that every time I have been here, some of these women were waiting for a pregnancy test like I am today. Some of them were pregnant like I am today. Had they also brought someone with them who could not be seen?

When the nurse is done drawing my blood, I ask her what time I should expect the call, and she tells me I'll hear from them in the late afternoon. She wishes me luck in a voice so soft that it is almost a whisper, as if she does not want anyone or anything to overhear us.

I am at home in my bedroom in the late afternoon when I answer the phone and a woman's voice says, "Your test was negative. You'll need to schedule a follow-up with the doctor before continuing to try. I'll transfer you to schedule an appointment."

The word "negative" hits like a thin needle jabbed into the soft spot behind my ear. I listen while a recording about minimal stimulation IVF plays. The recorded voice is cheerful, even a little excited.

"Minimal stimulation didn't get us shit, bitch—" I respond to the recording, but a real woman's voice interrupts me.

"Hello? Hello?" she says.

"Oh, sorry," I say.

"Do you want to schedule an appointment?" she says, as if the first word I said to her was not "bitch."

I try to say yes, but a gurgling sound comes out. The last thread holding me together snaps somewhere in my throat.

"Do you want to call back?"

"Yes," I manage. "Yes."

I walk up the stairs and into my bedroom, taking the phone with me. I crawl into our unmade bed and wrap myself in layers of down. It is not cold, and I start to sweat.

I call Reginald at work and tell him that I am not pregnant.

"I'm so sorry. I'll be home as soon as this meeting is over. Okay?"

I try to answer, to tell him there's no need, but my words, caught between sobs, are not making sense.

I hang up and scream until I am gasping for air. My nose fills with snot, and I can no longer scream and breathe at the same time.

I promise myself no more hope—no more belief, as if the problem is not my body, but my belief in its ability to reproduce. But it is one thing not to believe in a god, and another not to believe in the past. I am not ready to let go of my ancestors—the idea that bonds of family across generations of the dead and the living could be the marrow of the spiritual.

I pick up the phone and dial the fertility clinic to schedule a follow-up with the doctor who believes in aliens.

My maternal cousin Thalia, who is studying at the local college, stops by our house to eat dinner with my family. I am six years old. Everyone, including my brother, makes their own plate, sits down at the kitchen bar or the nearby table, and begins eating one by one. My father hands me a plate and I sit down next to Thalia. We eat while my mother asks Thalia about people in the nearby town where she grew up.

After a few minutes, Thalia puts her fork down and glances at me. "Wait, y'all. We forgot to say grace."

My father keeps eating, but everyone else looks up from their plate as if Thalia has said, *Hey, we forgot to do the hokey pokey.* We never say grace before eating.

Everyone lowers their eyes and waits for Thalia to speak, but she doesn't. My father mumbles a "Dear heavenly father . . ." like the preacher says when he prays at church, but the words get caught in the food in his mouth and it comes out, "Tear evely partner." I giggle.

"No, no," Thalia says, and we all look up. "Let's let San say it. San, sing that prayer, the one I heard you do last time. You know, the one you had just learned at school."

Everyone smiles now like they have finally been let in on a joke. Thalia covers her mouth to stop herself from laughing.

I know that the song makes them laugh, but I am not sure why it is so funny since no one laughs when we sing it at school before lunch. I shrug and launch into the prayer song with a country-and-western twang.

Oh, the Lord is good to me,
And so I thank the Lord
For giving me the things I need,
The sun, and the rain, and the apple seeds.
Oh, the Lord is good to me.

I sing, just as I do at school, but with one difference. Instead of closing my eyes, I keep them wide open.

CHAPTER 10

I am sixteen years old. I walk through the house like a ghost, talking to myself because no one here talks to me. In my head, I replay disagreements I had at school, trying to think of quips I might have said if I had been someone else. I think of scenes from movies and music videos, imagining myself in different roles and different worlds. As I make my way through the hallway, I repeat the words that small-town white teenagers say in movies: "God, I can't wait to get out of here." This line is one that I mean, because I am suffocating in this place.

At school, I am one of the "niggers." The white people we go to school with are not supposed to call us this aloud. But when they are angry, the poorest whites mutter the word under their breaths, and the poorest Blacks try to beat their asses before a teacher can pull them off. The rich whites do not have to call us anything because they can make us invisible whenever they want. They have all-white high school sororities and a whites-only country club where our Black uncles become their uncles, serving them drinks and cleaning up after them. They live on land designated for whites by the federal government before their parents were born. At school, we play sports with them and lead them to championships. In return, we get to hold one or two spots on the student council and the cheerleading squad. But if the white kids were to be seen with us after school in a car or at a party, they would forever be damaged goods. The boys would be called drug fiends and the girls would be considered stretched-out whores, shared around by Black men only.

Meanwhile, our Black world is a pressure cooker, where we fight one another like gladiators who know they will die. I do not know how to fight so I carry my majorette baton foolishly believing that if attacked I will wield it like a sword to protect myself. I realize it is just a toy when a strong girl with teeth as big as a sheep's blindsides me in a hallway before class. Though I do not know why she chooses me in particular, the glee the attack causes among Black students with no-name sneakers worn as thin as the knees of their jeans makes the lines of battle more apparent to me. It is the children of the desperately poor against the children of teachers and factory workers with "good jobs." I wonder aloud with my friends stupidly, "Why do they hate us . . . what did we ever do to them?"—never realizing that ignoring them instead of hating them back was the worst insult we could have dealt, as lethal to their humanity as the nonchalant toss of a white girl's hair onto our desks. But I cannot see any of this because I do not understand the why of this social landscape and my place in it, and I have no time to question or ponder. I am busy trying to make girls with sandpaper hands think I am a fearsome thing so that they will not hit me. I have no idea that hitting is the least of the many harms that could be done to a Black girl. I fail to anticipate the mental combat of rumors and innuendo—the quiet warfare in which a lethal whisper lands with the precise violence of a missile. The word "whore" begins to follow me through the hallways because I have been in search of something that feels like love. A Black boy uses the inside of my body like a batting cage. I consider ending my life, but I am not ready to die. I want too many things whose names I have yet to learn. I fixate on a new life that I will start in college, where no one will know me.

I am passing through the hallway talking to myself about wanting to leave home for good when my mother steps into the hallway to face me. Her hands are balled fists by her sides. "You think you're so smart, don't you? Where do you think you're going to go?"

I startle as if a mountain lion has jumped into my path. Her words pierce the cloud I have been floating in and rage shakes my body and mind awake.

"College!"

"You can go to college right here like your sister did."

I should just walk away. I have already discussed college with my father, and he has agreed that if I want to go away, he will help me. He has seen what happens to the Black people who get degrees at the local university and end up working in the mall because there are no places that will hire Black professionals here. My mother is not in charge of anything but where to put the coffee table. Still, I am angry and confused that she would want me to stay in this place where she knows I can never be free.

"Why would you want me to stay here?" I say. "Just because that's what you want? We are different people."

"What do you mean different? What are you trying to say about me?"

"I want to go to a city, where there are things to do besides gossip about other people."

"And you think that makes you better than me? We so different, huh?"

"What are you so mad about? We want different things because we are two different people."

"And what do you think there is to do that's any different from here?"

I do not know the answer to this question, so I say, "Places to go and do things, see things. Anything would be better than here."

"You'll be back! Just like all the rest of 'em!" she says, spit trailing behind her words. "You'll end up right back here!"

Cassandra?" I open my eyes and see a smiling woman in blue scrubs. I am sitting high up on a surgical table that is shaped like a chair. My feet are in stirrups. The nurse is at eye level with me even though she is standing. I look down at the beige tile floor to figure out how high up I am. But before I can check, I see a flash of red on a white pad between my thighs.

The nurse reaches for my feet to remove them from the stirrups, but I stop her with my hand.

"Are you okay?" she asks.

I look down at the pad between my legs where my blood has formed a jagged map of a place unknown.

"It's normal to have some bleeding," she says.

I do not have the energy to explain that this is my third egg retrieval and I have never seen red blood or any other sharp visual evidence that eggs were taken out of my body. So I nod at her and try to smile just a little so she will know I'm ready to get up.

She removes my feet from the stirrups and helps me sit up. I move to put one foot on the floor, and pain strikes like someone has left thorns inside me. I freeze at the realness of my body. I want to lie down and curl into myself, but I do not want to stay here in this room with shackles shaped like stirrups.

The nurse extends her arm and I press down on it to stand up. I hobble forward leaning on her and we make our way down a hallway, with her stopping every few steps to make sure that I am steady. I keep my eyes on the floor, nodding and walking like a movie monster. Reginald is waiting for me in the curtained room. He helps me onto the bed where I am supposed to rest, but I am in too much pain to do anything but wait for the doctor. When she enters the curtain, she says through a soft smile that she retrieved three eggs. Reginald beams at me and I look back with a cautious smile that says, *Three is better, but not a lot.* As if reading my mind, he answers, "That's three times more than we've ever had." His warm joy fills the curtained room and I inhale it until three feels like hope waiting to transform into the flesh.

The next day a nurse calls in the morning to tell me that of the three eggs retrieved, one egg did not fertilize. Another fertilized but appears to have stopped growing. The last egg is continuing to grow.

On the third day, I go to the clinic to have the still-growing embryo and the one that may have arrested put inside me.

For nine days after the transfer, I walk on my toes without meaning to. On the tenth day, I go in for a blood test and later a nurse calls to tell me that neither of the embryos will become a real baby.

I hang up and call Reginald, who is at work. His voicemail picks up, and I hesitate as I reach for a word that does not exist. There is no single word for "not pregnant," or at least no word that does not rely on the word "pregnant" or its synonyms. There is "unpregnant," which the *Oxford English Dictionary* indicates is no longer in common usage. There's "nongravid," based on the term "gravid," which means heavy or heavy with child. There are no true antonyms for pregnant: "barren," "infertile," "aborting," "miscarrying," "delivered."

I hang up and he calls back. I settle on one word. "No."

I am in my first year of college when I return to my dorm room to find my roommate standing in front of the mirror putting on her earrings. She looks at my reflection as I stand behind her and sucks her teeth. "Your dad called again," she says. "He said if you don't call back this time, you can forget about him sending money." She animates her voice to let me know that he was yelling. I can read the disgust on her face, but it is directed at me, not him.

She talks to her mother regularly on the phone and her voice is the same as when she is talking to friends. This seems to be normal at the women's college we attend. The women sprinkle their sentences with "my mom said" or "my dad thinks."

These intimacies fascinate and repel me. I spy on these relationships every chance I get, perusing dormmates' family vacation photos, peering into care boxes sent by their mothers, trying to get a glimpse of cards attached to birthday balloons sent by dads. I try to imagine what it would be like to experience relationships that are more speech than silence with my parents. I struggle to think of topics we might talk about. I want to dismiss the women who talk about their parents like they are friends. These girls are weak and needy.

I feel my difference so sharply that I create another difference to distract from it—a pronounced white southern accent, like the one I spoke in as a small child but that had long since worn off after I entered high school and made more Black friends. Nevertheless, I lean into the self I create, based on a character from a popular television show: a Black southern belle so doted on by her parents that even her speech connotes isolation from the real world. But because I absorb the accents around me easily, I am unable to maintain the charade for more than a few weeks.

I wait for my roommate to leave and call my father. He answers, "Hey, baby," like usual. We talk as if he did not just call and reprimand me via my roommate for the fact that I never call home. He asks how I am doing, and I say fine. I ask how he is doing, and he says fine. He asks if my classes are okay, and I say yes. There is a pause and he lowers his voice. "You know, your mother worries about you when you don't call. Let me put her on the phone."

My mother says hello and asks how I am doing. She does not ask about classes. She tells me that she is fine. Then she lowers her voice, "You know, your daddy worries about you. You need to call home more."

"Okay," I say.

But I am drained by this call. It is hard to use words without also communicating, to avoid anything that might indicate that we are people with feelings and interior lives. The phone feels heavy in my hand.

"Okay, then, bye," my mother says. She hands the phone back to my father.

"Be good, baby. Daddy is so proud of you." He cannot say "I." It is as if "Daddy" is another self who stands mute, next to him.

Just before he hangs up, there is a pause where the "I love you" and the "I miss you" are supposed to be.

• • •

I go home for the summer after my first year of college. My life is caught between an old world and a new one. I am sitting on my mother's bed after using the phone next to it to chat with a friend from college. My mother walks in, and my anger at her boils over.

"Why haven't you ever said 'I love you' to me?"

My mother stands over me with a genuine look of confusion on her face. "But you already know that," she says. "Why would you need me to say anything? We're paying all this money for your college."

She is vexed by my question, and I am vexed by hers. I begin to sob and my body shakes. Her body goes rigid, and she takes a step away as if I might attack her. Then she moves toward the door. She stops in the doorway and looks back over her shoulder. "You have to learn to be stronger than this," she says.

"This is being strong," I yell after her. "Silence is not strong." But she keeps walking down the hallway as if she does not hear me.

When my father comes home, I do not communicate any of my disappointment about this lack of intimacy to him. To demand intimacy from him would be to breach the contract between us—to force him to see me as someone with feelings all my own, rather than as the antidote to his loss. The door to this kind of intimacy closed twelve years before I was born, and if he ever loved in the way that I wanted to be loved, he would certainly never do it again after losing so much and so many. His past, his grief is like white noise, a fuzzy, staticky sound that muffles our emotions.

Instead of asking him for more, I vow that one day I will be different with my own child.

• • •

I have a new IVF doctor. He talks about acupuncture, immune sys-
tems, and something I do not understand called intralipids. When I
talk, he smiles with perfect porcelain veneers and looks into my eyes.
He has disguised his clinic to look like a spa. I wonder if he is a bit
kooky like Dr. K.—if intralipids are his aliens.

I see the acupuncturist before the procedures. She taps needle
after needle into my body as I sink into the stillness that acupuncture
demands.

When she is done, she leans over me and whispers, "I shouldn't tell
you this. It's early, but I'm pregnant—five weeks."

I lie there, a hostage shaped like a porcupine.

"I'm telling you because these techniques worked for me. My husband has horrible sperm count. I can recommend herbs for your husband too."

I do not believe her. Anyone who has suffered through infertility
knows that news of a pregnancy feels like bloodletting when you cannot get pregnant.

I try to explain to her that our problem is not sperm but eggs, and
that eggs are a much bigger problem, but as I begin to talk, I feel a
needle behind my ear shift and I purse my lips.

She places a heat lamp near my feet, turns out the lights, and leaves
the room.

I lie on the table, my body still, but every wild thought in my mind
runs free. I try to imagine hands on my belly, the hands of gods, spir-
its, long-dead grandmothers, aunts, and uncles who know where babies come from. But my mind wanders, and I think of women who

dress up as nurses and steal babies from hospitals. I am not crazy enough to do this, but I can see the tender thing that snapped in their brains—the moment when they went from being women who wanted children to being mothers without children.

I return home from the spa clinic with two embryos in my womb and skin freshly pricked with acupuncture needles.

This time I do not wait for the faint voice over the phone to tell me if I am pregnant or not. Instead, I do the thing that every single IVF doctor has asked me not to do. I buy a stack of pregnancy tests, and each morning, I pee on a stick. A friend who has two children conceived through IVF tells me that she could never have done this—that it would have been torture to read those negative sticks day after day. But I am through with disembodied voices saying "I'm sorry" over the phone. I want to find out for myself, disappoint myself before anyone else can.

I pee on the stick and while I wait for the result, I picture myself running down the stairs, test in hand to show two lines to my husband.

When the time is up, I stare at the little glossy test window, but hope fucks with my vision, making me think I see faint pink lines that could grow bolder in the days to come.

I show one to my husband. "Do you see it?" I say. He stares at it, searching for something that is not there.

I sit on my bed and pick up the folder from my nightstand. The glowing hot pink of the death certificates still shocks me as much as it did the first time I saw them. My fingers flip through the sheets, proving that what happened was real, not just something I imagined.

I have already done internet searches for information on the accident with no results. The certificates are all I have to explain the absence that haunts me, despite never having known my ancestors' presence.

My eyes light again on a line in my grandmother's certificate that says "Occupation: Domestic." A reminder that whoever prepared these documents thought that my grandmother must have belonged to someone other than herself. Had she perhaps done domestic work and no one had told me? Or had the preparer, a Mrs. Aycock, consciously or unconsciously found a way to distinguish her work, in a time when the expectation for middle-class married white women was to stay at home, from the less respectable work of Black women?

I call home and my father answers. I tell him about the certificates.

"Domestic? What? Who put that?" His voice rises with anger as if the certificates were written hours ago.

"Whoever prepared the documents."

"That's ridiculous. Mama never worked as no domestic. She farmed and when they gave that up she got a job up here at the school in the cafeteria. She wasn't no domestic."

"And your wife and sister?"

"Naw. That's just white folks. They put that down 'cause they were Black women." I am about to ask another question when he says, "Your mama wants to talk to you."

"San?" she says. I answer and her voice turns into a half whisper. "What are you doing? Why are you asking all this?"

"I need to know," I say.

She makes a clicking sound in her throat that says, *Can't you just leave well enough?*

"Your daddy says it was in the newspaper. But I don't know how you get that old stuff."

"I'm coming home," I say more to myself than to her.

"Good. That would be nice. Now I got to get over to the beauty shop. Let us know when you coming. Love you." Her last two words sound like a computer-generated voice, reminding me that while she says this because I once demanded it, it is a compromise. There is no "I," because these are not her words but mine, words that I've taught her to say, words that she believes she shouldn't have to.

I hang up and buy a plane ticket to Alabama.

My parents pick me up at the airport in Huntsville, and we drive down a highway with homes, farms, and shacks scattered along its edges. If Alabama has an official color, it should be the bright orange shade of the dirt commonly called red clay. It is ugly and beautiful at once—too bright for nature and as messy as finger paint, staining everything it touches. It shows through the sparse grass on country lots and leaves the asphalt highway with a bright burnt cast where there should be pale grays and blues.

My parents are chatty with happiness as they try to catch me up on what's happened. My father points out places where the last tornado flattened the houses and crops like a monster from a Japanese film. My mother talks about friends from their church—someone is recovering from surgery, another's daughter just got married, and yet another has cancer.

They pretend that they do not know the reason for my visit—I am here to look at injuries that my father has spent years covering. Shame creeps into my stomach. I finger the death certificates hidden inside a folder in my bag to remind myself that the story I have come for is also mine.

I am eight years old. I am playing with the kids next door when my stomach begins to feel uncomfortable. I tell Bunny and Leah that I have to go home. When they ask what's wrong, I tell them about the feeling in my stomach—that it does not hurt, but something is wrong with it.

"Are you hungry?" Bunny asks.

I think for a minute. "I don't know," I say. "What does that feel like?"

"You've never been hungry before?" they say. "Ever?"

I shake my head and remember a teenage cousin who'd complained that at my family's house he never had a chance to get hungry because my father was always cooking the next meal.

I walk home and enter through the kitchen, where my father is frying a chicken. He has not had a drink yet. He is wide-eyed and alert.

I ask him when the food will be ready.

"You hungry?" he says.

I hesitate. In our house, hunger is serious—so serious that my parents have to tell jokes to talk about it. They laugh about when they were little kids, fighting siblings for the last piece of meat. My mother cannot eat an orange without telling me that when she was little, she and her siblings only had oranges when they received them as Christmas presents from their parents. My father is not as open about the pain of childhood hunger, but it is most evident in the things that he refuses to make or eat, popcorn and hot cereals, foods that the poor use to fill their children's stomachs when there is nothing else to eat. Now our kitchen is always stocked to the brim with fruit, meat, and leftovers.

I sit down at the bar, spinning left then right on the barstool, while my father races around the kitchen as if my life depends on a ham sandwich. When he is done, he puts the plate in front of me. After the first few bites, we talk because this is the only place we ever talk, with his eyes on the hot grease popping out of the pan, the TV in the den blaring in the background. Here, we can pretend that what we say does not matter and that the past is not one giant wound. I ask him questions about his life as a child, whether his family kept horses, what his mother taught him to cook, how old he was when he learned to drive. Sometimes, I ask about his navy travels to the Caribbean and South America. He answers and somewhere along the way he pours himself a drink. His eyes grow droopy, and his answers become musical, peppered with slow "oh wells" and "sometimes" and the humming of songs that I do not know.

I know the limits of our conversation, firm as the walls of a conquistadore's fort. We do not talk about the terror of being a Black boy in the South, and we do not talk about the accident that killed his family. As long as I stay in bounds, everything will be fine.

I finish my sandwich, and he asks if I want more to eat.

"No," I say. "Thank you. This was really good."

You hungry?" my father asks. He is in the kitchen, holding the refrigerator door open. I am sitting nearby at a kitchen counter, spinning myself back and forth on a barstool, until I remember that I am thirty-seven years old and stop myself.

I tell my father that I am hungry, even though I am not sure I am. My stomach is pregnant with nervous anticipation as I prepare to ask him questions that I wish I had written down.

He pulls a large container of ribs out of the refrigerator, along with a bowl of sweet corn and greens. He makes me a plate with more food than I can eat and pops it in the microwave. The sharp, sweet scent of barbecue sauce fills the room.

He no longer drinks when he cooks. His doctor has explained to him that the painful gout he developed in his legs could be alleviated if he stopped drinking. But he is also someone else now. He is an elder, an official position of leadership at the church he attends weekly for adult Sunday school and worship service. I am not sure which happened first, abstinence from drinking or regular churchgoing. But the man who drank Pabst Blue Ribbon beer and Old Forester whiskey until he sank unconscious into a recliner is gone. While I do not miss that man whose grief leaked all over this house, this new man is often unfamiliar to me. Sometimes, his phone rings all day with calls about church business and he rushes to answer every call. Prior to this, I have never known my father to willingly talk on the phone for more than a few minutes to anyone. Now he smiles and recounts the person's question and his response after each call. At first, I wonder at his desire to help run a church after helping to run a plant for so long. But then I remember my mother's words: *We have to have our own churches because that's the only way Black folks can be in charge of anything. White folks won't let a Black person tell them what to do.* At church my father has a community that respects him, not because a white person put him in charge, but because they chose him.

He still does not talk about God to me. And though I imagine that he must do so when he teaches adult Sunday school, his lessons as recounted by my mother seem more practical than spiritual, and always delivered with a humorous dose of candor. *You know John tells them like it is. The other day they was all complaining about the young folks, talking about how they all party all the time. John said that we were all the same way when we were young, but we just didn't have as much money and cars as kids today. He told them they were complaining like they hadn't done all the same stuff. If they didn't do something, it wasn't because they were better but because they were too broke to do anything. Rita got so tickled at John saying that. And you know the rest of them shut up that ol' talk then.*

My father puts a plate in front of me, and I let the flavors of barbecued ribs and sweet corn soothe me. While I eat, my father moves around the kitchen preparing the next meal even though this one hasn't even been eaten.

When I finish, fear creeps up from my stomach to my throat and I involuntarily begin to turn back and forth on the stool again, until I brace my hands against the counter. I do not want to hurt my father, but I am afraid that any words that cut through time will also cut him. I struggle for a beginning, something that will not be a land mine that will shatter us both. But how do you ask someone about the day their family died?

His hands move in and out of the refrigerator gathering the eggs and buttermilk.

"Daddy," I say. "I have a question about the death certificates."

He stops and looks up at me with his own questions in his eyes.

"They list the place of residence for your sister, her husband, and San as North Chicago."

He puts the items on the countertop and opens a cabinet, searching the shelves. "Yeah. Maggie and them were living up there when it happened." His voice is matter-of-fact, like we are talking about a neighbor who moved away.

"I didn't know they lived in Chicago."

"Naw, not the big city Chicago. They lived in a little town called North Chicago up by Waukegan. Most folks around here just call that whole area Waukegan. They had been up there for a couple of years by then. Robert went up there for work. They were visiting here when the wreck happened."

Something splits like a seam along my chest. "Visiting" is Black southern for a summer vacation. As a child, "visiting" was the only kind of vacation that my family and all the Black people I knew took, traveling to relatives in St. Louis or Philadelphia. Visiting was always an exciting reunion where cousins became friends and adults stayed up all night talking and laughing. Visiting was a celebration. There is no such thing as a good day to lose your family in a car accident, but a reunion should never end this way.

On the counter, my father lines up each ingredient for cornbread—buttermilk, eggs, cornmeal, oil, and shortening—like schoolchildren on their way to recess. I search for a different kind of question, this time to protect not just him but myself from the past.

"What was your brother-in-law Robert Ray like? Did y'all always call him by his whole name like that?"

My father surprises me by smiling like someone is tickling him. "We called him that to distinguish him from another Robert in the family. He didn't mind either way though. He was the easiest-going man you could imagine." He describes a man who was calm, quiet, and steady—the opposite of his wife, a skinny woman with a fiery temper that could make her seem crazy when someone crossed her. My father's smile softens, but his eyes are still warm with love as he talks about Robert and Maggie. "They balanced each other out," he says. "He was the best. Just the best."

In June of 1960, my aunt Maggie and her husband, Robert Ray, traveled home to Alabama with their two daughters, Liza and San. They drove over six hundred miles in their new Pontiac from North Chicago, Illinois, to another small town, Sheffield, Alabama. If they made this trip on today's interstate highways, it would take them nearly ten hours. In 1960, before the completion of the system of highways that we now know as interstates, the drive would have been significantly longer, taking them through big cities like Chicago and tiny towns like Henderson, Kentucky. But unlike today, when they could stop at any number of bathrooms, restaurants, or hotels, their stops would have been short and few. *The Travelers' Green Book, 1960,* a booklet that provided Black travelers with lists of businesses that served Black people, notes just seventeen towns in the entire state of Indiana, the halfway point of their trip, where they could have found a gas station, restaurant, or rooming house that would serve them.

No one in my family has any memory of having ever seen a *Green Book*. At its height, just twenty thousand copies were published per year out of New York City and sold through mail order, Black-owned businesses, and Esso service stations. In the part of rural Alabama where my family came from, where the closest thing to a Black-owned business was sharecropping, access to the publication would have been limited. And besides, no southern Black person worth their salt would have been convinced that a little book could serve as adequate protection for a trip through the Midwest's and the South's sundown towns, where signs were posted saying no Blacks after sundown. The Black writer John A. Williams marveled that white travelers had no "idea of how much nerve and courage it requires for a Negro to drive coast to coast in America."

Despite its mission of helping Black travelers find services, even the *Green Book* came with a disclaimer, explaining that while the listings were "carefully checked . . . publishers cannot be responsible." They asked that patrons who experience "unpleasant or unsatisfactory service" report it to them. Hidden between the lines of this genteel request was an implicit condition: you may report if your Black ass survives the "unpleasant" encounter.

Because they faced hostility and the threat of violence merely for attempting to move through the American landscape, many Black families like mine traveled exclusively to visit family, whether for pleasure or necessity.

Maggie and Robert Ray had to plan carefully the first time they made the trip, consulting friends and family members to schedule safe stops, and pack food, water, and even full gas cans before they left to minimize the need to stop. They may have gone off route to find relatives in St. Louis to stay with before returning to their travels or taken turns napping in the car.

The family arrived safely at the home of John T., who was not yet my father, and his wife, Willodene. He had recently convinced his parents, Bernice and Bluitt, to give up sharecropping and move in with him in a rental house in town. There were also two little boys, Davy and Hal, one each belonging to either of Maggie and John T.'s older brothers, who were visiting too.

They all ate together scattered about the crowded living room. The adults drank and laughed and told stories that made them feel safe.

Everyone in the extended family took turns sneaking looks at the almost four-year-old San, with her flame-colored hair and reddish-brown skin. Finally, someone said it aloud: Where did that hair come from? San was used to people staring at her like she was wearing a sock on her head. Liza, big-eyed and thin like her mother, sat steady and quiet next to San on the floor, eating at the coffee table with the boys.

When the kids were done, Willodene served them ice cream and joined them at the little table. At nineteen, Willodene had yet to get pregnant, despite two years of marriage. John T. had come to believe that he was not able to produce children, but they did not talk about it because there was no use in talking about something that was out of their control.

When it was time to go to sleep, the adults made up the sofa and set pallets on the floor. The next morning, they all had breakfast together and my father headed to work, even though it was Saturday. Reynolds Metals Company had only recently started hiring Blacks into good jobs and he could not risk giving the supervisor a reason not to hire any more.

A few hours passed before everyone was dressed and ready to travel to Robert's family in Russellville, twenty miles away. When it was time to go, Bernice explained to the boys that there was no room in the car and they would have to stay behind, but a neighbor would check on them. When the littlest, Davy, begged to go with them, she promised that if he would stop crying, she would bring home his favorite food, fresh strawberries. Davy smiled so hard that it looked like the whole crying episode had been a trick. Everyone but the two boys climbed in the car and waved goodbye.

After that day, Davy would never eat strawberries again.

CHAPTER 11

"If you have questions, you really should ask me," my mother says.

I am in the den reading on the sofa when she sits down at the other end, wringing her hands.

"You shouldn't talk to him about it. Just ask me, and I'll tell you what he told me about it. Can you imagine losing everything like that?" She is trying to sound like she is giving directions, but anger makes her voice squeak like the strings of a toy ukulele.

She is trying to protect her husband from her child and simultaneously make herself the only source of knowledge about an event that happened before she knew my father. How much of this story is hers to tell or withhold? How much knowledge had their relationship borne?

"You aren't writing anything about this, are you?"

"No. I just need to know. Don't you understand that this is already a part of me? It's not just his story."

She presses her lips together and shakes her head. "You sure you not writing anything?"

"Why do you keep asking me that? I told you I need to know."

"Why now, then? Why do you need to know now?"

Words are spinning in my head: I need to know because I am infertile. I am grieving the loss of a child who never existed. And at the same time, I am grieving the people whose ghosts have haunted us since I can remember being alive. I do not want to torment my father by pointing to the injuries that we cannot heal. But I do want to re-create the dead. Have a real child, just as he did, that could contain this grief and promise that we would not have to be completely changed by a wreck—promise that we are not a wreck.

I cannot tell my mother any of this. A year earlier, I mentioned to her that Reginald and I were trying to have a baby. She winced at the word "trying" as if I had invited her into my bedroom to watch. Even that little knowledge was an unbearable intimacy.

Though I once explained that I could not travel to Alabama because we were doing IVF, I did not tell my parents about the painful procedures, the incessant doctors' visits, the disappointing diagnoses, the embryos that had failed. I never explained that I was grieving my own body, once defined as healthy, now condemned as insufficient, incapable of the very thing that sustains human life. I kept my grief to myself and made it my own fortress because it felt wrong to burden those who were already aggrieved, wrong to mourn a child who had never lived when real loss had stalked our family.

Without that information, it was impossible to make her understand the dark waters that had swallowed me and carried me home to this house.

So instead of telling her any of this, I ask her to tell me about the wreck.

She tells me a story about ironing clothes, about how materials were different back then, thicker and stiffer so that heavy irons were required to get the wrinkles out. She was ironing all afternoon and listening to the radio when a man's voice announced a terrible wreck on Highway 43. He warned people to stay away from the ugly scene and mentioned that there had been casualties, white and Negro.

She kept the radio on all day, waiting to find out who these unlucky Negroes were. She wouldn't learn their names until the next day when she saw them in the newspaper. The article said some of them were from Sheffield, where she had lived most of her life, but she wondered if this information was a mistake because she didn't recognize the names. Then she got to the last name listed with the word "Negro" behind it, "Willodene." That was the name of the girl who had just started working at the high school where she also worked. The girl had been young, a little plump, and looked pretty in her clothes. A good-looking tall man came to pick her up every day.

My mother picked up the phone to call a friend to tell her that she knew the girl who had been killed and to find out more about what happened.

She drifts back to me in the present, her eyes narrow with anger. "You know your daddy had to make all those funeral arrangements and pay for them by himself? He did. The rest of them, his brothers and sister, didn't pay one dime. Don't tell him I told you that. He don't like to talk about it. But it's true."

"How did you know that? "

She shoots me a hard look.

"Well, when exactly did you meet?" I say.

My mother looks away and tells the story that she has told me before of how they met when she was visiting the hospital with a friend. The friend had made it sound like she was dating my father. So when he called that evening, my mother refused to talk to him. He insisted that he was not dating her friend. She told him that she would not talk to him until her friend confirmed that what he said was true. My father hung up and called the friend and a few minutes later my mother received a call from the woman admitting that she'd only been joking about dating my father. My father called again later, and my mother accepted the call.

My mother's voice grows animated as she tells the story, and she looks at me with a vaguely satisfied smile. "I wasn't going to talk to him if he was dating my friend." she says.

"Why was Daddy visiting in the hospital?" I say.

"He was visiting his daddy. "

"Why was Daddy Bluitt there?"

"He was still there from the wreck."

"The wreck had just happened?"

She nods and squeezes her hands together, bouncing them as if she is keeping time with music.

"Did you realize who he was? That he was the one whose family died?"

She looks straight ahead at the wall in front of her. "I knew he'd been through a lot. Losing his wife and his family like that. Can you imagine?"

I cannot imagine any of it. Information about the timeline of their relationship swells like a balloon in my belly, pressing on my diaphragm until my breath grows short.

"You know that wasn't the first time he saw me though. He told me he saw me walking down the street one time, and I remember it too 'cause he was sitting on the porch with his brother Conrad and his wife, Belle. I had on a red skirt and white blouse, and I could see them watching me, but I didn't know them and wondered why they was staring so hard. Then later on John told me that Belle said to him, 'Now, John T. that's what you need. A girl like that.'"

My mouth falls open.

Questions form and crash into one another in my head. *What were you thinking dating a man who'd buried his wife a few weeks before? And why did everyone seem to think that what my father needed was a new wife? And didn't you worry that he needed more time to heal?* But this last question seems to shake me out of the inside of my head. It was 1960. What real help was there available to any trauma survivor? And even if there had been treatment, it wouldn't have been available to a Black man in the Jim Crow South who'd only recently managed to get his parents out of a cotton field. I was asking twenty-first-century questions; 1960 may as well have been 1860.

"Did you worry that—"

"I knew," she cut me off, "that he had to be strong to make it through all that."

"Did he talk to you about it?"

"He told me what happened."

I search for the words to ask her if my father processed his feelings with her, but again she calls him "strong"—the answer to my question. "Strong" to her means that my father did not talk to her about his hurt, or cry over dinner, or roll on dirty sheets shouting the pain until someone was willing to hold his body still. And if he'd faltered at the sight of a girl with woolly red hair like San's, or orange lipstick, the color his wife wore, my mother would not have tolerated disintegration. *You got to be stronger than this.* She would have shown him how to tamp pain down like dirt over a grave so you can walk over it on steady legs.

My father turns on the TV in their bedroom, and my mother goes to him as if he called her.

I think about a man who lived in the neighborhood when I was a child. The man's wife died suddenly. Shortly after, people began to claim they'd seen the man circling his car five times before getting in and jumping as gracefully as a child over cracks in sidewalks. Most surmised that grief had driven the man mad. My mother scoffed at this idea. She recalled that many years before, the man had stopped by the school classroom of a friend, a home economics teacher, and stared at a mannequin head that had slipped out from under the skirt of her worktable. The man left abruptly. Later someone mentioned to the teacher that they'd run into the man, and he'd accused her of letting white women hide under her worktable and peep at him. Most people never learned of the man's delusions, a relative miracle in a small town where there was little to do but gossip. My mother credited the man's wife for helping him remain a respected member of the community. *That man didn't go crazy. He was always crazy. Folks just didn't know 'cause his wife kept him from going too far off. She was really the only thing holding him together. A lot of men need a woman to hold them together.*

My mother never said exactly how the woman had held off the man's madness. And I never asked because I was frightened of the man who lived close by and the idea that mental illness could be like the objects you see in the rearview mirror—always closer than they appear. But now, I wonder what if anything had the wife done, and did my mother imagine that she had done the same thing? Had she pulled my father into her world of drapes and coffee tables before he drifted too far? Had she found a way to hold him together?

I think about how best to ask her this question, but she does not come back. I remain on the sofa waiting for her return even though I know we have reached an impasse, and the impasse itself is the answer to my question.

* * *

The next morning as I finish my breakfast at the kitchen bar, I tell my parents what they already know. "I am going to head over to the library."

My father puts a dish in the dishwasher and says without looking up, "Oh, I'll take you there, baby. Just let me finish this real quick. Won't take me but a minute."

A voice that can only be heard in my head is shouting no. But the voice stays inside because his proposal is not an offer, something that can be accepted or rejected. It is an offering, a sacrifice to which he is already committed. Whenever I am home, my father offers to "take me" places, drive me to see a cousin, or to a mall, or one of a handful of small historical museums. "Take me" means spending time with me, to find out what I am interested in, and sometimes to serve as a guide to a place where I no longer live. "Take me" means to take care of me. But today is different because I am going to the library to read about things that he cannot say.

My mother, sitting on the sofa with a cup of coffee in one hand and a newspaper in the other, puts the coffee down and taps her manicured nails on the arm of the leather sofa. She looks up at my father and turns to face me with lips pressed so tight they look sewn together. She does not need to say, *Your father is going to get hurt and it will be your fault*. I can hear it as her hand bounces faster, making a sound like kitten heels running on linoleum.

Whenever I have been able to name the thing that I want, my father has always treated my desire like hunger he must sate, my want like a cut that he must heal. This is the real reason why I have waited my whole life to ask him directly about the wreck—not because I feared that he might refuse me, but because I knew that he wouldn't. He would attend to my faint scars and ignore the blood gushing from his own body until his pain would have nowhere to live but in drink and dreams.

My father looks up from wiping the kitchen counter, noticing that I have not moved. "You ready, baby? Go on and get your shoes on. I'm about done here."

I get up to grab my shoes, but I keep my eyes on my mother. Her eyes move from my father to me, and she shakes her head before returning to her paper. For a moment, I see what she sees: a man who was once a wounded thing draped over a recliner chair calling dead people's names, and a woman-child too selfish to stop asking questions that could undo a man.

He reaches for his keys and I slip into my shoes before following him to the door. I want to turn back and tell the pounding in my chest to find somewhere else to go. But to do so would be to say the thing that we are not saying, the thing that lives in my mother's fingers that tap, tap, tap on the arm of the leather sofa—that this is not just a trip to the library, that this journey is dangerous, and that we may become other people, changed in ways we can't know now, by the time we return. But there is no point in saying it. I have no right to tell this man who has trekked through cotton fields and the thick heat of a metal plant that he cannot come to the library to research the accident that killed his family. I cannot treat him like a child by saying, *Watch out, you'll hurt yourself*, so instead I say, "Are you sure? I could be there for a while."

"Aww, I don't mind," he says.

We arrive at a redbrick building tucked away in the old downtown. I follow him to the front door and fear pulls my shoulders to my ears as I look at the place where I will hurt my father. But he moves as he always does, his tall body loping with a soft bounce between each step. As he holds the door for me, his mouth bends into a closed smile and I can feel something like joy radiating from him. On the one hand, it makes no sense, given why we are in a library on a pretty Saturday morning, but this is my father who takes pleasure in helping me. His love has always looked like this—doing, rather than talking. When he recounted the wreck over the phone, explaining the details exhausted him. He told me the order in which his family died, but offered no words about how he coped with deaths dropping like bombs all around him. In lieu of his story, he had pointed me to the newspapers. Now he wants to help me find them—to walk with me on this path and at the end hand me my family's story like a gift wrapped tight in birthday paper.

Historical research is never a neat and tidy path. Information reveals itself more like a city street after the melting of winter's last snow. Everything seems ordinary until you fall into a pothole that wasn't there a week ago and your body slams into the ground. If you are lucky, you keep going with wary eyes on the road. But other times, especially when you are Black and researching Black people in the past, the impact knocks the breath out of you so cleanly that you can see the hot mist leave your body. By the time you crawl out, you are no longer just you because your brain cannot keep separate your body and the bodies of Black people who died because they were Black. So you exist in two planes, the present and the past, aware that you are sitting in the cool of a library that was never intended for the likes of you.

Inside, a librarian directs us to the cabinets filled with microfilm of the local newspaper. I open a cabinet and my father is suddenly at home in the neat rows of boxes organized by date, trailing his finger along the labels so fast that he lands on the box we are looking for before I do. He hands me a box marked 1960 and we sit down in front of a brand-new microfilm machine. I fumble with loading the film. After a couple of false starts, I press a button and 1960 rolls by us. It was an election year and pictures of John F. Kennedy and Richard Nixon are sprinkled between stiff-haired white beauty queens, Black students sitting at lunch counters, and lingerie sale ads. A whole black-and-white world scrolls by each time I press my finger on the button.

When we get to June, I slow down, until my father tells me to stop.

June 25, 1960. On the front page is a tall structure, lengths of metal twisted together like giant snakes reaching upward in an embrace. The thing towers over a group of men. The only sign that the tangle was once separate cars is a tire sticking out on the left, making this part of the thing look like a leaning cyclops.

My father holds up a finger in front of the screen as he reads the article.

My stomach is heavy, pressing on my bowels, and my breath catches somewhere between my clavicle and my throat. New information spins in my head: The accident was on the front page of the newspaper. Photographers took pictures of the scene and the newspaper printed them. I am looking at a photograph of the car they died in. Because of me, my father is looking at it too.

The Florence Times June 25, 1960
[Front Page]
Four Dead, 6 Injured in Horrifying Colbert Crash
Lauderdale Couple Killed Instantly in 3-Car Smash

A crushing three vehicle accident left a twisted mass of wreckage and a Lauderdale county man and his wife and a Negro woman and child dead this morning on Highway 43 five miles south of Tuscumbia.

At least 6 other persons were injured.

Killed instantly were Mr. and Mrs. Harry Howard Morris, route five, Florence.

Hands and feet and other bits of human body were strewn over the incline where the accident occurred, producing a scene of horror. The top of the woman's head was sheared off.

An un-identified Negro woman and a small Negro child were also among the victims. One was pronounced dead upon arrival at Colbert County Hospital, while the other died a short time after arrival.

The accident occurred around 11 o'clock where four lane construction work was in progress. It involved a GMC dump truck loaded with road surfacing material, apparently traveling north down-grade, a 1960 Corvair in which both fatalities were riding, and a 1959 Pontiac with Illinois license plates.

The Corvair and Pontiac were both traveling south.

The driver of the truck, and at least seven passengers in the Pontiac were rushed to local hospitals by three ambulances.

Their names and the extent of their injuries were not immediately available at press time.

The truck was turned over and the Corvair completely flattened. The Pontiac was completely demolished.

No details of the wreck were available at press time.

Even though he is reading the article for the first time, my father seems to adjust seamlessly to 1960. He explains that the death toll is not complete because the newspaper was an evening paper and Maggie and Robert died after the paper went to press, and his mother died ten days later. He says nothing about the fact that the white couple killed made the headline and the Black people, our family, were reduced to "unidentified Negro woman" and "a small Negro child" who had also been killed. He does not mention that the phrase "both fatalities" refers to the white couple only as if the Black people by virtue of being Black were already dead anyway.

I lag behind, trying to process both the graphic descriptions of mangled bodies and the racism so evident in the account. The magnitude of the loss was so unimaginable that I had never conceived of it taking place in a real world, where everything from where you bought ketchup to when you stepped off a sidewalk was determined by race. To see evidence both of their deaths and of their oppression makes it feel like they have been killed twice.

I try to catch up to my father's finger as he runs it along the article, but he is too far ahead. My eyes wander back to the description of the scene: "Hands and feet and other bits of human body were strewn over the incline where the accident occurred, producing a scene of horror."

A voice in my head repeats the description like a serial murderer's mantra: *Hands and feet. Hands and feet. Hands and feet.*

Though we sit side by side, the gap between us grows wide and deep. My father is looking for the facts—a day, June 25, 1960; a place, Highway 43 in Colbert County, Alabama; an event, a truck hitting a car that then hit another car. While he runs his finger along facts, I reel from them. People reduced to hands and feet. The story of the bodies is at once too much information and too little. I did not come here in search of bodies. I came for stories that would explain him and me, and the house made of grief that made me. But now there are bodies where there should be stories. This morning, I was afraid of hurting my father. But now, sandwiched between the white fluorescent lights and thin carpet, I am the one hurting without the strength to run from the thing that hurts me. I am sinking, like an invisible hand is pressing a lever on my chair.

My father says that there will be more information if I scroll to the next day's paper. But when I open my mouth to answer, I suck in air. I must have forgotten to breathe a few seconds ago because all I can focus on is filling my lungs to capacity. I am relieved when a second breath is enough to sustain me because I do not want my father to have to take care of me, a grown woman, toppled by the mention of hands and feet.

My father gestures for me to pull the knob to make the newspaper roll forward. His face is neutral, but the angle of his body, leaning forward as he gestures, tells me that he is excited that we have found these newspaper accounts. The man with me now is a different man from the twenty-something-year-old that this story happened to. That young man whose family was changed by a wreck could not see this future—sitting here with his daughter in a library. That young man was probably ready to die himself. But this one knows that his life continued, that he became more than that tragedy that made people stare and whisper about his colossal loss wherever he went.

I have come here in search of the other man, the young one, to find out what happened to him and how he survived it. But that young man lives in the gap between the old man and this newspaper.

I pull the knob and the newspaper creeps forward.

• • •

Your legs carry you from the hospital entrance to the desk where a white woman sits. You tell her your family was in a wreck. She points you to the colored waiting room and goes to find a doctor.

You stand next to the crooked COLORED sign, because your body will not let you sit down even though the waiting area is far too small for your six-foot-four body to pace. An elderly colored woman dozes across from you.

The doctor arrives and looks back and forth from you to the old woman. You tell him your name and that your family was in the wreck.

"The young Negro man—"

"That's my brother-in-law, Robert," you interrupt the doctor.

"He died soon after arrival. And the smallest of the two girls . . ."

"That's my niece, San."

"She was dead on arrival."

"My god. My god," you say as your legs that refused to bend for you to sit down when you arrived now give way and you slide down the wall, landing in a deep squat.

The doctor is still talking. Something about attempting to treat one of the young colored women, but she also expired soon after arrival.

You nod, but you are still trying to make sense of the words "attempted" and "expired."

"Wait," you say. "Which woman?" Is it your wife or your sister?

The doctor looks at the clipboard in his hand, confused. He gestures to a Black nurse and she comes over. "Can you get the name of the girl in the wreck, the one who's going into surgery?"

So one of them is alive, your wife or your sister.

A shrill sound, soft at first, then louder, comes from the old woman. She lets out a church moan and rocks to music that no one else can hear.

The doctor looks over at the woman and asks you if she is a family member.

But you do not answer because your mouth no longer makes words. You lean your head against the wall behind you to keep it from rolling on the floor. You do not mind the old woman, but the doctor's voice sounds like it is coming through a tiny tube and you need him to just stop talking, if only for a minute. You are about to tell him this when you hear him say something about "the older child," your niece Liza, and the "two oldest Negroes," your mother, Bernice, and your father, Bluitt. For a moment, you think that the doctor is saying that they are dead too. But no, he is saying the opposite, that even though they were injured, they are going to be fine. That they were "lucky."

His tone says that you are supposed to be grateful, relieved. But you are waiting for the nurse to come back so you can stop alternately wishing that your wife or your sister is alive, because if one is alive, it means that the other is dead.

The old woman stops moaning and lets out a low buzzing sound like a bee trapped on the wrong side of a window.

"Can I help you?" the doctor says to her. "Are you waiting for someone?" But the old woman doesn't even look up at him.

You squeeze your eyes shut. When you hear the nurse's voice, you look up and see the spotless underside of that crooked-ass COLORED sign.

• • •

You are going to identify a body, but you do not know whose body. You have a new name, "informant." You tell someone that the body on the table is your wife. It is not your wife, but a body that looks vaguely like the one that she was alive in this morning. The face is swollen and dented like it is a hurried child's line drawing. But the hair is darker than your sister's, the body is rounder than hers. You wait for someone to ask if you are sure, like you saw in a movie. But the nurse asks instead if you would like to be alone. You shake your head no because you do not know how to be with this body on a table.

The nurse tells you to follow her and she leads you to the colored ward where your mother is sitting up in a bed looking at you like you are the one with the black eye and a bandaged forehead.

Her arms reach for you and she sobs into your neck. You hold her, but not too tight because you can feel the bulky bandages wrapped around her ribs.

She calls your name again and again: "John T., oh, John T."

A lie flies out of your mouth before you can say anything else. "I'm all right, Mama. I am all right."

She tells you that orderlies took your daddy somewhere to try to make him go to sleep and the doctors were doing some X-rays on little Liza, but they said she was all right. The baby, San, is dead. But they wouldn't tell her anything else.

She asks about Maggie and Robert and Willodene and you tell her that her daughter-in-law and son-in-law are dead, but that her daughter is going into surgery and the doctor said she would be all right.

Your mother sobs, her chest and head bouncing like she is having

a seizure. The colored nurse comes over to say that Bernice needs
to rest.

You nod and stand to go, but your mother grabs your hand and pulls
you down onto the edge of the bed.

"I need to tell you what happened," she says. "Right now. Before
they try to tell it different."

Robert Ray was driving everyone to Russellville on Highway 43.
There was construction and the road had been cut down from the
usual four lanes to two. They were traveling uphill when a white sports
car approached from behind and tried to pass by in the opposite lane.
A large dump truck came over the hill and hit the white car head-on,
knocking it into Robert's car.

She asks you if you understand. You nod, but she launches into the
story all over again as if you had said no.

"Do you understand?" she repeats. "They must not have realized
that lane was for oncoming traffic. They probably thought it was a
passing lane. It wasn't marked good. Do you know what happened to
the person driving that white car?"

You do not know, but from her description, you know that some part
of her has to know that whoever was in that white car must be dead.

"You better go call your brothers and sister. Let 'em know so they
can start heading this way."

You walk by the whites-only phone booth like it does not contain a
public phone. You drive home, but you will never remember how you
got there. You do not sit down because what would be the point? Instead, you go to the phone that hangs in the kitchen and hesitate because you are not sure who to call first. You dial the first number that
comes to mind. When you tell your wife's mother that her daughter is

dead, she weeps without words. You need to say something, so you tell her the story your mother told you about the wreck, reciting each detail because you do not know what else to say. You call your brother Conrad next, and he screams as if you have stabbed him with the word "wreck." You had hoped to ask Conrad to call your brother James and sister Judy, so that you could go back to the hospital and check on the others. But Conrad's wife takes the phone from her husband and explains how to reach your brother James's army base in Texas. You call your sister Judy and tell her that your wife, San, and Robert Ray are dead. There is a moment of silence until you call her name, and she sobs your name back. You ask her if she needs money to get home because you cannot listen to any more sobs. You leave a message for your brother James at the army base. As you say the words "wreck," "killed," and "surgery," you are grateful that the stranger on the other end of the phone seems to feel nothing but the desire to preserve your words in cold, neat print. The man reads your message back to you without emotion as if it were a weather prediction.

When you are done with the calls, you head back to the hospital. You do not know that in just a few hours you will have to call them all again.

The June 26, 1960, front-page headline reads "Wreck Death Toll at . . ." and lists the dead by name beginning with the white couple and concluding with my family. Each of my family members' names is followed by the word "Negro." While the white woman is referred to as "Mrs.," my father's wife and his sister are referred to simply by their first and last names, followed by "Negro woman." The article concludes with 154 words on the white family, where they were from originally, the church they belonged to, the man's occupation, their survivors, and funeral arrangements. There is no further mention of my family.

Three photos of the wreckage dominate the front page of the June 26 newspaper. My father points to the top two photos, telling me which twisted piece of metal was once Robert and Maggie's Pontiac and which ones had been the Corvair that belonged to the white couple.

A large crowd stands in the foreground and background of the photo. They are all white men, not so much surrounding the wreckage as they are standing in it, staring into the broken vehicles, with their hands on their hips and in their pockets. They look with chins tilted downward, owning the scene of death with their eyes and trampling it with their feet. I hate them for looking, for feeling the power to look. And yet, like them, I am also looking, consuming photographs of that which no one should be allowed to see.

I rest my eyes on the third photo, on the bottom of the page. It is the only one that does not include the crowds. A right shoe, a leather oxford still laced up, lies on the ground next to the open door of the Pontiac.

The caption reads:

"The left shoe of Robert Ray, Waukegan, Illinois, Negro driver of an ill-fated 1957 Pontiac remains almost perfectly in place on the floorboard of his shattered automobile in the aftermath of the grueling collision, five miles South of Tuscumbia, at 11 a.m. Saturday. Several hundred persons gathered at the scene of the smash-up."

I cannot make out the shoe that the caption refers to because this part of the photo is too dark. But the oxford on the ground is clear. It curves as if the missing foot were still in it. The shoe is big enough to belong to a man and yet small enough to have belonged to a woman. One of them, Maggie or Robert, or maybe my grandmother, had slipped their foot into this shoe and gone through the mundane task of tying its laces that morning only to fly out of it like a doll swung by an angry toddler.

I turn to my father to search his face for pain, but he is reading, his lips wet and slightly parted, his face luminous in the screen light. He offers corrections as he reads: "San was not five years old. She was three, almost four. Me and my wife lived at 2505 Hatch, not 2502. Robert and Maggie lived in a little town called North Chicago, right by Waukegan, but more Blacks lived in North Chicago back then. Robert went up there for work."

His finger stops moving on the screen and he frowns at it.

"They got it all wrong. That ain't what happened. They done got this all wrong."

My eyes follow his finger to a paragraph that reads: "As near as could be determined by the Highway Patrol and other officers who helped investigate and control traffic at the scene, the Pontiac driven by Ray hit the Corvair carrying Mr. and Mrs. Morris in the rear, knocking it over into the left hand or Northbound lane of traffic and directly into the path of the truck."

My father taps the screen and repeats, "They got this all wrong!" His voice is loud—too loud for the library—but there's only one person nearby, a white man also sitting at a microfilm machine. He remains still, staring at the screen before him, pretending he cannot hear my father's rising voice.

My father stands up and puts his hands on his hips. He walks a few steps away and then back, with his eyes on the blue carpet.

"Mama told me that the Corvair was trying to pass and the people in it didn't realize that what was always four lanes had been cut down to two because of the construction. See, the site wasn't marked off right. The dump truck came over the hill and hit the Corvair, knocking it into Mama and them." He sits back down and shakes his head at the screen.

"Do you understand what I'm saying? They got this all messed up."

I tell him that I understand, and he looks at me with soft eyes, like he is surprised to see me sitting next to him. His face relaxes.

"What else do you want to know, baby? I'll tell you."

I rest my finger on the shoe in the picture and look at him, unable to name the thing that I want to know and yet sure that I need him to acknowledge this—to admit that we are both here in the after, looking at an empty shoe that someone he loved, someone I would have loved, had tied, on an ordinary morning in the before.

The Florence Times June 27, 1960

[Front Page]

WRECK FATAL TO 6

WORST ON RECORD IN SHOALS DISTRICT

Truck Driver Improves But Others Critical

Negro Victims Still in Danger

James J. Crisler, 35-year-old Town Creek truck driver appeared in relatively good condition today at Colbert County Hospital, but three Negroes, critically injured in the Muscle Shoals area's "worst on record" highway accident remained in very poor condition today.

A check of Highway Patrol records for the Florence Post which comprise Colbert-Lauderdale-Franklin [Counties] showed that the previous highway death toll in one accident occurred last December in Franklin County when five died in an accident on Alabama 24 near Belgreen. Lauderdale had previously reported four killed in a single mishap and in 1945 26 persons were injured, but none killed in a bus accident in Colbert.

Still listed as critical today after the Saturday three-vehicle [accident] on U.S. 43 South of Tuscumbia were Bluit[t] Jackson, 50 of 2505 Hatch Boulevard, Sheffield, his wife, Bernice Jackson, 50 of the same address and seven-year-old Liza Ray of Waukegan, Illinois, granddaughter of the Jackson couple.

Killed in Saturday's wreck which occurred when a Pontiac and Corvair traveling the same direction, South on 43 collided then were both struck by a GMC dump truck traveling North and going down-grade were:

Harry Howard Morris, 49, of Rt. 5, Florence and his wife Mrs. Betty Sue Morris, 47, of Rt. 5.

Robert Ray and his wife, Maggie Jo Ray, Negroes of Waukegan, Illinois.

Sandra Ray, five-year-old daughter of the Ray couple and Willodean [sic] Jackson, Negro woman resident of 2505 Hatch Boulevard, daughter[-in-law] also of the Jackson couple.

Hundreds of motorists stopped at the scene of the accident, five miles South of the intersection of U.S. 43 and Alabama 20 Saturday and viewed the remains of the accident, which was absolutely vicious in nature.

The truck driver managed to tell patrolmen that the first thing he was able to see was the Corvair driven by Mr. Morris as he descended the hill with his truck loaded with re-surfacing material. He said the Corvair suddenly appeared in his lane of traffic and he didn't have time to do anything.

Highway Patrol officers stated that there definitely were three separate impacts in the wreck. They indicated that the 1959 Pontiac driven by Ray apparently hit the Corvair knocking it into the path of the truck, and that the truck hit the Corvair, then continued downhill to smash into the Pontiac.

There were no eyewitnesses to the accident, however, other than those who were actually involved.

The local wreck was the worst of a series of accidents in Alabama over the weekend which left 16 persons dead.

Two other multiple vehicle accidents helped mount the toll for the State, and the three accidents accounted for all but four of the 16 deaths.

The one in Colbert was the most tragic, leaving six dead.

We search the obituary sections of the newspaper, but we cannot find funeral announcements for any of my father's family members.

Confused and frustrated, he recites the dates of their deaths and funerals as if his certainty will make the obituaries appear.

"I know I buried Willodene on the Wednesday after the wreck. I had to wait to bury Maggie, San, and Robert because his parents were waiting for more family to arrive. Mama didn't die until July."

Numbers float in my head: Five dead. Four adults and one child. Three funerals, over a period of twelve days.

Now I understand why my father complained profusely whenever anyone postponed the burial of a loved one for more than a few days: *Black folks always letting bodies sit because they can, instead of just getting it over with.* He had endured almost two weeks of funerals.

The white man sitting a few chairs down from us leans back in his chair and turns in our direction.

"I don't want to offend y'all or nothing. But is the person whose obituary you're looking for African American?"

I recognize this man even though I have never met him before: a library hobbyist, a white man who spends his days in public libraries, reading histories and newspapers. He speaks with a heavy southern drawl, pronouncing "African American" one syllable at a time in that way that white people who fear that the word "Black" might be perceived as an insult do.

"Well, I don't want y'all to take offense, but back then they didn't put the African American obituaries in the same section. They put them in a Thursday column called . . ." He pauses and swallows. "'News about Negroes.' I really hope y'all don't take no offense."

"Oh yeah. They sure did." My father makes a face like he's just found a long-forgotten sock covered in dusty mold.

"Things were different back then," the man says in a whiny voice, as if pleading with us to let this word "different" mask the daily humiliations of segregation and make them seem like random differences instead of a rabid obsession with proving white superiority.

My father thanks him and turns back to the microfilm machine. He presses a button and headlines that all seem to read "Negro Prowler" and "Negro Rapist" fly by. He stops at a small section in the back of the paper, "News about Negroes."

The article is a cramped list of weddings, church concerts, cotillions, club events, honors, and funeral announcements nearly hidden amid ads. It is written in the style of a society page, complete with announcements of out-of-town guests. Black people mentioned here are Mr. and Mrs. or Rev. and Sgt. Before I can ask why Black people's names have titles of respect in this section, my father explains that it was written by a local Black woman.

The obituaries are at the bottom of the section. A paragraph explains that Willodene was buried the day before this column was published. Since the accident was on a Saturday, and she was buried the following Wednesday, there would have been no way to announce her funeral until the day after; the Negro column only appeared on Thursdays. The article notes that Maggie, San, and Robert would be buried the following Saturday.

Strange relief enters me when I see my father called "husband," and Willodene's family called "mother," "father," "sister," "brother," and "Mr. and Mrs." It takes only a few minutes to read the tiny column, but I linger on this oasis, not ready to return to the white people's newspaper.

At Willodene's funeral, you sit on the front pew trying to tune out the preacher who talks too much. You have warned him to keep this short, and he has agreed to honor your wishes. But neither he nor you expected a packed church on a Wednesday, just four days after the wreck. Word had spread fast in this place where there was little to no news most days. When you led the family procession to their seats, you saw that the church was spilling over with young women Willodene had gone to school with. They looked at you with pink eyes that they dabbed at with tissues. And you had tried not to look back. When you sat down, you could feel a church full of eyes boring into your back, waiting for your body to fold like a marionette without a puppeteer. You try to disappear from your body by thinking of chores that need to be done at work, food you should bring to your mother in the hospital, and the whiskey you will pour for yourself and your brothers as soon as you get home.

But the preacher's voice, slow and loud, like he is the official town crier to the hard of hearing, breaks through and brings you back to the casket that sits in front of you. He talks about the things everyone already knows—how young she was, the fact that she'd never had a child. Then he tells a lie: how we should trust in God because all of this was his plan. You glance around, wondering who else sees through that awful deceit. If there were a god, and you are not sure there is, he must have been looking the other way on June 25. There is no good reason that your wife's body is lying in a casket. And there was no divine plan for your niece to lose her parents and her only sibling. No god worth his salt would plan that. The only reason you do not shout the truth is that you need this funeral to be over and so do your siblings sitting on the pew behind you and your wife's parents and her sister who sit next to you.

The preacher begins to stomp back and forth in the pulpit, trying to scare somebody into getting saved, but fortunately there are no takers. The invitation, however, is the signal that the funeral is almost over. He prays and you bow your head, disappearing again. When you raise your head, you hear her, one young woman who wails like she is an old woman who has had enough of this world. Then the women are all weeping at once, their sounds vibrating every wood surface until the church hums like a bell rung minutes ago. You cannot cry with them because you have too much to do, more funerals to plan, hospital visits to make. But you are relieved that someone is crying for Willodene so you do not have to.

At the graveside, Willodene's mother puts her arms around your neck. When she lets go, Mr. Wilhite puts your right hand in his own and covers it with his other hand, squeezing gently at first and then harder and harder as tears run down his face. You wait for him to say something, any of the empty things that people have said to you since the accident to reassure you that everything will be all right even though nothing will ever be all right again. But Mr. Wilhite doesn't say anything, just makes a sound deep in his throat that confirms that you are both in hell now and there is nothing to be done about it but wait in hell.

You are standing next to the open grave when a pang of shame surprises you. You know that Willodene's death was not your fault. But the children she did not have, the grandchildren the Wilhites will never have, this you believe is your fault. You have no proof of anything, but why else would a bride who wasn't twenty years old yet be without children? It had to be your fault. You took something unnamable from her without ever meaning to, a legacy, the proof that she was here. You know that it was better that she left no child behind when she died. But you also wish that she could live beyond you and the eventual fading memories of two old people. No one forgets the young people who die, but eventually their memory is reduced to a warning to other young folks about what could kill them if they aren't careful.

A quick prayer and someone is throwing dirt on her casket. Willodene's sister hugs you and you walk toward your car so fast that your brothers and sister can't keep up. Too many weeping faces try to stop you, but you make your way out, dodging apologies and "god bless yous" until you are sitting behind the wheel of your car, glad that you insisted on driving yourself when your brothers offered. You still regret that there will have to be two funerals instead of one. But if you are going to sit on a pew again in two days in front of three caskets, one of them tiny enough for a three-year-old, you cannot let anyone stop to talk to you now.

The Florence Times July 6, 1960

[Page Two]

COLBERT WRECK CLAIMS VICTIM NUMBER SEVEN

Negro Woman Dies as Result of Injuries Suffered in Tragic June 25 Collision

Colbert County counted its seventh victim today from the June 25 highway accident on U.S. 43 five miles South of Alabama 20.

The latest to die as a result of injuries sustained in the three-vehicle crash was Bernice Jackson, 50-year-old Negro woman, resident of 2505 Hatch Boulevard, Sheffield. Her daughter[-in-law], Willodean [sic] Jackson of the same address, another daughter, Maggie Jo Ray, a son-in-law and granddaughted [sic] had succumbed earlier from injuries received in the wreck.

The Jackson woman died at 11:45 a.m. Tuesday at Colbert Hospital after being in critical condition for the past 11 days. She had suffered fractures of both legs, head injuries and shoulder fractures in the accident.

All three survivors of the crash remained in Colbert Hospital today with one of them still listed as critical.

He was Bluitt Jackson, 50, husband of Bernice Jackson and also a resident of 2505 Hatch Boulevard. Jackson is suffering from head and internal injuries.

A granddaughter, 7-year-old Liza Ray, remains confined with head injuries and a broken arm, but her condition is listed as "improved."

Also still confined, but in good condition is the truck driver, James H. Crisler of Town Creek, who suffered fractures of the chest region, cuts and bruises in the mishap.

According to Highway Patrol records the death toll from the single wreck is the worst on record for Colbert County or the Muscle Shoals district of Colbert-Lauderdale-Franklin.

The complete list of dead from the wreck now includes:

Harry Howard Morris, 49, Rt. 5 Florence.

Mrs. Betty Sue Morris, 47, Rt. 5 Florence.

Sandra Ray, five year old Waukegan, Ill., Negro girl.

Willodean [sic] Jackson, Negro woman resident of 2505 Hatch Boulevard, Sheffield.

Robert Ray, Negro resident of Waukegan, Illinois.

Maggie Jo Ray, Negro woman resident of Waukegan, Illinois and wife of Robert Ray and mother of Sandra Ray.

Bernice Jackson, Negro woman resident of 2505 Hatch Boulevard, wife of Bluitt Jackson, mother of both the Ray woman and Willodean [sic] Jackson and grandmother of the two Ray girls.

The death toll stemmed from a three-vehicle accident involving a 1960 Corvair occupied by Mr. and Mrs. Morris traveling South on 43; a 1959 Pontiac, traveling South and being driven by Robert Ray and a large GMC dump truck coming downhill and being driven by Crisler, who was hauling road re-surfacing material.

Highway Patrolmen said at the time of the wreck that the Pontiac apparently struck the Corvair from behind in an effort to pass, spun it in front of the truck which then hit both vehicles in turn.

On July 5, you return to work. The superintendent has told you that you can take as much time off as you need. But you cannot take a chance on losing this job.

Money is not the only reason you are back at work. If you did not come here, you would be moving back and forth between the hospital and your house that is too quiet for the living. Your brothers have gone back to their homes out of state. Your sister who was living with Maggie and Robert in North Chicago has decided to stay with you, but she is always at the hospital, sitting with your family. Her willingness to be there allows you to go back to work.

The other linemen sneak looks at you, their forced smiles begging to know why you are in a metal plant when you just put half your family in the ground. If they said what they were thinking, that you needed to take more time, you could tell them the truth: if they sat in front of four caskets in the span of a week, there would be no such thing as time as they understand it, an idea with hard edges, beginnings and endings, and a whole language to support the lie of it, like "on time," "pastime," "bedtime," "lunchtime." You would tell them that time is really an ugly seeping thing that bleeds in all directions. You wake up expecting to see your wife lying next to you even though she is already dead. Then you remember when you saw her swollen body lying last in the hospital. They would tell you that time heals, and you would call them liars and fools. Time is more like a train that changes tracks, going forward one minute and backward the next, until the passengers have forgotten which way they should be moving.

Your mother knows all this and that is why she was the first one to say you should go back to work. She knew that you would not go without her permission, and she gave it to you without provocation because she knew that you would never ask. You wanted to thank her, but you knew it would only embarrass you both to admit how much you needed to return to the plant. You came back, not just to be busy, but because work has a clock that counts down each shift, telling everyone when to start working, when to break, and when to stop altogether. Here, you can pretend that time is real.

The call comes around midday, just like the last one. This time, when a white man comes to get you, you do not wonder if it is a mistake. Your father, who has been in a coma since the wreck, must be dead. When you went to see him, he looked like he was already dead, lying flat and still as a fossil. When you pressed the doctor, who insisted that your father would survive, the doctor had finally admitted that the old man's condition was critical.

When you pick up the phone, you hear your sister crying.

"You need to come, John T. Mama is dead."

Her words make you lose your balance, and you reach for the desk to steady yourself. "Mama?"

"Yes," she says.

"What happened?"

"I don't know. Please hurry."

You and your sister sat with your mother the night before. She was tired but glad that her granddaughter was doing better, grateful that Liza would survive and go home with her when they were both released. When your sister had worried aloud about your father's condition, your mother had joked that nothing could kill old Bluitt Jackson because he was tough as a mule.

When you arrive at the hospital, you find your sister sitting next to your mother's body. You reach for your mother's shoulder as if to wake her, but stop yourself.

"What happened?" you say. "What happened to her?"

Your sister's whole body shakes.

The same doctor who had told you that your sister was dead approaches and introduces himself as if he has never met you. He explains that Bernice's body was so compromised by the wreck that she could have succumbed to any number of internal injuries.

You urge him to explain exactly what happened to your mother. What killed her? How could a woman who had been conscious and talking since the day of the wreck end up dead ten days later? And when would your family stop dying? You tell your sister to go to little Liza. You go home to call your brothers. You tell them to come back to Alabama as fast as they can because you are not going to wait one more day than necessary to have another funeral.

On the way home from the library my father and I joke about the nervousness of the white man who didn't want to "offend y'all or nothing."

"Looked like he'd already pissed on himself by the time he asked the question," my father says.

"And what did he think two Black people in a library on a Saturday morning were going to do if they were offended? Shoot him with the staple gun?" I say.

We talk about this one white man who had somehow managed to have a clue and be clueless at the same time. But we laugh hard enough for all the white people who are more concerned about being accused of racism than they have ever been about actual racism.

Laughter makes me breathe and the hard knot I have felt in my stomach all morning falls open with a click like a combination lock.

"I'm glad we could get that stuff," my father says, tilting his head toward the pile of newspaper copies in my lap.

"Me too," I say.

"I hadn't thought about 'News about Negroes' in years. Wasn't that something, 'News about Negroes' right there in the damn newspaper.

A shame. Make sure you ask your mama about it. I believe your mama used to type that column up for the lady that wrote it sometimes."

I nod, wondering if he is looking for a way to include my mother and thus get her approval of our research. Since retirement they have settled into a silent closeness, so conjoined that they attend each other's doctors' appointments. Though they never say "I love you," their communications are sprinkled with special consideration for each other. *Let me get you some ice cream. Did you remember to take your blood pressure pills? Let me get your glasses for you.* They no longer argue over lamps and drapes, not because they have more money, but because meeting each other's needs and desires is the safest way for them to express love. After fifty years of marriage, a casual agreement to purchase new wallpaper has become an expression of their commitment to take care of each other.

As we pull into the garage, it occurs to me that this easy comfort that shapes their lives together is what my mother wants to protect. They are the couple moving quietly through the grocery store reminding each other of ketchup and eggs, and I am the baby in the produce section, snatching a grapefruit from the bottom of a pyramid, leaving the floor covered in bouncing fruit. And still I am not satisfied, because the things I want are not sold in the grocery store. I have come with sharp-edged words and pointed them at two people who have been avoiding them for fifty years. *Your father don't like to talk about it but . . .*

As I walk into the house, I brace myself to face my mother, the evidence of my desire in my hands. I will tell her that my father is all right, that I have brought her husband back to her, changed but also intact, because this man is stronger than most people will ever have to be. Then I will follow my father's advice and ask her about "News about Negroes," giving her some of her power back by letting her be the conduit to information about the past.

But as soon as I see her rushing back and forth between the kitchen, the dining area, and the den, I realize that I will not do any of these things because my mother's anxiety has found a solvable problem to focus on.

"I have to get to my hair appointment," she says, agitated. "And I can't find my keys. Help me look for them."

My mother goes to the hairdresser every two weeks and her hair looks exactly the same when she comes home as it did before she left. Yet she grimaces now like she needs to get to an emergency room. She does not seem to notice the stack of papers I tuck under my arm to free my hands.

My father and I slip back into my mother's world, a concrete place where keys are always lost and there is no time to ask what happened back then because there are things that need to be dealt with now.

We search the bar counter and the dining table, all covered in decorative place settings, brass chargers topped with plates and fancy ringed napkins, brass flatware, and goblets. My mother has made a hobby of curating the table settings to look like the ones in home decorating magazines. But she seems not to understand that the point of table settings is for real people to eat at them. Our family has always pushed the settings aside at mealtimes and, when finished, put them back as best we could. The busy visual displays are magnets for clutter and a Bermuda Triangle for keys and minds.

Nearby, my mother paws at the inside of her purse.

Minutes pass as we all look, and then she says, "Found them!"

My father sits down in his recliner and shakes his head left and right. "What good is a pocketbook too big to find anything in?"

My mother rushes to the door, no longer caring about the research trip she'd tried to protect her husband from that morning.

At the sound of the garage door going up, my father turns on the television, and I go to my room and put copies of the newspaper articles in the folder with the death certificates. I pack the folder in my suitcase and lie down to breathe.

When I awake from an unintended nap, I go back to the den where I left my father resting. He glances up at the clock. It has been hours since my mother left.

"Your mama must have gone to the mall after her hair was done. Surely her hair didn't take that long."

He heads into the kitchen to make dinner. I follow him and sit down at the bar to watch. I wait until his fingers are covered in raw ground beef to ask.

"Who informed you of the accident?"

He salts the meat and frowns.

"I don't really know who it was, probably the police that called. I had to go to work that day. A guy came and got me and told me I had a call. I really thought it was a mistake. I hadn't been working there but a year or so. I got on the phone and a man asked me if I was John T. Jackson. I said yes. And he said your family's been in an accident and they were taken to the Russellville hospital. But whoever it was had it wrong. They took them to the Colbert County hospital right by where I worked."

"So how did you find them?"

"I got in my car and drove west on Highway 43 to get to Russellville.

Then all of a sudden the traffic stopped. The police had everything blocked off and cars were sitting with nobody in them like in a parking lot right there on the highway. Everybody had got out to look at what happened. I parked and went to find the police to let me through. I told a white man I needed to find the police and he said they weren't letting anybody through because of the accident. I told him it was my family and I needed to get through to the hospital in Russellville. He looked at me funny and said the ambulances didn't go to Russellville. They went the opposite way where I'd just come from. I asked him if he was sure and another man next to him said yeah, all the ambulances went to Colbert County Hospital, not Russellville. So I got back in my car and headed back the way I came."

He does not say anything about what he saw at the scene of the accident. But the newspaper description rolls over our conversation like a teleprompter reel: "Hands and feet . . . scene of horror."

My father's hands move faster, kneading and squeezing the meat as it drips blood onto the countertop. But he is also standing in a crowd, walking through glass and metal that crunches under his feet. He is too tall to avoid seeing the spire of metal towering above him and the pieces of bodies that were sacrificed scattered on the ground.

I want to do my mother's trick, to find a safe question that will bring us both back to this world, like how tall was Maggie, or what color was your mother's hair. But I am not my mother.

CHAPTER 12

I have known Liza all my life without realizing that she was also in the wreck. Someone, my grandfather perhaps, must have mentioned that she'd been there. But I cannot remember anyone saying, *Can you believe it? Little seven-year-old Liza survived—it was a miracle*. The magnitude of her loss—the death of her mother, father, and only sibling in a single day—must have made the idea of miracles or divine intervention seem absurd. Liza's life was a gift with no sender.

I tell my father I'd like to talk to Liza about the accident and the next day we climb into the car with my mother and my sister, who has just arrived from Atlanta, and we make our way to Russellville, which is twenty miles away. My sister asks questions that all seem to begin with "Whatever happened to so-and-so," and my mother offers long explanations of divorces, illnesses, and deaths.

As the car climbs a steep hill, my father interrupts. "Right up here is where it happened. See, they were coming over the top of this hill, and the other car was trying to pass them. Then the dump truck came over the hill the opposite way and knocked that Corvair right into Mama and them."

My stomach seems to float up, pressing hard on my diaphragm as we cross the peak. I have passed over this spot more times than I can count, visiting relatives or gravesites in Russellville. But not once had he said those words that he delivered now with soft matter-of-factness: *Here is where it happened*.

My sister looks at me, her drawn-on eyebrows twisting like bait worms. She opens her mouth to say something, but I cannot hear her.

I turn back trying to see the spot in the road again, but it's too late. It has already disappeared behind the hill.

We pull into Liza's dirt yard and a medium-size brown dog circles our car, barking. I am about to get out, but my mother insists that the dog is a vicious pit bull. My father honks the horn, and Liza walks out the front door laughing at our caution.

"This dog won't do anything," she says. "Y'all come on in." She throws her head back and laughs again, and she is beautiful. Her eyes are so large that when she turns them the shiny whites seem endless. Her skin is smooth and brown, without makeup. She has a tiny waist, long, thin limbs, and the kind of large, full breasts that I prayed for as a teenager but never got.

As soon as I am out of the car, she hugs me. I hug her back and guilt rains down on me as I see over her shoulder my hand holding the folder filled with death certificates and newspaper articles.

I tell her I knew her dog was friendly, and I speak to him in sing-songy baby talk. He steps back and eyes me like he is sure I am going to steal something. My mother laughs and says he is trying to figure out why my voice is so much like Liza's. But I know better. I am trespassing here to ask for memories that don't belong to me, and he seems to know it.

We follow Liza into her living room and sit down. We all chat for a while, asking about different relatives.

Finally, we go silent, and my father looks at me, waiting.

I push down my fear. "Liza?" I say. "I've been doing some research on the wreck. Would you mind if I ask you a few questions about what happened?"

I wait for Liza's pleasant expression to drop like a mask, but she is still smiling at me. I search her face, looking for some sign that she realizes I have just handed her a shovel and told her to dig up her family's graves. But she looks back, interested, like I am talking about the distant family of a long-dead neighbor, someone she loved but had already said her goodbyes to.

"Of course I don't mind. But you know I don't remember anything about it, San."

"You don't?" My father sits up and moves to the edge of his chair.

"No. I can't remember anything about it."

"But you would have been seven years old by then," my father says.

"Really? I don't remember any of it."

My mother launches into the one story that she knows about that day—the story of my first cousin Davy who wanted to go on the trip to Russellville and whom my grandmother persuaded to stay behind by promising him strawberries. "Do you know he told me that he never ate strawberries again after that day?" my mother says.

Liza gives my mother the reaction she is looking for. She puts her hand on her face and says, "Oh my goodness."

"Do you know exactly what happened? Did anyone ever tell you?" I ask.

Liza shakes her head and looks at my father.

He tells the story of that Saturday morning from the beginning, why her family had come to Alabama, why he wasn't there that morning, the construction site, and the collisions between the dump truck and the cars. His words and matter-of-fact tone are identical to when he explained to me what happened that day. With his calm voice serving as a buffer between the violence of that day and the present, it is not so much a story as a recitation of his mother's testimony.

Now Liza is the one inching forward to the edge of her seat, her forehead a shifting map of what-ifs as she processes all the events that led her family to that stretch of highway. Her eyes begin to move between my father's face, my face, and the floor, as if she is looking for somewhere for this information to go, but like water it keeps flowing, spreading, and creeping onto surfaces that cannot hold it.

"I didn't know that Daddy Bluitt remembered all that. He never told me," Liza says.

"Naw, Mama told me. Daddy didn't remember anything."

"But she died. How could she—"

"Mama lived for ten days after and she was sitting up talking the whole time."

"Oh, Uncle John T.," Liza says, the weight of it all knocking her usually high voice down a whole octave.

I am fourteen years old and standing in my front yard with Liza, who is in her early thirties, and her two little girls, who must be around four and six. They are wearing their Easter dresses, gifts from my mother. They are holding hands and grinning. The oldest is all eyes and looks so much like me that even I can see the resemblance. The littlest is doll-like, with a round face, a button nose, and happy eyes. The girls look at each other, communicating in a silent language of smiles and glances that only they understand.

My mother snaps photos of them and says, "Aww, ain't they pretty" over and over again. But they are more than pretty. They are dazzling. They are not like me. At their ages, I tore through the world, running through briars that ripped my flesh, never stopping to wipe the blood.

They move about the yard together like toys come to life—curious and grinning, investigating the earth and consulting each other like old ladies.

I take the girls to the backyard to play with my little dog, Tux. But they are afraid of her. I encourage them to pet her. Dawn rubs her head while Tux stands. But Cadence, too little to know how to pet a dog, bangs on Tux's back with a stiff hand. I should stop her, but I don't want to make her any more afraid of dogs than she already is. Tux swings her head around and snaps at the air. Both girls stand and step back. Dawn points at Tux. "It bites! It bites!"

I try to quiet her, to convince her that the dog is gentle and that if it wanted to bite, it would have, rather than striking at the air.

But it is too late. She knows there is danger and she pulls her sister away.

Liza, can you tell me about your mother?" I say. "What was she like?"

Liza stares at me blank-faced. "I don't remember her."

"What?" my father says a little too loud. "You don't remember your mother?"

"No. I don't remember my parents at all. Sometimes I think I remember something about our house, like a room, but I can't remember them."

"What about your sister, San? Do you have any memories of her?" I say.

"No. I don't remember her either."

My father puts his hands over his eyes and runs them down the sides of his face. "Well, I'll be," he says.

I hand Liza two photographs, one of her and her sister, San, and another of her own mother at the age of three.

"I've seen this one," she says, pointing to the photograph of her and her sister. "But who is this other little girl?"

"Your mother."

"Really?" she says, smiling at the picture.

I hand her the folder and she flips through it while my father warns her that the news articles are all wrong.

Liza stops at a large front-page photo of the wreck.

"It really is a wonder that I survived, isn't it?" she says in a soft, airy voice.

"Mama saved you," my father says. "She covered your body with hers."

My mother presses her lips into a half smirk. She has never heard this detail, and her lack of sentiment, her no-nonsense clear-sightedness, will not let her believe it. I also have doubts. How could anyone shield another person while flying through the air? But unlike my mother, I see the gift in the lie. Whether she believes him or not, Liza nods at my father, accepting his offering, a memory of being loved by a family that she cannot remember.

I am still a teenager when my mother tells me that Liza's daughter Cadence has cancer. Everyone I know who had cancer is dead. But they were grown-ups. I struggle to make the connection between their old bodies and little Cadence.

My father says we are going to visit Cadence in the hospital, and he drives me and my mother two hours to the Ronald McDonald House, a charitable organization that helps sick children who cannot afford treatment. We find her in a large, dim room that looks like an old-fashioned hospital ward with rows of small beds along the walls. Sick children lie in the beds while their families huddle around them. The walls are covered in life-size drawings of a grinning Ronald McDonald and his gang of happy burger-eating characters.

Liza spots us and waves us over. She smiles and hugs us as if this is an ordinary visit to her house, rather than a bedside visit to a child with cancer.

Cadence smiles from her bed and closes her eyes. I am relieved to see that she still has a head full of thick hair.

"She's just had a treatment," Liza says. "It really takes a lot out of her."

"Oh, I can imagine," my mother says. But nothing in this room of hollow-eyed children languishing on tiny beds is imaginable.

Liza offers us chairs. My mother and I sit, but my father refuses. He rocks back and forth on his feet near the end of the bed as if his only job is to be ready to escape this place.

My mother gets out just a few sentences before my father says we should go. Liza insists that we don't have to rush off, but my father says he wants to let Cadence rest.

My parents had called this trip "going to visit Cadence in the hospital," but I know that is not what this is. We did not come all this way to visit, but to make visible the love and support that words cannot hold. Our presence is all we have to give. So after Liza and Cadence have seen us, we say goodbye and make our way out of this room where Ronald McDonald grins over dying children.

. . .

I am in graduate school when my mother calls to say that Cadence's cancer is back. She is thirteen years old, but I picture her as she was when she was a very little girl falling in and out of consciousness at the Ronald McDonald House.

I am consumed by the idea of her suffering, the cruelty and unfairness of it. But I am sure that she will survive. My mother calls just days later to tell me that Cadence is dead.

Both of my parents say that there is no need to come home for the funeral, but I ignore them and drive to Alabama from Georgia in stunned disbelief.

At the funeral, a children's choir sings over a small casket. Liza sits at the front of the church with her arm resting on her daughter Dawn's shoulder. Their bodies are completely still as if they too have died. A preacher says things about youth and the mystery of God's plans, compelling us to accept Cadence's death without requiring an understanding of a being greater than us. Then he launches into a hard sell for baptism, warning us that damnation will follow death without it. Hatred for him sets my belly and shoulders on fire. I have never been more sure that God is a lie.

While Liza flips through the papers in the folder, I spot a glass cabinet filled with Barbie dolls still in their original boxes in her hallway.

"Where did you get those?" I say, pointing.

She looks back over her shoulder. "Oh, the dolls. They were Cadence's. She loved collecting them."

I step into the hallway to take a closer look at the never-opened dolls with their glossy hair and rubbery legs still attached to the box.

"Ain't that something?" my mother says. "She collected all those?" Her voice is light, admiring, even though she would rather have cut her own hands off and put them in a display cabinet before she would have put boxes of plastic dolls out in her own home. This is what grief looks like when it takes up residence in your house. Ordinary objects become artifacts frozen in another time. They look the same, but they are transformed in ways that the body can feel. I step back into the living room.

"Where did you go after the accident? I say to Liza.

"Here," she says. "To this house with Mrs. Ray."

Everyone seemed to call Liza's paternal grandmother Mrs. Ray. Though I must have met her as a child, I have no memory of her.

I look around the neat little house with its low ceilings and shiny wood floors. Liza still lives in the house she was brought to after the accident.

"Do you remember anything from that time?" I say.

"One thing," Liza says. "Aunt Judy came here to visit me after I came home from the hospital. I was so happy to see her. She had been staying with us in Illinois before the wreck. I knew her, and I hadn't spent much time with Mrs. Ray. When Judy left, I started to cry. And Mrs. Ray whipped me for crying. I can remember that."

My sister lets out a gasp.

Liza looks at her with a sad smile on her face, but her luminous eyes are bright and clear. "Old folks just didn't know any better back then."

One corner of my father's mouth bends down and stays so still that his face looks paralyzed.

I nod at Liza, not because I agree with her excuse for her grandmother, but because I am not in a position to judge a woman who had just lost her son, daughter-in-law, and grandchild all in one day. Mrs. Ray had beaten Liza and also beaten back the past in the process. Not on purpose, but the result was the same. Liza's grief had nowhere to go and so her child brain that could not process the triple loss had crammed the accident and everyone it killed into a shoebox, burying it so deep that not even the adult Liza could find it. She would remember this new trauma, the sound of a switch before it ripped at her flesh still sore from the wreck. But June 25, 1960, and everything before it was gone.

Liza's "thank yous" follow us all the way to the car. When my father backs out onto the dirt road, Liza is still waving from the yard. The mutt next to her is no longer barking, but he eyes us in a way that says, *You are trespassing.*

As he drives down the highway, my father says to me, "I'm glad you gave her those things. She needed them, and you could see she was glad to get them."

"Yeah, she needed that," my sister agrees. "Nobody had even told her a thing about it." She stares out the window as if she is talking to the highway. "And Mrs. Ray just beat her." She shakes her head. "I guess old people didn't know any better back then and didn't have a way to learn any different."

The weight of Liza's story fills the car and we fall silent because there is nothing to be done for a fifty-year-old wound.

But my mother casts a look of disapproval at me. And I think I understand why. Liza's mind had managed to forget the wreck and I had
gone to her house and burdened her with it. In Liza's house, grief stands
still in plastic boxes marked Dream Fantasy Barbie and Evening En-
chantment Barbie. Why would she ever need another relic of death?

My mother hums through the silence. After a few minutes she asks
my sister if she remembers a woman who used to go to our church.
Then they go back and forth as my sister tries and fails to place the
woman. My mother's voice is casual, but she worries her hands like
she is applying an invisible balm. "You do know her. Had a sister
named . . . Let me see, what was her sister's name? I think they called
her Dodie. John, you remember her, don't you? San, well, you might
not remember 'cause she was a lot older than you. But you probably
knew her little brother. Let me see, what was his name?"

My sister sighs.

But my mother will not stop. She keeps reciting names and demanding everyone's recognition as if an acknowledgment of the familiar is the only thing that can thin the air in the car enough for us all to
breathe again. She forms a linked chain made of names: Sheila and
Cece, Jimmy and Blue, Nel, and Willie Mae. And whether we remember these people or not, each name tugs at us, pulling us back to the
mundane before we float any further into a past that does not love us.

Finally, my sister says, "You talking about Lisa's cousin?"

And my mother lets out a sigh of relief. "You know, I forgot they
were cousins on their daddy's side. Well, she works at the mall now
and she called me to tell me that the suit I liked is on sale now. Y'all
want to go to the mall when we get back? Jason. That was his name,
San. He'd a been along with you in school. He would be her little
brother."

I do not know who she is talking about, but I know when I am being called home to safety even though I refuse to go.

As we move along the highway, I look for the spot where all of our lives changed—where the other San died and my life became possible. Every time I feel the car climbing a steep hill, I try to memorize the place, to map it as if knowing will fill all the absences of my life. But I can never be sure because every hill feels like it is the one.

CHAPTER 13

O n Tuesday, August 2, 1960, more than a month after the wreck, the *Florence Times* newspaper published its standard weekly list of all hospital admissions and dismissals. My grandfather's name appeared under dismissals: "Bluitt Jackson, Sheffield, Negro."

I am six years old and in my room when Daddy Bluitt calls me like he does every day to come to the den and bring my socks with me. Today he says my name, "San," but I am never sure if he means me or the dead one. Some days he calls me Maggie, and other times, Liza. I answer to all these names.

In my room, I grab my socks and follow him down the hallway as he limps to the den and sits down on the sofa. I sit down next to him with my foot in his lap and hand him my socks. He stretches out a sock and examines it to locate the heel. Then he slips it on my foot and straightens the seams for a long time with his shaky fingers. When he is satisfied that the sock is perfect, he tells me to give him my other foot and he repeats the process. He does this for me every day, even though I am old enough to put my own socks on.

When he is done, he tells me to go put my shoes on so he can take me to the store.

I stuff my feet into my shoes and follow Daddy Bluitt out the door. We hold hands and I feel his body shifting like a sideways rocking horse as we walk down the street. Three blocks later, we enter the cool of a small convenience store.

"Pick out what you want," he says. He chats with the clerk about the weather as I choose between individually wrapped pieces of pink bubble gum and green apple Now and Laters.

After I've made my selection, I put it on the counter and he pays.

Outside, I unwrap the Now and Laters and pop one in my mouth. I chew the sticky candy all the way home, its sweetness bursting in my mouth. When one melts, I pop in another. There is no need to save them, because tomorrow Daddy Bluitt will tell me to go get my socks, put them on my feet, and take me to the store again.

On the day that you bring your father home from the hospital, he yells for your mother to bring him his socks. He is sitting on the edge of his bed, staring at the wall as if he could see his wife on the other side folding laundry.

"John T.," he says, agitated. "Tell your mother I said to bring me my socks!"

You consider nodding, even pretending to get socks from your mother so that your father can live just a little longer in a place where the worst thing that could happen is your wife ignoring you. But the doctor was clear that pretending would cause more frustration and eventually madness.

"Mama is not here, Daddy," you say. "Remember what I told you? She died."

Your father frowns at you like you have poked his arm with a fork. "What did you say, boy?"

"There was a wreck, Daddy. You were in it too."

He tightens his mouth and shakes his head at you like he has raised a fool.

"John T., go ask Willodene what Bernice did with my socks."

"Willodene is dead," you say. "She died in the wreck too. Don't you remember? We talked about this at the hospital."

Your father's eyes widen and he begins to shake as memory and then grief find their places in his body.

I am seven years old, eating breakfast with Daddy Bluitt while my mother runs back and forth gathering her things for work.

When she is finally out the door, he waits to make sure she hasn't forgotten anything. When he is sure that she is gone, he limps into the kitchen and pours me a cup of coffee with cream and sugar. This is how we start our summer days together.

Behind us the TV is blaring commercials.

I sip and wait for him to tell a story.

"You have to watch out for cats. Did I tell you about the time one tried to suck my breath?"

I shake my head no, even though I have heard this story and other bizarre tales of near death from him almost every day that he takes care of me in the summers while my family is at work.

"I was asleep when that thing crawled on top of me and started sucking my breath. They do that, you know. Try to suck all the air right out of you. It almost killed me."

"How'd you stop it?"

"I woke up just in time and knocked that cat off of me so hard it flew right into the wall. And do you know that scoun jumped right up and ran off like lightning." He slaps his hands together and pulls them apart. "Gone just like that. But that's why you can't keep no cat around. They'll try to kill you every time."

It is midnight when you get home from the evening shift at your job. Your father and sister are asleep. You climb into bed, and just as you start to drift off, someone screams. You jump out of the bed and run to the kitchen still in your underwear. Your father is standing there looking back at you.

"Daddy, what's going on?"

"I can't find Bernice. Your mother is gone." He limps past you into the living room and down a hallway.

You follow and watch him open the door to the closet and wait for his wife to jump out of her hiding place.

"Daddy, listen to me. Mama is dead," you say, trying not to yell.

He closes the closet door and walks into the living room.

"She didn't make it back last night? I got to go look for her." He swings the front door open but stops at the threshold as if the door were still closed.

You resist the urge to shake him, and instead take a deep breath before saying, "Mama is dead, Daddy. She is not coming back."

"No, son. I'm talking about your mama. Bernice should have been back by now."

You tell him again that your mother is dead, and this time you list all the names of the dead: Bernice, Willodene, Maggie, Robert, and San. All dead.

The words break over him, bending his body forward, and he grabs the doorframe. When you walk over to help him, he looks up at you with hurt eyes.

You walk him to the couch and you both sit down while your family dies all over again.

I am thirty-eight years old when I ask my father about Daddy Bluitt's story of the enormous needle the hospital staff put inside his back.

My father cocks his head at me. "When did he tell you that?"

"When I was little, too many times to count."

My father laughs. "He didn't remember a thing. He was in a coma. His legs and hips were messed up so bad that the doctors kept him in a coma while he was healing. That's why he limped like that. But I don't know anything about a needle."

"Do you think the memory might have come to him later?"

"Naaaah. It's possible he mixed it up with that time he got bitten by a spider years before. I think they gave him a shot then."

"But he told me over and over again—a story about two men holding him down while a doctor inserted a huge needle in his back."

"I'm sure he felt like that's what happened. Might have even dreamed it. But his mind was different after the wreck."

"Different how?

"It was months before he could even remember who was dead. I'd have to tell him again and again. But even after that passed, he still got confused. That's why I had to settle the lawsuit. My lawyer wanted to take it all the way to court, but he wanted Daddy to testify. There was no way he was gonna be able to testify, and I didn't want to put him through that."

The Florence Times June 25, 1961

[Front page]

$400,000 IS SOUGHT FROM 1960 WRECK

Seven separate suits asking an accumulative total of $400,000 damages have been filed in Colbert Circuit Court in connection with Alabama's worst traffic tragedy of 1960. ·

Howell Heflin and Harold Hughston, Tuscumbia attorneys, filed the suits Friday on behalf of members of a Negro family, five of whom died in the June 25, 1960, accident on U.S. 43 south of Tuscumbia in which a total of seven persons died.

Named as defendants in the suit were Burgreen Construction Company of Athens, Ala., Burgreen Asphalt Company and Howard E. Morris, administrator of the estate of Harry Howard Morris.

Harry Howard Morris, a Church of Christ preacher, and his wife were also victims of the two-car and truck collision, five miles south of Tuscumbia.

Only two Negroes, Bluitt Jackson of Sheffield and his granddaughter Liza Ray, survived the truck accident in addition to the truck driver, James H. Crisler.

Five of the suits are filed in the name of John T. Jackson administrator of the estates of Sandra Ray, Maggie Jo Ray, Burnice [sic] Jackson, Robert Ray and Willodene Jackson, all victims of the crash. Each of these five suits asked damages in the amount of $50,000.

Another suit finds Louise Ray, guardian of Liza Ray, young Negro girl injured in the mishap, suing for $50,000 for personal injuries suffered by the child.

The other suit, brought by Bluitt Jackson, elderly Sheffield Negro, asks $100,000 in damages for personal injuries suffered in the mishap.

In count one of the three-count complaint in one of the suits, the plaintiffs list their allegations as to how the May 25 [sic], 1960 accident happened.

They contend as follows:

COUNT ONE: "The plaintiff suing as administrator of the estate of Willodene Jackson, deceased, claims of the defendants, the sum of $50,000, as damages for that heretofore, on, to wit, the 25th day of June, 1960, the plaintiff's descendant Willodene Jackson, who was also the wife of the said John T. Jackson, was a passenger in a Pontiac automobile being driven by Robert Ray in a southerly direction on U.S. Highway 43, a public highway, at a point, to-wit: 5 miles south of the City of Tuscumbia in Colbert County, Alabama.

"Then and there the said Harry Howard Morris was driving a Chevrolet Corvair in a southerly direction and attempting to unlawfully pass said Pontiac automobile on a hill. Then and there James H. Crisler, an agent, servant or employee of Burgreen Construction Company, a corporation, and Burgreen Asphalt Company, a corporation, while acting within the line and scope of his employment, was driving a 1955 GMC two and one-half ton truck at an unlawful and high rate of speed in a northerly direction and came over said hill as said Chevrolet Corvair automobile was attempting to pass the said Pontiac automobile. Then and there the said Harry Howard Morris sharply drove the Chevrolet Corvair automobile into the path of the Pontiac automobile and suddenly applied his brakes causing said Pontiac automobile to hit said Chevrolet Corvair in the rear and knock said Chevrolet Corvair into the said two and one-half ton GMC truck, which was then and there traveling at an unlawful and high rate of speed.

"Then and there also after said collision occurred between the said Chevrolet Corvair automobile and the said GMC two and one-half ton truck, another collision occurred a few seconds later between the said Pontiac automobile and the said GMC two and one-half ton truck.

"Then and there the said Harry Morris and said James H. Crisler so negligently operated the respective motor vehicles which they were driving so as to cause said collision."

My father does not remember the last time he had to explain to Daddy Bluitt that their family was dead. At some point, Daddy Bluitt stopped searching the closets for his wife, ceased complaining that his daughter-in-law had misplaced the spatula, and quit wondering aloud why his daughter and her husband never came to visit anymore.

I am little. The theme to *General Hospital* is playing on the television as the credits scroll on the screen. Daddy Bluitt steps into the kitchen and grunts as he bends over and pulls out my daddy's whiskey.

He pours some into a glass of soda and puts the whiskey bottle back in the cabinet. He sits down at the bar in the same place where he drinks his coffee and tells me to head on into the den and turn the TV to whatever I want to watch.

I flip through channels while he sips. I settle on *The Flintstones*, but over Fred Flintstone's booming voice, I can hear Daddy Bluitt calling his wife by her name. "Now, Bernice," he says, "you know that Luke should know better than that." He is trying to explain something to her about *General Hospital*, but I cannot understand because there are too many half-spoken words that drip like tears from his mouth.

When he is done, he walks over to the sofa and sits down.

"I'm not asleep," he says. "I'm just resting my eyes."

I do not know if he is talking to me or her, but he snores and smiles while I watch my show.

CHAPTER 14

Back in New Jersey, I sit on the sofa next to my husband and show him the newspaper articles. I tell him everything I learned about the accident and its aftermath. I talk and talk as if the telling will make sense of the world and save us both from it.

"But do you feel like you learned what you needed to know?" he says. The question surprises me because I have never articulated to him exactly what I needed to know, and yet the urgency in his words lets me know that I do not have to explain. The "what" is a stand-in for many things at once: who, how, why, and more. This is why he puts the emphasis on the word "needed," as if to say, *Whatever it is, it is important to me because you needed it.*

I mumble a yes and a no. I found out what happened, saw the place where lives ended and mine became possible. But there was also no amount of knowledge that could ever be satisfying. The story of what happened could not be known as an object or studied into submission.

I tell him about Daddy Bluitt looking in a closet for his wife and all the old women who searched my six-year-old face looking for dead ones. The search was never fully over for any of us. We were all carrying our ghosts with us.

If we have a child, biological or not, this will be their legacy too. It will become theirs as much as it is mine and my father's. This is not the information I went looking for, but it is what I needed to know.

He nods, and I see the little boy who found his father dead in a living room chair and ran next door to borrow a car to get his father to the hospital, even though at twelve years old, the boy did not know how to drive.

My last IVF is a medicalized version of the film *Groundhog Day*. I do nothing that I have not done before. I lie on papered tables, wear bulbous tissue caps, and shiver in backless gowns.

On the day of the transfer, the doctor hands me pictures of two embryos. I pass them to my husband without a word. I will not moon over possibility.

The new doctor looks at us both and nods his understanding. He is different from the other doctors. He makes no promises, mentions no aliens, and offers no hippy magic. He has been an IVF patient himself and he knows the dangers of hope.

I lie on a table and watch a screen that shows the ashy black sky that is my uterus. My abdomen cramps and a bright dot flies across the screen like a comet and disappears.

I spend the evening on bedrest. This is where I am when I get a call from my mother. Her sister, who was admitted to the hospital just yesterday, is dead.

Days after the embryo transfer, I travel home and arrive in Alabama on a hot fall day.

The funeral is a debacle. In a church packed with family and friends, a preacher rants about my aunt as a troubled woman who was abused and rejected by her parents, and who in turn did the same to her own children. He accuses my aunt and my grandparents of failing as parents and as people. This is his eulogy of my aunt. The church fills with whispers, but we all sit as if we are being held hostage by a madman.

One of my aunt's daughters, already sobbing, begins to shake. I walk over to her and ask if she wants me to do something and she says yes.

I approach the front of the church, unsure of the protocol but focused on a simple task, to make a fool sit down. I enter the pulpit and explain to one of the sitting ministers that the family would like the preacher to cease immediately.

As he approaches the preacher, whispering in his ear, I turn and see my parents in the front pew, a mime's wall of thin, airy space between them. My father sits like a figure in an eighteenth-century painting. His face is stern, unreadable, and his body is straight and still, skills he must have taught himself sitting in front of too many caskets.

Though my mother is dressed in something shiny like a gushing mother of a bride, she is as still and quiet as fog in this growing chaos of murmuring women and fidgeting men. She looks not at the pulpit, but instead straight ahead, having already disappeared the ranting preacher in her head. She is the woman who refused to let grief swallow my father whole, the one who never asked too many questions and who demanded gray silence in place of tears. Her dammed-up hurt helps my father to engineer his own dams. She is the one who made me possible.

The preacher says something about refusing to hide the truth. I approach again and make it clear to the pastor that he must make this man sit down, or I will.

I stand and wait, this time staring at the preacher but seeing my mother out of the corner of my eye. *She was really the only thing holding him together. A lot of men need a woman to hold them together.*

I glare at the preacher, and like my mother, I refuse to stand for weakness, for ranting, for self-indulgence or madness. In this moment, I understand her choice not to examine every bit of hurt and loss too closely, to instead bury it deep and tamp the ground smooth as quickly as possible. I want to suffocate grief like the rest of life depends on its impossible demise.

The preacher bows his head and limps to his seat.

After I return to New Jersey, I head to the drugstore to purchase a pregnancy test. If hope has to die one more time, it will die with just me and a stick.

I walk past Reginald without a word on my way to our third-floor bathroom where I can count on total privacy. Assuming that the test will be negative, there would be no need to tell him at this point. He can grieve once after the blood test instead of twice like me.

I pee in the cup, dip the stick in, and resolve to face failure. I do not plan for the second blue line that appears instantly. Two clear lines, one test line that indicates the test is working, and another that indicates I am pregnant.

I am no longer here, no voice, just sound, and something that feels like wings flying. Then I am downstairs in front of Reginald. I am talking but no words are coming out, just squeaky sounds, like a cat toy. My whole body begins to cry.

"What's wrong?" he says.

I shake my head no and hold up the stick. But he does not under-stand. He reaches for me with sad, limp arms.

I manage to release the words trapped at the back of my throat. "No," I say and pull my body away from him "We are . . . I am pregnant."

A tiny smile appears at the corner of his lips, but his eyebrows re-main knitted together. "But the blood test isn't until—"

"I know, but . . ." I hold up the stick again. "Two lines. It says I'm pregnant."

He smiles a strange toothy grin. His eyes seem to look through me instead of at me. He starts to say something, but he stops. And I know what it is because I feel it too. Fear. Not scared of having a baby, but scared of not having one—scared that the test is not the real truth. What if this expensive stick I just peed on is wrong?

I shake off my fear and say it again. "Pregnant!"

He glances down at the stick and smiles. "It's a good sign. But shouldn't we wait?"

I am about to tell him everything I have read about home preg-nancy tests, that false positives are rare, that yes, sometimes the body produces hormones because of ectopic pregnancies or chemical preg-nancies, situations where the embryo was not in the right place to survive and develop, but just thinking about the test in these clinical terms is enough to bring me back to the ground. He is right. Only a blood test and more blood tests would tell us if this pregnancy would result in a baby.

We sit down on the sofa holding each other like we are loose sails that could blow away.

We cannot be further from the old sitcom scenario where the calm wife surprises an unwitting husband by telling him that she's pregnant and then laughs at him as he runs around the room, unsure of whether to get her a glass of water or a pillow.

Reginald will never be that silly man and I will never be that smug, smiling woman.

For nine months, we are twin pendulums swinging between joy and fear. We hold our breath at every blood test, urine test, and ultrasound. Every time we wait for the nurse to find the heartbeat, we prepare ourselves for death in the pause before joy. But catastrophe does not come.

The baby's heartbeat is loud, full of the rhythmic knocking sounds of a construction site.

We do not name the baby or find out its sex because these acts would require imagining a future. We call it Lub-dub, a quiet imitation of the sound we hear coming from its heart.

I do not tell my parents that I am pregnant until an ultrasound technician measures the baby's head and limbs. If there is a loss, I want it to be mine, and not my father's.

My mother answers the phone. She lets out a "what" that is not a question but an exclamation, and calls my father to the phone.

When I tell him that I am pregnant his voice goes high and he laughs as joy spills over his edges.

He does not say congratulations because he is from a generation of Black people for whom a baby is not an accomplishment but a mysterious gift. He is happy and he searches for words and sounds to convey this. "Aww, baby! Ain't that something? A baby."

We are new in this moment, glowing with love and anticipation for someone we have not met but who is already part of us.

As my baby grows inside me, a secret thing also grows inside my father deep in the marrow of his bones. Cells are dividing, multiplying, a quiet cancer that neither he nor anyone knows is there.

In a year, he will be working outside when he feels pain deep in his rib cage. His doctor will tell him he has a broken rib, but this makes no sense because all he did was reach above his head. At the hospital, nurses will wrap his chest and send him home, a partial mummy, to rest. But his rib will not heal and another one will break, and then another. My father will crumble from the inside, and no one will know why.

At a subsequent visit to the emergency room, a new doctor, a Black man, will insist on running new tests. He will figure out in twenty minutes what the other doctors didn't even investigate. My father has multiple myeloma, a cancer of the bones that affects twice as many Black people as white.

After numerous warnings from friends that we should abandon our plan to bring home the new baby by ourselves, I reluctantly ask my parents to stay with us. When they arrive at my home to help with the new baby, I am thirty-nine weeks and my belly looks like it is going to explode with a thousand babies. My father's cancer flourishes unseen.

While I wait for the baby to arrive, my parents give themselves jobs.

My father shops for groceries and cooks as if the smell of bacon will make the baby curious enough to come out of my body. My mother puts on makeup and colorful summer outfits each day just to wash laundry and scrub my house. She washes so much laundry that a pipe breaks and spills water into my kitchen. Then both of them labor over this new broken thing and the water that spills from it.

While the baby waits patiently for two weeks more inside my body, my parents never talk about when the baby will come, the uncertainties of birth, or who might be inside. Instead, they work as if their survival as well as mine and the baby's depends on the sustained movement of their wrinkled hands across kitchen counters, tables, floors, and laundry baskets.

At my week forty-one obstetrician visit, the doctor says there is nothing to worry about. He assures me that the medical practice will wait for the baby. He tries to send me back home, but I ask for a fluid check—one last ultrasound to make sure that the baby has everything it needs. He indulges me, and tells me I can leave as soon as the ultrasound is over—he does not need to see me again today.

The ultrasound tech smiles wide at me when I waddle into the room. I am big enough and pregnant enough that she does not bother with the game face she usually wears when she is checking to make sure that a fetus is alive.

I lie down on the table and let her place a glob of warm jelly on my giant egg-shaped belly. She looks at the screen and puts her game face on. She is not allowed to tell me why, but she sends me back in to see the doctor.

In the examining room, the doctor is washing his hands. He looks over his shoulder at me and reaches for a towel. "The baby is fine, but the fluid it needs is low. We need to give you a drug tonight to open your cervix and we'll induce birth in the morning. You'll need to be at the hospital by seven p.m. tonight. You won't be able to eat after that time. So have a good meal today with your husband. It will be your last one with just the two of you for a long time." He smiles. "Tomorrow, you'll be a mother."

I hang on to this seesaw of words: "The baby is fine, *but* . . ." I know that most inductions lead to C-sections, but I am not worried about my own body. I do not care if they pull the baby out of my ear. I am thinking of the baby's body. Plus, the doctor is wrong. I am already a mother.

Reginald and I go out to eat alone, smiling and talking fast like the people we are: people who are happy and terrified at the same time. On the way home to grab my bag and head to the hospital, our tire goes flat. We manage to pull into a tire center, and Reginald jumps out of the car to ask the mechanic how fast he can change the tire. The man is shaking his head no just as I emerge from the car looking like an emergency about to happen. The mechanic goes from shaking his head to waving his arms to direct Reginald to pull the car into the garage. Twenty minutes later, the mechanic emerges from the garage sweating like he has birthed his own baby, and we drive away.

We arrive at the hospital on time. Nurses lead me to a room and explain how to arrange the hospital gown. They do not know that the gown has been my uniform for almost two years of infertility treatments.

I put it on and climb onto the bed, assuming the identity of the patient.

Dr. S. arrives and explains that he will give me a drug to make my cervix open for the baby to come out.

"You should get some sleep," he says. "Tonight will be your last chance at good sleep for a long time."

I smile and roll my eyes, knowing that there is no way I will be able to sleep while waiting for my baby to be born.

"It really is important that you rest tonight. I can give you a sleep aid."

I say okay, knowing that it will be the only way I will sleep.

A nurse attaches monitors to my belly. As she finishes, another nurse shows up with the sleeping pill. I take it and drift off.

When I wake up in the night, my belly feels like a watermelon being dashed against a hot sidewalk. A woman is screaming. She is close, probably in the hallway or in the room next door.

I need to go to the bathroom. I sit up and feel something tethering my body. There is no time to figure out what it is because the pressure in my bladder is building. I rip sticky patches off my body and stand up. But I am dizzy and the left side of my head feels like it is still asleep.

Reginald stands next to me, reaching for my arms as I tilt left and right walking to the toilet like a broken windup toy. Something is beeping. In the bathroom, I order Reginald to go away. I fall asleep as soon as I sit down. The sound of the door opening wakes me. A nurse runs in looking about like she has lost something. She helps me back to the bed and I sit on the side with my feet on the floor.

"You have to stop taking off these pads," she says. She reattaches each one to my body. I tell her that I still feel like I have to pee, even though nothing is coming out. She ignores me and instructs Reginald: "Don't let her pull these off again. Just roll the machine with her if she needs to walk." I drift off while I am still sitting on the edge of the bed.

I wake up lying on my side. Someone is still screaming, and I feel like I am in an insane asylum where they put women who won't behave.

The pain and pressure in my belly drive me back to the bathroom. Reginald drags the monitor beside me. This time when I kick him out of the bathroom, I see fear in his eyes. I am the woman who has been screaming.

I sit and nothing happens, but I feel myself falling asleep and call for him. He helps me up and checks the toilet to make sure our baby is not floating around in it.

As I head toward the bed, I fall asleep standing up. Reginald wakes me and helps me back to the bed.

I sleep again and wake to nurses rushing into the room. They say that the baby's heartbeat is accelerating. But when they arrive, the baby calms down as if it is saying, *Nanny nanny boo boo, I just fooled you!* This happens two more times.

The third time, one of the nurses says, "This is a crazy baby."

Though I can barely stay awake, I shoot her a look that says, *This baby is smarter than you.*

When morning comes, I am just the pain. I labor, but my body does not open. There is nowhere for my baby to go.

Another doctor arrives and tells me that it's time to get this baby out. She is going to perform a C-section.

I will remember: a needle in my back, hands that hold me still, my parents sitting in a waiting area with tight worried smiles as I roll by on a stretcher, the bitter smell of antiseptic, the color blue, my body rocking from side to side like a Christmas ham cut with a dull knife. A screaming mouth—so open that I can see the flesh trembling in the back of her throat.

"Meet your daughter," someone says.

A daughter.

My daughter.

At the hospital, my daughter and I drift between being one person and two. She teaches my husband to do her bidding while I am still in the recovery room waiting for the feeling in my legs to return. He rolls her to me in a bassinet, its squeaky wheels no match for the angry music box in her throat.

"What are you doing here? You're supposed to meet me in the room. I cannot feel my feet yet."

He looks at his daughter as he talks to me. "The nurse said she's hungry and that I needed to bring her to you now. I asked her how that was possible. She was just born. How could she be hungry?"

The nurse next to me suppresses a laugh. One day, he and I will joke about how silly he sounded as he tried to make logical sense of a baby's needs. But now, I marvel at how unchanged he is by the past twenty-four hours. He still divides human experience between the possible and the impossible. Meanwhile, I am completely transformed. My body has been split open, a whole person yanked out of it, and a doctor has literally pasted the halves of me together. Possible and impossible are now irrelevant categories. What matters is my baby's cry that crawls inside me, taking up residence where her body once was. I am hers, even before my legs tingle with life again.

I look at the nurse and she nods as I open my gown. She places my daughter on my chest and cups my breast, pointing the nipple at her mouth. My daughter latches on with a grip so tight that I am sure she is the first baby born with shark's teeth. I feel pain, but not like the thin slash in my belly that will always remind me of a street fight. The pain in my breasts is at once sharp like needles of straw and dull as a strike with a wooden spoon. I lie still on the edge between tolerance and love. And just like that we are one warm body again.

We spend our first night together like this. Reginald changing her and handing her to me. Her sucking and drifting. Me letting the strength of her mouth pull me inside her, gritting my teeth until I am gone. This is the thing that our bodies will remember even when our conscious minds cannot.

The nurse tells us to keep track of the baby's wet diapers to make sure that she is consuming colostrum, the thick liquid that the breasts produce before the milk arrives. The suggestion that my daughter could be just suckling rather than eating frightens me, snatching my trust in this thing that feels right. But on day two of my daughter's life, my breasts grow hard in the shower, and I become a sprinkler, milk shooting from me onto the tile walls. I climb out still dripping with water, milk, and soap. I pick up my daughter and press her to my body. She opens her mouth wide and shakes her head until she feels the tip of my nipple against her lips. She sputters at first, then drinks until the tension in my neck lets go and there is no longer any separation between her desire and mine. We drift together, muscles relaxing into dreams.

All day and night nurses come to check our vitals. They ask me if she is my second baby. They tell me that she cannot be my first baby because I am too good at this. They say that I am "a natural." I am too tired to argue with them. But I do not trust this word that assumes that we are nothing more than our biology. "Natural" is a mean measuring stick, one that made Black girls wrong just for living: too fast, too fertile, not fertile enough—always broken, always on the other end of those old southern phrases "fixing to" or "getting ready to get ready" but never just right.

One day, I will tell my daughter that this body that nurtured her also required a scalpel to get her out. The body that orgasmed like starbursts also refused to conceive. The body that couldn't get pregnant also rained milk like rice at a wedding. My body was a long story marked by contradictions that no one could explain, though everyone pretended to. And one day everyone will pretend to know what her body means too.

I will tell my daughter that the body is a story that does not end with the body. That we carry others from room to room on our backs, calling out the names of our dead in our sleep, and that this is why I have given her a new name of her own. I will teach her the other names in due time.

When I come home from the hospital three days after my daughter's birth by C-section, I do not have to do anything but feed my baby. All day, my father cooks and sends meals to my room via Reginald or my mother. Biscuits with coffee gravy, crispy chicken wings, fried sweet corn, and warm peach pies that ooze with love that cannot be spoken. I eat it all and pass it on to my daughter in my breast milk. My daughter grows and I heal quickly.

As she brings warm food to my bed on a tray, my mother catches a glimpse of my nipples, raw, red, and swollen with pain. She gasps an

"Aww, baby!" so tender that were it not for the disgust in her eyes, I might think she is talking to my daughter.

"Don't that hurt?"

I nod and tell her that I have made an appointment with a lactation consultant. The confused look on her face reminds me that this job exists because medicine told a whole generation of mothers that their milk was not good enough.

"She'll check the baby's latch and make suggestions about how to heal my breasts."

My mother glances around the room as if she is looking for something that might help. I pick up a salve and rub it on my breast, more to calm her than to help me.

"Can she have a bottle?" she says.

I tell her that I want to make sure my daughter is established on the breasts first.

She makes a pained face at me like I am eating a bug.

As she leaves, I try to imagine her with me when I was a newborn. I see her hands, tense with the labor of diapers and bottles. But then I remember the newborn baby she once pretended to breastfeed and the gauzy wall of fabric that stood between his mouth and her breast. I cannot picture her sinking willingly into the vulnerability of broken skin and drunken love.

When I am done eating, I bring my daughter downstairs to my father, and he holds her while my mother tries to use the baby's ears to gauge how dark her fair skin will get when she grows older.

"I think she'll be about San's color. What you think, John?"

My father mumbles a noncommittal answer but never takes his eyes off his granddaughter.

• • •

My daughter is one year old when my mother tells me that my father has cancer. Instead of thinking about what it would mean to me to lose him, all I can think about is that my loss will also be my daughter's and that she might not remember him.

I travel to Alabama where I find my father sucking the air like it is thick with blood. His doctors have been trying, but failing, to get Medicare to approve an oxygen tank. His body is shrunken in height and girth and curves like a spoon.

I take him to the doctor for his treatment and on the way back we stop at the pharmacy. He is too weak to get out of the car, so I drop the prescription at the pharmacy counter and return to the car to wait with him.

"I am not afraid to die," he says. "I have led a good life."

I clamp my mouth shut as a voice inside me screams, *You have not had a good life! You lost most of your family, including your nineteen-year-old bride and almost four-year-old niece. That is the opposite of a good life.*

But he talks about owning a home for his children and being able to educate them, things that were beyond his imagination as a boy picking cotton on someone else's land. He is not a two-car, one-dump-truck wreck on Highway 43. He does not remember or choose to re-member the drunken naps when he called out a dead girl's name and I answered. He remembers a good life.

When my visit ends, I am pulled in two different directions: to stay and care for my father, an act that he would never allow, or to go back to my life in New Jersey where I care for my child. I kiss him goodbye and leave him sitting in the spot where I braided and decorated his hair when I was little. I do not expect to see my father alive again.

I travel to Alabama every few months with my daughter. When my father holds her, I worry that her weight will break his fragile bones, but to him, she is worth more than the risk. Besides me and my husband, my father is the only one my daughter allows to hold her. The stillness of his sick body calms her. She hides her face in his shoulder when my mother speaks to her in loud baby talk. He rocks her in his recliner and she falls asleep wrapped in his thinning arms.

When he is not holding her, he treats death like a new job—a thing to prepare for and thus labor over. He buys my mother a new car so she will never have to buy a car herself. He chooses and purchases a silver casket in the same way that he shopped for the car, weighing price and aesthetics and knocking on the hood. He selects a drawer in a mausoleum and writes his own obituary.

In this way, he seems like the man I knew who tended his gardens and cooked all day. But now he lives with constant pain he does not talk about. He tells me only that he is fine or feeling better. But when I am there with my daughter, I see him grimace as he leans forward on his walker to get out of the chair.

I maintain my silence as well, never mentioning that I have had doctors insert a frozen embryo left over from the previous IVF into my womb. When I call him to tell him that I am pregnant, I let him know that my mother-in-law is coming to help us before he can offer to do the very thing that he cannot do anymore: take care of me. We both pretend that the plan has nothing to do with his failing body.

"Oh, that makes sense," he says. He turns to my mother. "Reginald's mama is coming to help them since she didn't get to come last time 'cause we were there."

Then he talks about when he will make a trip to see the baby, a trip that we both know he will never make.

My second daughter arrives via planned C-section just before my oldest turns three. My body is ready for her, and I shape-shift into a breast-feeding mother, this time without pain because my breasts have already been toughened by a baby's pink tongue. When she is done eating, we are both satisfied, even though if it were a poem it would be too short.

My daughters meet for the first time on a hospital bed. When I ask my oldest if she remembers the baby's name, she points at her sister, but instead of saying the name I have practiced with her, she calls the baby by her own name. I start to correct her, just as her words hit me. This slippage is as near as I will get to a definition of family.

My father lives for six more years. My children are three and six when my father gathers his children to discuss his will. I send the girls to play with Reginald while I join my siblings and mother sitting around my father's lounge chair.

"I don't want no fighting over money like these other folks out here scrapping over pennies when somebody dies," he says. "Everything will go to your mother, and when she dies, whatever is left will be divided equally between y'all."

He tells us everything that is paid for, from the house to his casket. My brother sits at the kitchen bar, looking at the ceiling in a weak attempt to blink back tears.

"Boy, I don't know what you looking at that ceiling for. You the one that lives nearby so you need to be paying the most attention. Don't nobody know when or how they gonna die. I might die of this cancer, but I could be like that woman at church that took a nap and just never woke up. Ain't no way to know." His tone is so matter-of-fact that it sounds like he's talking about the pros and cons of something as mundane as peanut butter and jelly sandwiches.

My sister, mother, and I laugh, not out of nervousness, but because his characteristic irreverence makes him seem healthy and whole.

My brother does not laugh. He stands up and runs from the house to his car before my father can finish.

Part of me wants to run too, to a place where I do not have to perform the strong daughter. But I am unwilling to add to the suffering that I cannot heal. So instead, I ask questions—where can I find the car titles and insurance papers? We listen while my father answers with the certainty of a man who is too strong to die.

My sister calls while I am cleaning my attic. I decide to call her back later. Seconds later, my phone rings again, this time my husband. I answer and wait for him to say that my father is dead. Instead, my husband says that my brother has died. The steeliness I have honed in preparation for my father's death melts into confusion.

I call my parents, and my mother tells me that she arrived at my brother's house just before the paramedics covered his face with a sheet. *They think it must have been his heart.* She repeats the story, again and again, trying to convey a trauma that words will never re-create.

She puts my father on the phone and I ask, "How are you doing?" as if my brother has not just died.

"I'm doing all right," he says. But there are long gaps between his words. He says that he has to go, but he forgets to hang up the phone.

He wails so loudly that I can see him on his knees. "I can't," he says. "I can't take no more."

My mother tells him to stop. "Carrying on won't help nothing," she says. "John, you got to be strong. Ain't nothing else we can do."

Later my mother will mention a friend of our family who stopped by after she heard the news of my brother's death. *She was just a-blubbering, you know.* My mother is trying to convey how much the woman loved my brother, but she does not know how to talk about tears without some derision. She will never mention the animal sound that came from my father on the day his son died.

My brother's funeral is the last time my father will sit in front of a casket, staring at the space between the shiny metal and the preacher's head. He, my mother, and my brother's wife sit on the front pew still and dry-faced like they are at a car wash. The rest of us pack the church until it is standing room only and transform our bodies into one quaking, weeping thing.

Later, my sister-in-law will say with a curled lip that everyone was amazed at how calm she was at the funeral. *I don't know what they thought I was going to do. Break down all over everybody?*

For days, guests arrive at my parents' house, carrying dishes of food. My mother greets them and invites them inside. My father goes to his room to hide in his bed. He will never mention my brother's name to me again.

My six-year-old daughter knows what death is. When I return to New Jersey after my brother's funeral, she tells me that she is sorry about my brother. But the look on her face, like she is looking at a photograph of herself with a toy she cannot remember, tells me that she is not sure who we are talking about.

She had spent little time with my brother, who was always on his way to or from work when he visited my parents' house. But he had always scooped her up in his arms, carrying her and eventually my youngest daughter on his hip. I remind her of this, of the man with the six-foot-two frame she had run to every time she heard him arrive during our visits to my parents' home.

A look of recognition crosses her face. "You mean the one I love?"

I cry and nod. She looks down at the table in front of her. "Does this mean that Grandpa will die soon too?"

I tell her the truth. "I don't know."

The next day, I overhear her making a list of who is dead and who is alive. I am surprised when she says, "Grandpa's mom." I remember a day when I told her to stop playing with the clasp on her seat belt. She asked why she had to wear a seat belt. I explained the dangers and she asked if I knew anyone who had died in a car accident. I told her that Grandpa had lost his family, our family, in a wreck. She stopped playing with the seat belt and asked a follow-up question I do not remember because I was busy regretting my words. I did not want our family's loss to be a cautionary tale about seat belts. Whatever my answer was, she looked satisfied, like she understood something important.

I wanted to tell her wizened face about the hospital's colored ward where grown men and women separated surgical tools into colored and white piles, and that the newspapers that reported the wreck printed the word "Negro" after each of her ancestors' names. But the whole story of the wreck would have to be told in pieces, each one picked up so carefully that its razor-sharp edges wouldn't break the skin. I vowed to bide my time in sharing our losses, to tell my children about our family before I told them what happened to them.

Now, when she is done listing the dead and the living, I tell her the story of Bernice, the skinny woman who moved through the world with a team of petticoats swinging behind her, demanding that anyone who could not love her children at least have the respect to leave them be. *She didn't take no shit off white folks.*

My father's last full day in this world will be on the fifty-eighth anniversary of the wreck. My brother will have been dead for a little over a year.

We arrive in Alabama for our regular June visit a week before my father dies.

He spends his final days in June with my two daughters, the oldest not quite seven, and the youngest just four. He calls them "Grandaddy's babies" and "sugar dolls." When he greets them, they scream "Grandpa!" like a tiny cheerleading squad. They stay close to him like sentinels, giggling and readying themselves for the unknown. They sit in his lap and read to him while he listens and reacts with animated faces, interrupting a few times to say, "Y'all, look at this. Look at how these babies can read."

At night, after their bath, they go into the den in their pajamas to say good night to him and my mother. My mother admires their beauty. They give her an obligatory hug but run to my father, who pretends to be surprised at the awesomeness of their pajamas. He stretches his time to love them by discussing each detail, kittens, puppies, stripes, and hearts. "And look at that. Is that a pig with sunglasses?"

One night, I catch the four-year-old rifling through her suitcase and I ask her what she's doing. She answers, while still continuing her search, "Looking for pajamas so Grandaddy can see how cute I am."

My mother and I take my father for his weekly cancer treatment, but the doctor tells us that there is nothing more that can be done. My father's bones have broken down so much that their insides have been released into his blood. His kidneys are failing. My father sits in a wheelchair while the doctor discusses hospice care in an uneasy voice filled with southern "wells" and "ya knows" that lead to nowhere. When he runs out of filler words, the doctor asks my father, the man he has just told that he will die soon, what he thinks. My father cracks a half smile. "I think I'd like to live forever, but . . ." Just as the doctor points out the obvious, that living forever is not possible, my father interrupts him: "I'm gonna get home to my grandbabies now."

On the fourth day of our visit, my father begins to hallucinate. He sees a hot cup of coffee in his hands and asks me to take it from him so he will not spill it as he stands up. My performance does not pass muster, and he asks my husband to take it instead. Reginald reaches out with two slow hands, pretending the cup is so full that a drop of hot coffee scalds him, and my father is satisfied. Reginald sets the cup-that-is-not-a-cup aside and helps my father stand up and walk to his bed. But the pain in his body will not tolerate stillness. So he asks Reginald to help him walk back and forth from the bed to his chair every ten minutes.

My littlest, who likes to sit next to her grandpa, is not happy with these interruptions and follows him. When she does not come back, I walk to his room to find her. The two of them are sitting next to each other on the edge of the bed. His feet are on the floor and he is looking down, unaware of the little girl sitting next to him. His hands are pressing into the mattress like he is not sure if he is going to get up or lie down. Her tiny foot catches his eye. He frowns at it, squeezes his eyes shut, and looks again to see if his eyes are betraying him. How could a baby foot get in his bed? Would tiny hands appear next? *Hands and feet . . . hands and feet.* The four-year-old breaks the spell with her giggle. When he sees the smiling brown cherub face attached to the foot, his face relaxes and he laughs for the last time in this world.

ACKNOWLEDGMENTS

I wish to express my deepest gratitude to my mother for filling the silences of my childhood with the harrowing stories of hers. Her constant refrain of "It's really a wonder none of us got killed" made me feel like my survival was also possible.

I cannot express my appreciation enough for the amazing Suzanne Gluck, who believed in this project more than I knew how to. Since the moment she said, "We are walking down the aisle," my life has felt like the very best dream. I am forever grateful to her for making me part of the WME family.

Laura Tisdel can change a whole book with a single question. Knowing I could count on her deep insight allowed me to write like a writer instead of pretending to be an editor. I am so thankful for the gentle ways that she shaped me and this book.

Thank you to the entire team at Viking for putting a wealth of creative energy into making my story live as a book: Brian Tart, Andrea Schulz, Kristina Fazzalaro, Julia Falkner, Lydia Hirt, and Jenn Houghton.

Grace Han's cover design shattered me and put me back together anew. No wonder her name is Grace.

I am grateful to The College of New Jersey for providing me with financial support to write.

During the years that I worked on this book, I wrote a collaborative book, *The Toni Morrison Book Club*, with my friends, who also happen to be colleagues. Piper, Winnie, and Juda made a home for whatever I had to say, and when I let shame cut off my words they kicked it right out the front door. Their love pushed me to make this book a reality.

Many friends supported me on this journey: Sarah Chartock's questions and ideas shaped this book profoundly. She helped me figure out how to create community in a pandemic, and I feel certain that I'd have gone mad without her. Cari Brown is the friend I didn't know was possible. Our conversations about grief, love, music, and books sustained me. I will never stop being grateful for this friendship. Much thanks to Mayfield and Marleina for all the inspiring conversations about art and the world. Kelesha, Lisa, Kila, Catherine, Mekala, Farrah, Su, Hanifa, and the Wine Before Books Book Club carried this colored girl through when the rainbow was not enough.

There are so many writers, some of whom I have met and some who I have not, whose work made it possible for me to imagine this book. Roxane Gay's *Hunger* taught me the concept of a memoir of the body. She also generously interviewed me for a previous book and the seriousness with which she treated my writing gave me the confidence to send *The Wreck* out. Sarah Broom's *The Yellow House*, a memoir of her family and a city, made me understand that to tell Black stories I had to challenge the boundaries of traditional memoir. Jacqueline Woodson's *Another Brooklyn* cracked open the doors to Black girlhood for me when I could not bear to open them on my own. Natasha Trethewey's *Memorial Drive* gave me insight into what it means to write from "the wound that never heals." Jesmyn Ward swept me up and took me home, reminding me that Black people of the rural South are too important not to write about. Deesha Philyaw's *The Secret Lives of Church Ladies* set me on fire. Honorée Fanonne Jeffers's exploration of the free and unfree gave me a whole world to get lost in and reminded me that I am free enough to get lost. All of these Black women writers and more gave me literary shelter when my own stories were homeless. I am so grateful to be living, reading, and writing during their time.

My dear cousin opened her memory and its absences to me with abandon just for the love of family. I hope this book honors her and the ancestors we share.

My husband, Reginald, encouraged me to write before I was ready to call myself a writer. Though every writer should be able to count on a partner who is as invested in their work as he has been in mine, I know that such support is rare. I am thankful for all the times he reminded me that housework is a "poor yield" on my time.

This book would not exist without my little girls, whose courageous creativity made art feel like it was always within my reach. Playing and dancing with them reminds me that joy is a thing we make together.

My daddy is the reason for this book. I am so thankful for his willingness to walk with me into the past despite the pain it caused him. When I am at my most impatient with my writing, I try to picture him rolling out pie dough, adding water with wet fingers until it is soft enough to wrap around cooked peaches, but tough enough to turn golden in popping hot grease. Watching him in the kitchen taught me that life is not so much about making as it is about remaking and that there is no starting over because nothing is ever really over. Thank you for always believing in my power to remake a life, Daddy.